COPING
with
LIFE
CHALLENGES

COPING
with
LIFE
CHALLENGES

Chris L. Kleinke

University of Alaska, Anchorage

 Brooks/Cole Publishing Company
Pacific Grove, California

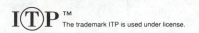
ITP ™ The trademark ITP is used under license.

Brooks/Cole Publishing Company
A Division of Wadsworth, Inc.

Printed in the United States of America

10   9   8   7   6

Library of Congress Cataloging in Publication Data

Kleinke, Chris L.
    Coping with life challenges / Chris L. Kleinke.
        p.   cm.
    Includes bibliographical references and index.
    ISBN 0-534-14424-1
    1. Adjustment (Psychology)   2. Adjustment (Psychology)—Case
studies.   I. Title.
BFK335.K59   1990   90-37189
158—dc20   CIP

Sponsoring Editor: *Claire Verduin*
Marketing Representative: *Tammy Stenquist*
Editorial Assistant: *Gay Bond*
Production Editor: *Linda Loba*
Manuscript Editor: *Betty Berenson*
Permissions Editor: *Carline Haga*
Interior Design: *Kelly Shoemaker*
Cover Design and Illustration: *Nani Hudson*
Art Coordinator: *Lisa Torri*
Interior Illustration: *Lisa Torri*
Photo Researcher: *Ruth Minerva*
Typesetting: *Dharma Enterprises*
Printing and Binding: *Malloy Lithographing*

Photo Credits

P.1, Robert Brenner/PhotoEdit; P.13, James Carroll; P.27, PhotoEdit; P.42, Bob Clay; P.55, H.Mark
Weidman; P.69, Cleo Freelance Photographers; P.84, Tony Freeman/PhotoEdit; P.98, Evan
Johnson/Jeroboam, Inc.; Pp.106-107, "Examples of Assertiveness, Nonassertiveness, and
Aggression," reprinted with permission from *Stress Inoculation Training*, by Donald Meichenbaum,
1985, Pergamon Press plc.; P.108, "Preferred and Disliked Influence Tactics" adapted with
permission from "Multidimensional Scaling of Power Strategies," by T. Falbo, *Journal of Personality
and Social Psychology,* 1977, *35*, 537-547. Copyright 1977 by the American Psychological
Association; P.111, Myrleen Ferguson/PhotoEdit; P.121, "Tactics of Manipulations," by D.M. Buss, M.
Gomes, D.S. Higgins, and K. Lauterbach, reprinted with permission from *Journal of Personality and
Social Psychology,* 1987, *52*, 1219-1229. Copyright 1987 by the American Psychological Association,
P.121, "Communication Styles," adapted from "The Role of Cognitive Appraisal in Self-Reports of
Marital Communication," by N. Epstein, J.L. Pretzer, and B. Fleming, *Behavior Therapy,* 1987, 18,
51-69. Copyright 1987 by the Association for the Advancement of Behavior Therapy. Adapted with
permission; P.128, Evan Johnson/Jeroboam, Inc.; P.142, Joan Liftin/ Actuality, Inc.; P.155, Richard
Hutchings/PhotoEdit; P.157, "Pain Rating Index" from "The McGill Pain Questionnaire: Major
Properties and Scoring Methods," by R. Melzack, *Pain,* 1975, *1*, 277-299. Copyright 1975 by
Elsevier Science Publishers. Adapted with permission; P.169, Richard Wood /Jeroboam, Inc.; P.172,
"Stressful Life Events," reprinted with permission from "The Social Readjustment Rating Scale," by
T.H. Holmes and R.H. Rahe, *Journal of Psychosomatic Research,* 1967, *11*, 213-218, Pergamon Press
plc. and "Stressful Events are Indeed a Factor in Physical Illness: Reply to Schroeder and Costa," by
S.R. Maddi, P.T. Bartone, and M.C. Puccetti, *Journal of Personality and Social Psychology,* 1984, *52*,
833-843. Copyright 1987 by the American Psychological Association; P.183, Evan Johnson/Jeroboam,
Inc.; P.199, Alan Oddie/PhotoEdit.

*To Anya and Alexander
and their grandparents*

Preface

●●

We are all confronted at times in our lives with problems and challenges. During times of stress, it is comforting to know you have skills and resources that will help you make the best of difficult situations.

Researchers have collected a wealth of information about how people cope with life challenges. They have directed their efforts toward answering the following questions: "Can different styles of coping be identified and measured? Are some coping strategies more useful for certain problems than others? How can I learn to cope more effectively with challenges that confront me?"

My purpose in writing this book is to communicate the findings of these studies to people not trained in the scientific jargon contained in professional journals. This book will give you an overview of what researchers have discovered about coping. You will read about coping responses you already know and about ones you don't know and will want to learn. You will come to appreciate the fact that you, as a human being, are adaptable. Your ability to cope is not fixed at birth. It is developed and perfected throughout your life. You need not be a passive bystander. Living is not always easy. But knowledge *is* power, and this book will hopefully empower you to gain a greater sense of control over the challenges in your life.

This book can be roughly divided into three sections. Chapters 1–3 provide an introduction to the concept of coping and explain a number of important terms. Chapter 1 defines the concept of coping and two terms that will be used throughout the book: primary appraisal and secondary appraisal. Several important topics are discussed, including the distinction between self-blame and self-responsibility, the pros and cons of avoidance, and common self-defeating behaviors. Chapter 2 focuses on daily hassles and how they affect us. The reader is encouraged to develop an attitude of mastery and self-efficacy. Chapter 3 describes eight skills that should be added to your coping arsenal: building a support system, problem solving, self-relaxation, maintaining internal control, talking yourself through challenges, developing your sense of humor, exercising, and rewarding yourself for accomplishments.

Chapters 4–12 focus on challenges people face at various times in their lives. Each of these chapters includes a description of useful coping skills. Chapter 4 teaches skills for coping with failure. Chapter 5 teaches skills for coping with depression. Chapter 6 teaches skills for coping with loneliness, shyness, and rejection. Chapter 7 teaches skills for coping with anxiety. Chapter 8 teaches skills for coping with anger. Chapter 9 teaches skills for coping with conflicts in close relationships. Chapter 10 teaches skills for coping with loss. Chapter 11 teaches skills for coping with aging. Chapter 12 teaches skills for coping with pain.

Chapters 13–15 take a somewhat different approach by describing the experiences of people who have borne up to difficult life challenges. Chapter 13 focuses on illness, preventive medicine, and health. Examples are given about how people cope with illness and health problems ranging from headaches to cancer and AIDS. Suggestions are given for developing an attitude of hardiness and developing a low-stress personality. Chapter 14 offers a tribute to people who have undergone injury and trauma. The reader learns about coping by appreciating the experiences of those who suffered harm from natural and human caused disasters. Included in this chapter is a discussion of post-traumatic stress disorder. Chapter 15 sums up the theme of this book by discussing coping as a life philosophy. A distinction is made between the psychological effects of helplessness and hope. The reader is encouraged to become a well-rounded person and to develop an attitude of self-preservation. The chapter concludes by highlighting the benefits perfecting your coping skills in this challenging and unpredictable world.

I would like to thank the following reviewers for their helpful comments and suggestions: Dr. Paul Bowers, Grayson County College, Texas; Dr. William Brown, University of Wisconsin at Eau Claire; Dr. Kenneth E. Coffield, University of Alabama-Huntsville; Dr. Philip Comer, West Virginia University; Dr. Bernard Gorman, Nassau Community College, New York; Dr. Peter Gram, Pensacola Junior College, Florida; Dr. John Lembo, Millersville University, Pennsylvania; Professor Alicia O'Neill, Monterey Peninsula College, California; Dr. Thomas K. Saville, Metropolitan State College, Colorado; and Dr. Gary Sherman, University of Wisconsin at Superior.

Chris L. Kleinke

Contents

• •

12 Coping with Pain 155

13 Coping with Illness and Maintaining Health 169

14 Coping with Injury and Trauma 183

1

What Does It Mean to Cope?

This book is about dealing with challenges, traumas, and hassles in our lives. It is about "keeping the faith," "hanging in," and managing our fears, hostilities, doubts, frustrations, and sadness. It is a tribute to people's adaptability and capacity to overcome adversity. My goal in writing this book is to teach a number of useful coping skills to use when confronted with life challenges. I also want to communicate a philosophy—a coping skills attitude toward life. That is, I want to communicate a belief that no matter how tough things seem, you can make a plan and survive. The value of a coping attitude toward life lies in its encouragement of personal growth. You can make your life interesting by mastering new skills and taking on meaningful challenges.

We will begin with a definition of coping and a description of how the coping process works. A good place to start is with the process of *appraisal*. R. S. Lazarus and S. Folkman (1984) define two kinds of appraisal: *primary appraisal* and *secondary appraisal*. When faced with a potential challenge or stress we first determine whether we are in jeopardy or danger. We ask ourselves whether this is something worth getting upset about. This is primary appraisal. Primary appraisal is concerned with our physical as well as psychological and emotional well-being. If we determine that we are in jeopardy or danger, we ask ourselves whether there is something we can do about it and, if so, what? This is secondary appraisal.

PRIMARY APPRAISAL

Let's say a company executive tells three of her assistants in a gruff voice that she wants to see them in her office "first thing next morning." What sorts of primary appraisals might the assistants make?

One, Tim, might think: "This means trouble. That gruff tone can only mean I did something wrong and that I'm in hot water. There's nothing I can do now. I probably won't sleep all night and I'll be really tired and anxious tomorrow."

Another, Lisa, might think: "Sometimes when the boss uses that gruff tone it doesn't mean anything and sometimes it does. I won't know until tomorrow if there is any trouble, but it will be in my best interest to be up on my facts and figures. And, just in case, I'll dress extra professionally tomorrow."

The third, Ed, might think: "If the boss sounds gruff, that's her problem. Her problems don't concern me, so I'll just pretend nothing happened and come in tomorrow just as I always do."

Note the different impact as well as the subjectivity of primary appraisals. Tim has appraised the director's gruff tone as a definite threat. Lisa has appraised it as a possible threat. Ed has appraised it as posing no threat. At this point we don't know whose appraisal is correct, but you would probably agree that Lisa's is most prudent. Tim is being a "catastrophizer," and by assuming the worst he will suffer a good deal of stress. Ed is being a "denier." He is not under any stress right now, but he may pay a price in the future. Lisa is taking the issue seriously, but is managing her stress by making concrete plans.

SECONDARY APPRAISAL

The above example also includes the process of secondary appraisal. If our primary appraisal tells us we are in jeopardy, we need to ask what we can do about it. Tim's secondary appraisal tells him he is facing a threat that is beyond his control. Lisa concludes there is a possible threat and she draws up a "battle plan." Because Ed assumes there is no threat, he feels no need for a secondary appraisal.

Primary and secondary appraisals impact on how we respond to a challenge or threat. It is in our best interest to make a realistic primary appraisal. We don't want to fly off the handle and panic, but we also don't want to ignore problems that are real. If our primary appraisal indicates reason for concern, we want to make a secondary appraisal that is adaptive. We would like to be able to say to ourselves: "This is a genuine problem. Things look tough. I've got to come up with some good plans. Let me dig into my bag of coping strategies and make plan A and plan B, and possibly plan C."

Most of the time our secondary appraisal will suggest some steps we can take to manage the situation. On other occasions we will determine that the situation is beyond our control and that our best plan is to "exert control" by not fighting a battle we can't win. There are times when it is better to be flexible and roll with the punches.

A DEFINITION OF COPING

Rose Kennedy was once asked about her reaction to the many tragedies that have befallen her family. She replied, "I cope." Coping can be defined as the *efforts we make to manage situations we have appraised as potentially harmful or stressful.* This definition of coping, which is adapted from Lazarus and Folkman (1984), has three key features: (1) It implies that coping involves a certain amount of effort and planning. Note further that this concept of coping does not include automatic or reflex responses to a challenge. (2) The definition does not imply a positive outcome. Some of our coping responses may work well for us while others may not. (3) The definition emphasizes coping as a process taking place over time.

The above features are important in a definition of coping because they allow us to study different styles and strategies of coping and to evaluate which ones work best in different situations. The goal of researchers has been to find out whether there are personality traits, beliefs, or ways of viewing the world that are more or less adaptive in various situations. After looking at what has been learned about these questions you will be able to distinguish effective coping strategies you can use in your life.

TWO GENERAL COPING STRATEGIES

Lazarus and Folkman (1984) identify two general forms of coping: *problem-focused coping* and *emotion-focused coping*. Problem-focused coping involves the attempt to understand and define a problem and to work out possible solutions. Problem-focused coping strategies can be outer-directed or inner-directed. Outer-directed coping strategies are oriented toward altering the situation or the behaviors of others. Inner-directed coping strategies include efforts we make to reconsider our attitudes and needs and to develop new skills and responses. Emotion-focused coping is oriented toward managing emotional distress. Emotion-focused coping strategies include physical exercise, meditation, expressing feelings, and seeking support.

We are more likely to engage in problem-focused coping when we feel there is something we can do about a problem or challenge. When a problem or challenge appears beyond our control, we rely more on emotion-focused coping (Folkman & Lazarus, 1980). In most situations, we probably benefit most by combining these coping strategies. For example, we can prepare for a job interview by practicing our responses to questions and choosing appropriate dress (problem-focused) and by being relaxed and maintaining a nondefensive attitude (emotion-focused). We can cope with difficult confrontations by keeping cool (emotion-focused) and using effective negotiation (problem-focused).

The distinction between problem-focused and emotion-focused coping provides a broad basis for understanding the concept of coping. It is also possible to define more specific coping responses, such as those discussed below.

RESEARCH ON COPING RESPONSES

Take a few moments and think about the most stressful event that has happened to you during the past month. With this event in mind, check how often you did each of the following things.

	Never	*Sometimes*	*Often*
1. Tried to see the positive side.	____	____	____
2. Took things one step at a time.	____	____	____
3. Stepped back to be more objective.	____	____	____
4. Took some positive action.	____	____	____
5. Exercised more.	____	____	____
6. Talked with friends.	____	____	____
7. Kept my feelings to myself.	____	____	____
8. Ate more, smoked cigarettes, or used drugs.	____	____	____
9. Refused to acknowledge problem.	____	____	____

The above coping responses were studied in a community survey (Billings & Moos, 1981; Holahan & Moos, 1987). You may have noticed that responses 1, 5, 7, 8, and 9 are emotion-focused and responses 2, 4, and 6 are problem-focused. Another way to define these coping responses is according to whether they represent an *active-cognitive* method (1, 2, 3), an *active-behavioral* method (4, 5, 6), or *avoidance* (7, 8, 9). Results of the survey indicated that women used active-behavioral methods and avoidance more often than men. Men and women did not differ in their use of active-cognitive methods. People who used active-cognitive and active-behavioral coping responses tended to be easygoing and less anxious. They also had relatively high self-confidence. People who were avoiders tended to be more depressed and anxious and they suffered greater physical stress. Avoiders also had fewer educational and financial resources and less family support.

In another survey of how people cope, married couples were questioned about their responses to four sources of stress: marriage, parenting, household finances, and work (Pearlin & Schooler, 1978). A number of coping responses were employed by people who suffered comparatively low levels of emotional stress. These coping responses included taking an active, self-reliant, problem-solving approach. Greater amounts of emotional distress were experienced by people who felt helpless, blamed themselves, and engaged in denial and avoidance.

A third group of researchers surveyed people on their experiences with various coping responses when faced with losses, threats, and challenges (McCrae & Costa, 1986). The most effective coping responses included seeking help, communicating feelings, taking rational action, drawing strength from adversity, using humor, and maintaining faith, self-confidence, and feelings of control. The least effective coping responses included hostility, indecisiveness, self-blame, and attempting to escape or withdraw from the situation.

A fourth example of effective and ineffective coping responses comes from a community survey in which people reported how they coped with a recent stressful experience, such as loss of self-esteem, concern for a loved one, interpersonal conflict, financial strain, health problems, and lack of success at work (Folkman, Lazarus, Dunkel-Schetter, DeLongis, & Gruen, 1986). People who reported satisfactory resolution of their stressful experience tended to cope by maintaining their composure and working out a plan and by using the stressful experience as an opportunity for personal growth. Those who did not successfully resolve their problem responded by being impulsive, aggressive, or angry or by ignoring the problem and downplaying its importance.

In yet another study investigating the relation between coping and emotions (Folkman & Lazarus, 1988), participants reported how often they used the following types of coping responses for a recent stressful event:

Confrontive coping: "I stood my ground and fought for what I wanted."
Distancing: "I went on as if nothing had happened."
Self-control: "I tried to keep my feelings to myself."
Seeking social support: "I talked to someone who could do something concrete about the problem."
Accepting responsibility: "I criticized or lectured myself."
Escape-avoidance: "I wished that the situation would go away or somehow be over with."
Planful problem solving: "I knew what had to be done, so I doubled my efforts to make things work."
Positive reappraisal: "I changed or grew as a person in a good way."

The respondents also reported which of the following emotions they experienced as a result of their response to the stressful situation: *worried/fearful, disgusted/angry, confident,* or *pleased/happy*.

After analyzing the correlation between the respondents' coping responses and their resulting emotions, the researchers reached the following conclusions: Planful problem solving appeared to be the most effective coping response because it was associated with the most positive emotions. Confrontive coping and distancing turned out to be the least effective coping responses because they were associated with the most negative emotions. Positive reappraisal was more effective for the types of problems faced by adults in their 30s and 40s. Seeking social support was more effective for adults who were 60 and older. Results for the remaining coping responses did not show a strong pattern, but there was no evidence they were particularly effective.

A final example of research on coping responses comes from a group of researchers who attempted to integrate studies on coping by devising a list of fourteen coping responses (Carver, Scheier, & Weintraub, 1989):[1]

Active coping *(personal correlates: optimism, confidence, self-esteem, low anxiety):* "I take additional action to try to get rid of the problem." "I concentrate my efforts on doing something about it." "I do what has to be done, one step at a time."

Planning *(personal correlates: optimism, confidence, self-esteem):* "I try to come up with a strategy about what to do." "I make a plan of action." "I think hard about what steps to take."

Suppression of competing activities *(personal correlates: none):* "I put aside other activities in order to concentrate on this." "I focus on dealing with this problem, and if necessary let other things slide a little." "I keep myself from getting distracted by other thoughts or activities."

Restraint coping *(personal correlates: optimism, low anxiety):* "I force myself to wait for the right time to do something." "I hold off doing anything about it until the situation permits." "I make sure not to make matters worse by acting too soon."

Seeking social support for instrumental reasons *(personal correlates: optimism):* "I ask people who have had similiar experiences what they did." "I try to get advice from someone about what to do." "I talk to someone to find out more about the situation."

Seeking social support for emotional reasons *(personal correlates: none):* "I talk to someone about how I feel." "I try to get emotional support from friends or relatives." "I discuss my feelings with someone."

Positive reinterpretation and growth *(personal correlates: optimism, confidence, self-esteem, low anxiety):* "I look for something good in what is happening." "I try to see it in a different light, to make it seem more positive." "I learn something from the experience."

Acceptance *(personal correlates: optimism):* "I learn to live with it." "I accept that this has happened and that it can't be changed." "I get used to the idea that it happened."

Turning to religion *(personal correlates: optimism):* "I seek God's help." "I put my trust in God." "I try to find comfort in my religion."

Focus on and venting of emotions *(personal correlates: low confidence, anxiety):* "I get upset and let my emotions out." "I let my feelings out." "I feel a lot of emotional distress and I find myself expressing those feelings a lot."

[1] Carver, C. S., Scheier, M. F., & Weintraub, J. K. (1989). Assessing coping strategies: A theoretically based approach. *Journal of Personality and Social Psychology, 56*, 267–283. Copyright 1989 by the American Psychological Association. Adapted with permission.

Denial *(personal correlates: pessimism, low confidence, low self-esteem, anxiety):* "I refuse to believe that it has happened." "I pretend that it hasn't really happened." "I act as though it hasn't happened."

Behavioral disengagement *(personal correlates: pessimism, low confidence, low self-esteem, anxiety):* "I give up the attempt to get what I want." "I just give up trying to reach my goal." "I admit to myself that I can't deal with it and quit trying."

Mental disengagement *(personal correlates: pessimism, low confidence, anxiety):* "I turn to work or other substitute activities to take my mind off things." "I go to movies or watch TV, to think about it less." "I daydream about things other than this."

Alcohol and/or drug use *(personal correlates: pessimism):* "I use alcohol or drugs to make myself feel better." "I try to lose myself for a while by drinking alcohol or taking drugs." "I use alcohol or drugs to help me get though it."

People's preference for these coping responses were correlated with personal factors including optimism versus pessimism, confidence versus low confidence, self-esteem versus low self-esteem, and low anxiety versus anxiety. The following coping responses were correlated with the most healthy personal factors: active coping, planning, restraint coping, positive reinterpretation and growth, and acceptance. Coping responses correlated with the least healthy personal factors included: focus on and ventilation of emotions, denial, behavioral disengagement, mental disengagement, and use of alcohol and drugs.

In general, we can conclude that it is most adaptive to cope with life challenges by taking an active, self-reliant approach that includes planning and problem solving. It is least adaptive to cope by avoiding and denying the challenge or by responding in an impulsive manner.

DISTINGUISHING BETWEEN SELF-BLAME AND SELF-RESPONSIBILITY

One insight you will gain from reading this book is that it is not helpful to cope with life challenges by engaging in self-blame. People who blame themselves when faced with threats and trauma tend to be less happy, less well adjusted, and more depressed than those who don't employ this self-defeating coping style (Kleinke, 1988; Revenson & Felton, 1989; Vitaliano, Katon, Maiuro, & Russo, 1989). Compared with self-blame, self-responsibility is a very different kind of coping style. Self-responsibility is *not* blaming or derogating ourselves for negative and unhappy events in our lives. Self-responsibility means developing our sense of self-efficacy and internal control (see Chapter 2) and making the effort to learn and practice coping skills such as those described in Chapter 3. Self-responsibility requires us to honestly determine when we are responsible (and not responsible) for the causes and solutions of our problems (see Chapter 15).

THE PROS AND CONS OF AVOIDANCE

We are all tempted at times to respond to life challenges with avoidance. Avoidance means not putting out the effort to cope when we should. Instead of heading off problems at their source, we ignore them and hope they will go away. Unfortunately, most challenges in life don't automatically disappear. While avoidance may reduce immediate anxiety, it will often result in greater stress in the long run because we never know when problems will catch up to us.

Avoidance is a useful strategy for coping with problems that don't have long-term consequences. It is often more adaptive to let brief irritations pass, rather than to get upset about them. There is no point in suffering stress from problems that will resolve themselves. But avoidance is not a good strategy for coping with life challenges requiring involvement. Under these circumstances, we need to control our stress by taking a coping attitude, reinforcing our feelings of self-efficacy (see Chapter 2), and using coping skills such as those outlined in Chapter 3 (Suls & Fletcher, 1985).

Another way to understand the pros and cons of avoidance is with the concepts of *monitoring* and *blunting* (Miller, S. M., 1987). Monitoring concerns the importance we attach to being alert, vigilant, and prepared for potential threats. People who are monitors exert a lot of effort to gain information about threatening events. High monitors read warning labels and safety information and collect facts about illness and health. They expend a lot of energy trying to anticipate what is going to happen to them. Low monitors live their lives without paying much attention to potential dangers. They wait until threats happen before reacting to them.

Blunting refers to our tendency to distract ourselves from feelings and emotions associated with danger and threat. Blunters are people who shield themselves from the emotional impact of negative experiences. They don't focus on what's happening inside their bodies. Nonblunters are sensitive to their emotions when faced with threat. They are in touch with their feelings during challenging situations.

Research studies have found that it is best to seek information (high monitoring) and be emotionally sensitive (nonblunting) when we are confronted with threats we can overcome (Miller, 1987; Miller & Birnbaum, 1988; Miller, Brody, & Summerton, 1988). When a potential danger is surmountable, it is advantageous to be vigilant and energized by heightened emotions. When faced with threats beyond our control, it is more adaptive to cope by allowing life to take its course. It is stressful to try to monitor every threat that might potentially affect us. People who do this are at risk of being hypertensive (Miller, S. M., Leinbach, & Brody, 1989). We need to direct our information seeking and emotional energies toward challenges where we believe we can be most effective.

HOW PEOPLE DEFEAT THEMSELVES

I will conclude this chapter by looking at some disadvantageous coping strategies. Knowing how people can defeat themselves helps us avoid their mistakes. R. F. Baumeister and S. J. Scher (1988) identified the following self-defeating behavior patterns: *primary self-destruction, tradeoffs,* and *counterproductive strategies.* Primary self-destruction refers to the intentional desire to harm oneself. It has its roots in guilt, remorse, and low self-esteem. Tradeoffs occur when a choice must be made between conflicting goals. Sometimes to avoid immediate pain or inconvenience, a person takes a course of action that turns out to be a poor choice in the long run. Counterproductive strategies are caused by poor planning and judgment. They are not intentionally chosen to cause self-harm. People use counterproductive strategies when they don't have the skills or insight to settle on a better plan.

Primary Self-Destruction

The most common primary self-defeating behaviors are outlined below. Check how much you agree or disagree with the following statements.

	Strongly agree	Agree	Disagree	Strongly disagree
1. I have done dangerous things just for the thrill of it.	____	____	____	____
2. Sometimes I don't seem to care what happens to me.	____	____	____	____
3. Often I don't take very good care of myself.	____	____	____	____
4. I usually call a doctor when I'm sure I'm becoming ill.	____	____	____	____
5. I seem to keep making the same mistakes.	____	____	____	____
6. I am frequently late for important things.	____	____	____	____
7. I do not believe in gambling.	____	____	____	____
8. I smoke more than a pack of cigarettes a day.	____	____	____	____
9. I usually eat breakfast.	____	____	____	____
10. I frequently fall in love with the wrong person.	____	____	____	____

These statements come from the Chronic Self-Destructiveness Scale (Kelley, Byrne, et al., 1985; Kelley, Cheung, et al., 1986). People tend to be more self-destructive if they agree with statements 1, 2, 3, 5, 6, 8, and 10 and disagree with statements 4, 7, and 9. People with high scores on self-destructiveness do not take responsibility for their own well-being. They have low feelings of internal control (see Chapter 3). They also do things that are not in their best interest, such as cheating, driving unsafely, and ignoring their health.

Examples of primary self-destruction include masochism, eating disorders, drug abuse, recklessness, and suicide. People usually know they are in emotional pain when they engage in these harmful behaviors but, unfortunately, they are not always ready or able to change.

Tradeoffs

Tradeoffs result in self-defeating behaviors when people opt to choose immediate pleasure or relief despite the long-term costs of health risk or anxiety. Some examples of tradeoffs include smoking, drinking, failing to wear seat belts, avoiding exercise, eating badly, neglecting health care, and using recreational drugs. Tradeoffs also occur when people choose safe but nonchallenging goals and when they allow excuses to stand in the way of achieving gratifications they could enjoy from more effortful accomplishments. People often make poor tradeoffs when they have not learned how to cope with failure (see Chapter 4).

Counterproductive Strategies

Counterproductive strategies result from poor insight and lack of judgment. They are often not very effective, and can be recognized by their rigidity. For example, when trying to solve a difficult problem or negotiate a sensitive issue, people sometimes hinder themselves by not using all of their options. They get stuck on one track and forget alternative solutions. Or they make demands from which they can't retreat. A successful solution or fruitful negotiation requires flexibility. In some situations it may be best to be firm. Other times, more may be gained by compromising or even allowing others to have their way. People who avoid counterproductive strategies know how to use a problem-solving approach like the one outlined in Chapter 3.

SELF-DEROGATION

Check whether you agree or disagree with the following statements.

	True	False
1. I wish I could have more respect for myself.	_____	_____
2. On the whole, I am satisfied with myself.	_____	_____
3. I feel I do not have much to be proud of.	_____	_____
4. I'm inclined to think I'm a failure.	_____	_____
5. I take a positive attitude toward myself.	_____	_____
6. At times I think I'm no good at all.	_____	_____
7. I certainly feel useless at times.	_____	_____

These statements come from the Self-Derogation Scale (Kaplan, 1970). People with a strong tendency to derogate themselves agree with statements 1, 3, 4, 6, and 7 and disagree with statements 2 and 5. People who derogate themselves are less well adjusted. They are anxious and depressed and have a hard time adjusting to life challenges. They are also more likely to experience physical and psychological stress and to become suicidal (Kaplan 1970; Kaplan & Pokorny, 1969, 1976a, 1976b).

Self-derogation results from the experience of growing up in a family or social group where it is difficult to get credit for engaging in appropriate behaviors. People with a history of rejection and nonacceptance often feel like underdogs and identify themselves as members of outgroups. Because they have failed to gain self-esteem and recognition by following societal norms, they sometimes become antisocial. Over time, the antisocial orientation can become the only way to maintain identity and self-esteem (Kaplan, Johnson, & Bailey, 1986; Kaplan, Martin, & Johnson, 1986).

It is understandable that people with a history of rejection would have a harder time learning adaptive coping responses than those who had good role models as they were growing up. It is difficult to have a coping attitude toward life when positive rewards seem beyond control. However, our own thoughts, feelings, attitudes, and behaviors are ours to manage in the best way we can. The coping skills discussed in this book are meant to increase your power over yourself. By increasing your personal sense of competence and effectiveness, you stand a chance of gaining more positive reactions from others.

SOME CONCLUSIONS ABOUT SUCCESSFUL COPING RESPONSES

What conclusions can we reach from research studies on coping responses? People who cope most successfully are those who are equipped with a battery of coping strategies and who are flexible in gearing their responses to the situation. Good copers have developed the following three skills (Atonovsky, 1979): (1) *flexibility:* being able to create and consider alternative plans; (2) *farsightedness:* anticipating long-range effects of coping responses; and (3) *rationality:* making accurate appraisals.

In this chapter we looked at a number of research studies analyzing the effectiveness of people's coping responses. Although these studies used somewhat different terms for their coping measures, they all agreed on the following conclusions:

> Successful copers respond to life challenges by taking responsibility for finding a solution to their problems. They approach problems with a sense of competence and mastery. Their goal is to assess the situation, get advice and support from others, and work out a plan that will be in their best interest. Successful copers use life challenges as an opportunity for personal growth, and they attempt to face these challenges with hope, patience, and a sense of humor.

> Unsuccessful copers respond to life challenges with denial and avoidance. They either withdraw from problems or they react impulsively without taking the time and effort to seek the best solution. Unsuccessful copers are angry and aggressive or depressed and passive. They blame themselves or others for their problems and don't appreciate the value of approaching life challenges with a sense of hope, mastery, and personal control.

We live in a society where people want easy answers to their problems—a pill, a quick fix, or a guaranteed solution that doesn't require much cost or effort. Successful coping does not result from discovering a single fail-proof response. It is an attitude and a life philosophy. Successful copers teach themselves to use primary and secondary appraisal for deriving coping responses best suited for a particular life event they are facing. You will learn more about how this process works in Chapter 2.

SUGGESTIONS FOR FURTHER READING

GOLEMAN, D. (1985). *Vital lies, simple truths: The psychology of self-deception.* New York: Simon & Schuster.

LAZARUS, R. S., & FOLKMAN, S. (1984). *Stress, appraisal, and coping.* New York: Springer.

MENNINGER, K. (1966). *Man against himself.* New York: Harcourt Brace Jovanovich. (Original work published 1938.)

TEGER, A. I. (1980). *Too much invested to quit.* New York: Pergamon.

2

. . . .

The Process
of Coping

This chapter builds on the concepts introduced in Chapter 1 to develop a model for understanding the process of coping. To lay the groundwork for this model, it will be useful for you to consider how you respond to daily hassles. Daily hassles are minor aggravating events. When considered alone, daily hassles don't amount to much. However, they can take a toll if we are under a lot of pressure or when they all seem to pile up at the same time. It has been recognized for some time that major life crises can significantly influence our lives (Dohrenwend & Dohrenwend, 1974; Holmes & Rahe, 1967). More recently, psychologists have documented the stresses caused by daily hassles (Kanner, Coyne, Schaefer, & Lazarus, 1981; Monroe, 1983). Although not as dramatic as major life crises, daily hassles are an important cause of stress. We are often not aware of how much such daily hassles can wear us out.

MEASURING DAILY HASSLES

Take a moment and think of the issues, fears, or desires that are a daily frustration for you. People responding in a survey said they most commonly experienced the following daily hassles (Kanner et al., 1981): concerns about weight and physical appearance, health of a family member, rising prices, home maintenance, too many things to do, property, investments, taxes, and crime. Other hassles listed were pollution, traffic, inclement weather, arguments, and rejections.

Another way to assess the daily hassles in your life is by responding to questions such as the ones below. At the end of each day, mark which of these daily life events happened to you. Then rate the events that happened on the following scale:

1 = occurred but was not stressful
2 = caused very little stress
3 = caused a little stress
4 = caused some stress
5 = caused much stress
6 = caused very much stress
7 = caused me to panic

Daily Life Events	*Score*
1. Performed poorly at a task	_____
2. Criticized verbally or verbally attacked	_____
3. Interrupted while talking	_____
4. Was stared at	_____
5. Was embarrassed	_____
6. Argued with someone	_____
7. Had car trouble	_____
8. Had difficulty in traffic	_____
9. Misplaced something	_____
10. Bad weather	_____
11. Money problems	_____
12. Heard some bad news	_____

Daily Life Events	*Score*
13. Experienced narrow escape from danger	_____
14. Was late for work/appointment	_____
15. Exposed to upsetting TV show, movie, book, news article	_____

The above incidents are a selection of the 58 daily hassles contained in the Daily Stress Inventory (Brantley, Waggoner, Jones, & Rappaport, 1987). This inventory is designed to give a daily reading of the effects of daily hassles on a person's life. You can derive a stress score by adding up the points you score for each event. Since some days are more stressful than others, it's natural for your stress score to change from day to day. But if your stress scores are consistently very high (5 or higher), chances are that daily hassles are getting the best of you.

HOW DAILY HASSLES AFFECT US

It has long been suspected that daily hassles can have a detrimental effect on our physical and emotional well-being. Recent studies indicate this is true. There is indeed a correlation between the number of daily hassles people experience and their symptoms of health problems and psychological as well as physiological stress (Brantley, Dietz, McKnight, Jones, & Tulley, 1988; DeLongis, Coyne, Dakof, Folkman, & Lazarus, 1982; Kanner, Coyne, Schaefer, & Lazarus, 1981; Monroe, 1983).

Researchers also found that the detrimental effects of daily hassles are lower for people with high self-esteem and good support systems (DeLongis, Folkman, & Lazarus, 1988). Later in this chapter you will learn how you can strengthen your self-esteem by building up your sense of internal control and self-efficacy. Good self-esteem helps us bear up to the negative effects of daily stress. In Chapter 3, you will learn about the benefits of developing a good support system. Support from others helps to alleviate the negative effects of daily stress on our moods and psychological well-being.

The fact that daily hassles and stress reactions influence each other has important implications for successful coping. The diagram in Figure 2.1 demonstrates the processes we go through when faced with a life event (Lazarus, 1984). This diagram has three key features. First, a life event (boss's gruff voice, traffic jam, rejection) is not a problem unless we appraise it as such (primary appraisal). The lesson here is that we want our primary appraisals to be realistic so that we attend to legitimate problems and threats but don't overburden ourselves with events that must be accepted as part of life. Second, when a life event is appraised as a problem or threat and results in stress, the negative effects of this stress can be moderated with a secondary appraisal that results in a self-perception of efficacy and competence. Third, a successful coping response will serve to further control and minimize stress. An unsuccessful coping response should prompt us to reappraise the life event or to try a different coping strategy. Figure 2.1 shows that coping responses must be flexible and that new coping strategies can be learned. As suggested in Chapter 1, it is always desirable to have a plan A, a plan B, and a plan C.

You now have a basic understanding of the concepts of primary appraisal, secondary appraisal, and coping. The remainder of this chapter will be devoted to a more detailed analysis of these important processes.

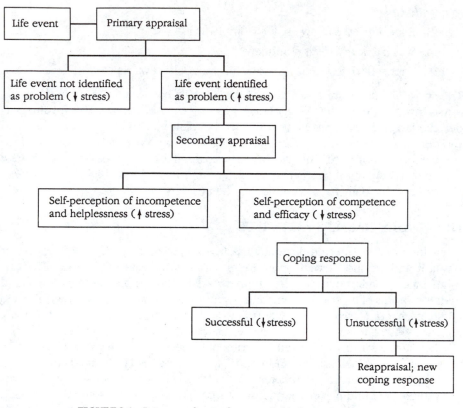

FIGURE 2.1 Primary and secondary appraisal in the coping process
Note: ↑ = increase in stress; ↓ = decrease in stress.

PRIMARY APPRAISAL

How can we learn to make realistic primary appraisals? A good place to start is by understanding the insights offered by Albert Ellis in his *rational-emotive* therapy (Ellis, 1962; Ellis & Harper, 1975). Ellis helps us appreciate the subjectivity of primary appraisals. He explains that people have more control over their primary appraisals than they might realize. Using rational-emotive theory, we can break the process of primary appraisal into three steps (see Figure 2.2). Step 1 consists of a life event, which Ellis calls the activating event. Step 2 is the appraisal of this life event. This appraisal arises out of our subjective belief system. Step 3 consists of the feelings, emotions, and possible stresses that are a consequence of how the life event was appraised. To explain it another way, the manner in which we appraise a life event has a significant influence on our emotions and feelings. Ellis's theory is deceptively simple. It is easy to appreciate how it works, but it is often difficult to apply in everyday life. For an example of how rational-emotive therapy applies to primary appraisal, consider a man who was just denied a promotion. The life event in Figure 2.2 is thus the denied promotion. What emotions would this person experience if he made the following appraisals?

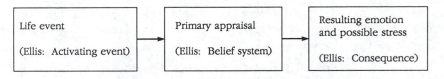

Life event	Primary appraisal	Resulting emotion and possible stress
(Ellis: Activating event)	(Ellis: Belief system)	(Ellis: Consequence)

FIGURE 2.2   The process of primary appraisal

Appraisal A: "I lost the promotion and that means I'm a failure. I'm no good. My life is ruined. I can never be happy without that promotion." Resulting emotion: _____.

Appraisal B: "So that's what I get for all my hard work. Stepped on! Those rotten executives think they are so high and mighty! They have no right to treat me this way." Resulting emotion: _____.

Appraisal C: "I'm very disappointed about losing the promotion. It's a setback for me, and I'll probably be upset about it for some time. But I know I have to pick myself up and find a new course of action." Resulting emotion: _____.

Appraisal D: "Not getting the promotion is no big deal. I don't care about what those executives think about me." Resulting emotion: _____.

Appraisal A would most likely result in depression. Appraisal B would probably cause anger. The consequence of Appraisal C is likely to be sadness and hope. The consequence of Appraisal D depends on its truthfulness. If the man really doesn't care about the promotion, the fact that he didn't get it won't have much effect on him. If he really wanted the promotion but is denying it, he will probably feel numbness in the short run and tension and stress in the long run.

The theory behind rational-emotive therapy is not new. In the first century A.D., the Greek philosopher Epictetus explained: "People feel disturbed not by things, but by the views they take of them" (cited in Ellis & Harper, 1975, p. 33). And William Shakespeare wrote in *Hamlet:* "There is nothing either good or bad, but thinking makes it so" (act II, scene 2).

Recognizing Irrational Appraisals

Primary appraisals are a product of our belief system. If we demand that others be perfect, we will be disappointed when they're not. If we insist on unconditional attention from someone, we will be hurt and angry when it is not forthcoming. Ellis shows us that people can learn to recognize when they are making irrational appraisals and that they can take steps to correct them. Consider the following appraisals (Ellis, 1962; Ellis & Harper, 1975):

"People who are important to me should always love me."
"People should never treat me wrong and they are bad people if they do."
"It's awful when things are not the way I want them to be."
"When things are uncertain I have to keep worrying about them."
"I must achieve success at all times."

Ellis points out that these appraisals are irrational because they are not realistic and are bound to result in negative experiences. Irrational appraisals tend to be absolute.

They can be recognized by their "shoulds," "musts," and insistence on perfection. The following irrational beliefs were identified in a series of research studies (Lohr, Hamberger, & Bonge, 1988).

Demand for approval: "I must be approved of and loved by all significant people in my life."

High self-expectations: "I must be thoroughly competent and adequate in all respects if I am to be worthwhile."

Blame-proneness: "If I (or others) am bad, wicked, or ignorant, then I (or others) should be blamed."

Emotional helplessness: "My unhappiness is caused by others or situations, and I have little or no ability to control my unhappiness."

Anxious overconcern: "If there's a chance that something dangerous or fearsome might happen, I should worry about it."

Problem avoidance: "It's easier to avoid than face certain difficulties and responsibilities."

Dependency: "I need someone stronger than myself to rely on."

Helplessness: "My past is an all-important determinant of my present behavior, and if something once strongly affected me, it will always affect me."

People who insist on these beliefs have problems in their lives because it is difficult for them to achieve satisfaction.

By learning to make more reasonable appraisals, we can moderate some of our negative emotions and reduce our stress. For example, assume that a woman's husband leaves her. How she manages this life event depends on her choice of one of the following kinds of appraisals:

"He is all that counts in my life. My life is worthless without him." (Depression)

"I can't bear to have him leave me. I can't stand being without him." (Desperation, panic)

"How can he do this to me? How could he be so thoughtless and irresponsible!" (Hurt, anger)

Any of these appraisals is likely to result in undue stress and suffering. The goal of rational-emotive therapy would be to help the rejected woman "tone down" her reactions by making a more adaptive assessment, such as:

"It hurts to have him leave me and I'll really miss him. But the pain of breaking up is part of life. Right now I can only feel sadness, but in time I'll be grateful for the life we had together and then I'll be ready to find someone new." (Sadness, hope)

Recognizing Maladaptive Schemas

Another way to understand irrational appraisals is by studying *maladaptive schemas* (Young, 1989). Schemas are patterns of thinking that determine how we perceive ourselves in relation to others around us. What kinds of roles do we play with others? Do we sometimes adopt beliefs about our interpersonal relations that are not in our best interest? All of the schemas described in Table 2.1 have disadvantages, and people who use them would benefit by giving them up.

TABLE 2.1   Maladaptive Schemas
••

A. Autonomy
    1. Dependence
       a. Definition: Belief that one is unable to function on one's own and needs the constant support of others.
       b. Possible thoughts: "I can't function on my own." "I need someone else to help me." "I can't support myself."
       c. Potential problems: Being passive, alienating others, underachieving.
    2. Subjugation/lack of individuation
       a. Definition: The voluntary or involuntary sacrifice of one's own needs to satisfy others' needs, with an accompanying failure to recognize one's own needs.
       b. Possible thoughts: "If I do what I want, something bad will happen." "I must sacrifice myself for others." "My needs are not as important as those of others."
       c. Potential problems: Feeling stressed and worn out. Inner feelings of deprivation and anger.
    3. Vulnerability to harm or illness
       a. Definition: The fear that disaster is about to strike at any time.
       b. Possible thoughts: "Something terrible will happen to me." "I worry about things going wrong." "I feel anxious and fearful."
       c. Potential problems: Anxiety, panic, hypertension.
    4. Fear of losing control
       a. Definition: The fear that one will involuntarily lose control of one's own behavior, impulses, emotions, mind, body, and so on.
       b. Possible thoughts: "I'm losing control." "I can't control myself." "Am I becoming unbalanced?"
       c. Potential problems: Anxiety and tension or rigidity and overcontrol.
B. Connectedness
    5. Emotional deprivation
       a. Definition: The expectation that one's needs for nurturance, empathy, affection, and caring will never be adequately met by others.
       b. Possible thoughts: "No one is ever there to meet my needs." "I don't get enough love and attention." "No one really cares about me."
       c. Potential problems: Anger, resentment, manipulativeness.
    6. Abandonment/loss
       a. Definition: The fear that one will imminently lose significant others and then be emotionally isolated forever.
       b. Possible thoughts: "I'll be alone forever." "No one will be there for me." "I will be abandoned."
       c. Potential problems: Loneliness, fear of making commitments.
    7. Mistrust
       a. Definition: The expectation that others will willfully hurt, abuse, cheat, lie, manipulate, or take advantage of one.
       b. Possible thoughts: "People will hurt me, attack me, put me down." "I must protect myself." "I'll attack them before they get me."
       c. Potential problems: Hostility, mistrust, aggressiveness.
    8. Social isolation/alienation
       a. Definition: The feeling that one is isolated from the rest of the world, different from other people, and not a part of any group or community.

(continued)

TABLE 2.1   *(continued)*

  b. Possible thoughts: "I don't fit in." "I'm different." "No one understands me."
  c. Potential problems: Isolation, loneliness.

C. Worthiness

  9. Defectiveness/unlovability
  a. Definition: The feeling that one is inwardly defective and flawed, that one is fundamentally unlovable.
  b. Possible thoughts: "No man/woman I desire will ever love me." "No one would want to stay close to me." "There's something inherently flawed and defective in me."
  c. Potential problems: Depression, low self-esteem.

  10. Social undesirability
  a. Definition: The belief that one is outwardly undesirable to others.
  b. Possible thoughts: "I'm a social outcast." "People don't like me." "I'm fat, I'm ugly, I'm boring."
  c. Potential problems: Loneliness, depression, low self-esteem.

  11. Incompetence/failure
  a. Definition: The belief that one cannot perform competently in areas of achievement, daily responsibilities, decision making.
  b. Possible thoughts: "Nothing I do is ever good enough." "I'm incompetent." "I screw up everything I try."
  c. Potential problems: Underachievement, rigidity, low self-esteem.

  12. Guilt/punishment
  a. Definition: The belief that one is morally or ethically bad or irresponsible and deserves harsh criticism or punishment.
  b. Possible thoughts: "I'm a bad person." "I deserve to be punished." "I don't deserve pleasure or happiness."
  c. Potential problems: Depression, low self-esteem.

  13. Shame/Embarrassment
  a. Definition: Recurrent feelings of shame or self-consciousness.
  b. Possible thoughts: "I'm humiliated by my own failure and inadequacy." "I am too inferior to get close to someone." "If others found out about my defects, I couldn't face them."
  c. Potential problems: Anxiety, self-consciousness, low self-esteem.

D. Limits and standards

  14. Unrelenting standards
  a. Definition: The relentless striving to meet extremely high expectations of oneself, at the expense of happiness, pleasure, sense of accomplishment, or satisfying relationships.
  b. Possible thoughts: "I must be the best." "I must be perfect." "I have to work harder."
  c. Potential problems: Hypertension, isolation.

  15. Entitlement/insufficient limits
  a. Definition: The insistence that one be able to do, say, or have whatever one wants immediately.
  b. Possible thoughts: "I should always get what I want." "I'm special and shouldn't have to accept restrictions placed on others." "I deserve immediate satisfaction."
  c. Potential problems: Impulsiveness, anger, alienation.

Changing maladaptive schemas is not always easy, especially if we have been using them for a long time. It is often necessary to treat these schemas as enemies that must be fought with a more realistic outlook on life. Some strategies for overcoming maladaptive schemas are suggested below (McMullin, 1986).

Counters

Counters are things we can say to ourself to avoid focusing on beliefs that are not in our best interest. Sometimes a counter can be a single word: "Nonsense!" "That's silly!" "Not true!" "Stop!" Or we can use a full sentence: "I don't need to be perfect as long as I do my best." "It is not realistic to expect everyone to love me." "Sometimes people don't treat me right, but that doesn't mean everyone is out to get me."

Alternative Interpretation

Maladaptive schemas often cause faulty interpretations of life events. It's useful to question our perceptions, particularly when facing stress and challenge. Here are some examples.

1. A man is not hired for a job he really wants.
   a. *Maladaptive interpretations*
      "I'm not worthy of the job. I'm no good."
      "Those people are unfair. They were out to get me."
   b. *Alternative interpretations*
      "There was tremendous competition and only one opening."
      "My qualifications are good, but someone else fit their needs more closely."
2. A woman is depressed over a recent personal loss.
   a. *Maladaptive interpretation*
      "I'm a weak person to let this bother me so much."
      "I'll never feel better."
      "Something is wrong with me."
   b. *Alternative interpretations*
      "It's natural to feel this way under the circumstances."
      "I need to give myself a break."
3. Someone treats you rudely.
   a. *Maladaptive interpretations*
      "I'm no good. I deserve being treated badly."
      "That person is rotten and deserves to be punished."
      "Everybody hates me."
   b. *Alternative interpretations*
      "That person was probably in a bad mood."
      "If people are nasty, that's their problem."
      "I know how to be tactful with all kinds of people."

Recognizing Worst-Case Scenarios

We all sometimes blow things out of proportion and make them seem much worse than they really are. When this happens, we need to take a reality check by asking,

"What's the worst thing that could happen?" This can be done by rating difficult life events from 1 to 10. Consider the low end (1 up) those events that you consider unpleasant but that you know you would survive. The other end of the scale would be events that you feel would be the end of the world. You want to use your coping skills to get your rating down to 5 or less.

Relabeling

R. E. McMullin (1986, pp. 26–27) suggests how we can gain a more adaptive outlook with the technique of relabeling. For example:

A person who . . .	could be called . . .	or could be called . . .
changes his or her mind a lot	wishy-washy	flexible
isn't orderly	sloppy, piggish	spontaneous, carefree
gets anxious	weak, cowardly	self-protective
is emotionally sensitive	sick, fragile	caring
isn't good at a task	stupid, inferior	hasn't practiced
pleases others	passive	likable
believes what others say	gullible	trusting
takes risks	impulsive	brave
gets excited	hysterical	exuberant
sticks to projects	compulsive	determined
gets depressed sometimes	neurotic	normal human being
is sure of something	conceited	self-confident
expresses one's opinion	egotistical	honest, assertive

Other useful strategies for maladaptive schemas include humor and talking ourself through challenges. These strategies are described in Chapter 3.

Making Rational Appraisals

One goal of rational-emotive therapy is to teach people to identify the consequences of their appraisals and to convince them to alter their appraisals for the sake of more livable consequences. Another approach is to have people practice adaptive appraisals *before* they are confronted with life challenges. Think of the last time you were interviewed for a job. What did you say to yourself during the interview? How would you have felt if you responded to the interview with the following sorts of negative appraisals:

"I can't think of a thing to say."
"I'm being humiliated."
"The interviewer doesn't like me."
"I sound like I don't know what I'm talking about."
"I'm freezing up."

Compare the consequences of the above negative appraisals with the consequences of the following positive appraisals:

"This is a job I want and my attitude shows it."
"I would be really good at this job."
"This place needs someone like me."
"I'm dressed right and well prepared for this interview."
"Having a job interview is a good experience for me."

Researchers have found that people who experience low levels of anxiety about job interviews have more positive appraisals and fewer negative appraisals than job interviewees who are very anxious (Heimberg, Keller, & Peca-Baker, 1986). The following chapters of this book suggest many situations where it will be useful to practice adaptive appraisals.

A third way to manage the process of primary appraisal (see Figure 2.2) is to alter our life events. Later in this book you will learn how to gain more control over your life by developing social skills, assertiveness, and strategies for negotiation. Remember, however, that there are many occasions when we can't control life events and must rely on making realistic, rational, and adaptive appraisals.

SECONDARY APPRAISAL

Secondary appraisal occurs when we ask ourselves if there is anything we can do about a life event we have appraised as stressful. The process of secondary appraisal depends to a large degree on our sense of competence, mastery, and self-esteem.

Check how much you agree or disagree with the following statements.

	Strongly agree	*Agree*	*Disagree*	*Strongly disagree*
1. I believe my problem is controllable.	____	____	____	____
2. There is something that can be done about my problem.	____	____	____	____
3. My problem is very important to me.	____	____	____	____
4. My problem is really not a big deal.	____	____	____	____
5. I am quite familiar with these kinds of problems.	____	____	____	____
6. My problem is something new to me.	____	____	____	____
7. I believe my problem is only temporary.	____	____	____	____
8. My problem will not go away.	____	____	____	____
9. My problem is not the result of anything I did.	____	____	____	____
10. My actions contributed to my problems.	____	____	____	____

	Strongly agree	Agree	Disagree	Strongly disagree
11. I know the course the problem will follow.	____	____	____	____
12. My problem is unpredictable.	____	____	____	____

These statements come from the Appraisal Dimensions Scale (Vitaliano, 1988). This scale measures six kinds of secondary appraisals:

Control: Statements 1 and 2. How much control do you feel you have over the problem?

Importance: Statements 3 and 4. How important is this problem? How much does it concern you?

Novelty: Statements 5 and 6. Have you experienced this kind of problem in the past or is it new to you?

Duration: Statements 7 and 8. Is the problem short-lived or something that will last a long time?

Causality: Statements 9 and 10. Did you cause the problem or did it result for other reasons?

Predictability: Statements 11 and 12. Can you predict the outcome of the problem?

As indicated in Figure 2.1, if we feel incompetent and helpless when facing a threat or challenge, we are not likely to come up with a suitable coping response. Our sense of competence and mastery is a product of our knowledge and experience in dealing with similar stresses in the past. It is also a state of mind. Two people with the same knowledge and experience can differ widely in their feelings of competence. Why is this so? To understand the secondary appraisal process more completely, it will be useful to learn about the concept of *self-efficacy,* which was defined by Albert Bandura (Bandura, 1977; Bandura, Adams, & Beyer, 1977). Self-efficacy is a useful concept because it explains how our ability to adapt to life events is determined by our thoughts and our actions.

SELF-EFFICACY

Measuring Self-Efficacy

Check how much the following statements apply to you.

	Strongly agree	Agree	Disagree	Strongly disagree
1. If I can't do a job the first time, I keep trying until I can.	____	____	____	____
2. When I set important goals for myself, I rarely achieve them.	____	____	____	____
3. I give up easily.	____	____	____	____

	Strongly agree	Agree	Disagree	Strongly disagree
4. When I have something unpleasant to do, I stick to it until I finish it.	____	____	____	____
5. If something looks too complicated, I will not even bother to try it.	____	____	____	____
6. It is difficult for me to make new friends.	____	____	____	____
7. I have acquired my friends through my personal abilities at making friends.	____	____	____	____
8. If I see someone I would like to meet, I go to that person instead of waiting for him or her to come to me.	____	____	____	____

These statements come from the Self-Efficacy Scale (Scherer & Adams, 1983; Scherer et al., 1982). People with high self-efficacy tend to agree with statements 1, 4, 7, and 8 and to disagree with statements 2, 3, 5, and 6. Statements 1 through 5 measure general self-efficacy and statements 6 through 8 measure self-efficacy in social interactions. People with high scores on self-efficacy are more assertive and outgoing and have higher self-esteem and a greater sense of control over their lives. High self-efficacy is also related to job success and educational achievement.

Developing Self-Efficacy

Self-efficacy refers to our expectations and confidence that the responses we make to life challenges can have a meaningful effect. People with strong feelings of efficacy face life challenges with energy and persistence. They keep trying new alternatives until they succeed or at least survive.

How does self-efficacy develop? Why do some people have greater self-efficacy than others? Self-efficacy comes from life experiences and from people who serve as significant models (Bandura, 1977). That is, we develop self-efficacy by observing how other people deal successfully with life challenges and by the kinds of teaching and support we received as we were growing up. Self-efficacy is built up by responding to life challenges with *action, flexibility,* and *persistence:* Action is essential because we learn best by doing. Flexibility encourages us to try new alternatives and to avoid getting stuck. We might not always succeed, but persistence will give us an attitude of survival.

How can we increase the self-efficacy we bring to our lives? Research by Bandura and his colleagues provides the following suggestions (Andersen & Williams, 1985; Bandura, 1977, 1989):

1. Live a life of goals. We can't develop self-efficacy unless we succeed at things and we can't succeed if we don't have goals. Make it a practice to have goals and give yourself credit when you achieve them.

2. Set goals with reasonable standards. They should be challenging enough to provide a feeling of satisfaction, but also realistic so we can reach them.
3. Seek out good role models. Role models don't have to be people we personally know. But they should be people who inspire a life attitude of competence and mastery.
4. Talk to yourself in a positive manner. If you are self-conscious about talking to yourself out loud, talk to yourself silently. Take time to "psych yourself up" and to think over good experiences and past successes.
5. Remember that success in reaching goals and overcoming life challenges depends on our willingness to exert sufficient energy and effort. Athletes are well aware of this rule when they say, "Winning depends on how much you want it."

COPING

We have learned that coping involves keeping our composure when faced with life challenges and working out an appropriate course of action. We also learned that there are no guaranteed coping responses that can be applied in all situations. Coping is a process where we use flexibility to respond with skills and strategies that best fit the demands of the situation. In Chapter 3 we will be introduced to eight coping strategies: using support systems, problem solving, self-relaxation, maintaining internal control, talking ourselves through challenges, using our sense of humor, exercising, and rewarding ourselves for accomplishments. These coping skills should be in everyone's coping arsenal. The remainder of this book focuses on specific life events that are potentially stressful in many people's lives. The knowledge we gain will help us to develop some useful strategies for holding our own when faced with these challenges, to feel good about ourselves, and to make the challenge part of a growth-producing life experience.

SUGGESTIONS FOR FURTHER READING

ELLIS, A., & HARPER, R. A. (1975). *A new guide to rational living*. Englewood Cliffs, N.J.: Prentice-Hall.
MCMULLIN, R. E. (1986). *Handbook of cognitive therapy techniques*. New York: Norton.

3

Eight Skills
to Add to Your
Coping Arsenal

In this chapter you will learn how to use eight skills that should be added to your coping arsenal and practiced for the rest of your life. These coping skills include using support systems, problem solving, self-relaxation, maintaining internal control, talking yourself through challenges, developing your sense of humor, exercising, and rewarding yourself for accomplishments.

USING SUPPORT SYSTEMS

One coping skill neglected by many people is the constructive use of a support system. You can test your support system by answering the following questions.

1. Are there people you can really count on to listen to you when you need to talk? If so, list their names.
2. Are there people you can really talk with frankly, without having to watch what you say? If so, list their names.
3. Are there people you can really count on to be dependable when you need help? If so, list their names.
4. Are there people who really appreciate you as a person? If so, list their names.
5. Are there people you can really count on to care about you, regardless of what is happening to you? If so, list their names.
6. Are there people you can really count on to support you in major decisions you make? If so, list their names.

These questions come from the Social Support Questionnaire (Sarason, I. G., Levine, Basham, & Sarason, 1983). The Social Support Questionnaire is scored by tabulating the *number* of support people available for each problem. A second social support score is derived by rating how *satisfied* people are with their support systems for each problem. Research indicates that people with a good social support system are less depressed and anxious and more optimistic about their lives than those with a poor social support system. Other studies show that people with a good support system are more successful at overcoming depression, adapting to injuries resulting in physical disability, maintaining self-esteem, and overcoming loneliness. There is also evidence that people with a good support system suffer fewer health complaints (Billings & Moos, 1985; Cohen, D. R., Sherrod, & Clark, 1986; Cohen, S., & Syme, 1985; Schultz & Decker, 1985).

A social support system satisfies our needs for nurturance and attachment, relieves stress, and bolsters our sense of self-worth, trust, and life-direction. In general, a social support system satisfies the following needs (Schaefer, Coyne, & Lazarus, 1981; Weiss, 1974):

Emotional support: This kind of support is useful when we need someone to confide in; when we seek reassurance that we are loved and cared about; when we want someone to lean on.

Tangible support: This kind of support is useful when we need assistance with a job or a chore; when we require aid, a gift, or a loan; when there is a problem we can't handle on our own.

Informational support: This kind of support is useful when we need information or advice; when some feedback will help us with a problem or challenge.

Social support systems are helpful in many ways. First, we can rely on support people for direct assistance in times of trouble. Second, the knowledge that we have a good support system provides a psychological boost when we most need it. When things are tough, we can take consolation in the fact that people care about us. Third, a social support system helps us feel accepted, loved, and valued. This security provides self-confidence when facing life challenges (Sarason, B. R., Shearin, Pierce, & Sarason, 1987). Finally, a social support system can provide companionship to make our lives more enjoyable (Rook, 1987).

How can we add an effective support system to our coping arsenal? Several points must be considered. First of all, it is important to understand that a strong support system has little to do with the number of people we know and a lot to do with developing special relationships that make us feel someone knows us and cares about us (Wethington & Kessler, 1986). Having a good support system is not related to being sociable and having many acquaintances. People who like to spend time alone can also have an effective support system to use when they need it.

A second fact is that building a good support system is a coping skill because it requires personal effort. It is not very effective to wait until others figure out we need their support. We must be willing to take the initiative. In the following statements, check the alternative that best describes what you would do in the situation described.

1. You are failing at a difficult task. Do you:
   a. Find someone who can teach you how to do it better?
   b. Keep working on your own?
2. When you are feeling lonely, do you call someone on the telephone to talk?
   a. Yes, I do call.
   b. No, I don't call.
3. If you are troubled by a personal problem, do you:
   a. Keep it to yourself?
   b. Discuss it with someone?
4. You need some important information. Do you:
   a. Look for it on your own?
   b. Ask someone for assistance?
5. After placing an order at a local sandwich shop, you realize you are 25 cents short. Do you:
   a. Cancel your order?
   b. Ask someone if you could borrow 25 cents?
6. You have to fill out some confusing, official forms. Do you:
   a. Try to find someone who can help you?
   b. Work your way through them as best as you can?
7. If you think you did badly on a project, do you:
   a. Wait and see how you did?
   b. Ask someone knowledgeable about it to give you feedback?
8. You are unsure about your career goals. Do you:
   a. Try to figure them out on your own?
   b. Seek someone who can help you clarify your goals?

These statements come from the SEEK Scale which was developed to measure how actively people seek social support (Conn & Peterson, 1989). Those who are most willing to seek support choose alternative *a* for statements 1, 2, and 6 and alternative *b* for statements 3, 4, 5, 7, and 8. It is a mistake to view the use of social support systems as a sign of weakness. Willingness to seek support from others when we need it actually gives us an increased feeling of competence and self-esteem, because we are taking action rather than passively waiting for things to get better.

Health Care Professionals

Of course, we want our support people to have a positive effect on our lives by providing support, setting a good example, remaining calm, being reliable, and not making unreasonable demands (Suls, 1982). If it turns out that friends and family members are not able to provide the support we need, it is wise to seek help from *health care professionals.* The value of health care professionals is that they are in a position to provide support without being emotionally drained. It is unfortunate that many people don't appreciate the fact that gaining support from health care professionals is a coping skill and not a sign of weakness (Sibicky & Dovidio, 1986). These professionals can offer the following kinds of assistance (Wills, 1987):

1. *Enhancing self-esteem.* The warmth, rapport, and sharing that take place when we work with a trained professional is a real morale booster. A good way to increase self-esteem is to take an active role in solving problems with the support of a person we trust.

2. *Maintaining self-confidence and motivation.* In order to confront life challenges it is necessary to maintain your confidence and motivation. A health care professional can give encouragement when we feel like giving up. Even though things may seem very discouraging at the moment, support from a professional will instill a feeling of confidence that we will find the best solution.

3. *Rational thinking.* A good deal of this book is devoted to the importance of rational thinking. Sometimes we need a trained professional to help us analyze our perceptions and expectations in an objective manner. Are we telling ourself things that are not in our best interest? Would some challenges in our life go more smoothly if we talked to ourself in a different way?

Another major focus of this book is on the value of learning new coping skills. Health care professionals are teachers. They can help us increase our options when responding to difficult challenges.

PROBLEM SOLVING

Check how much you agree or disagree with the following statements:

	Strongly agree	Agree	Disagree	Strongly disagree
1. I trust my ability to solve new and difficult problems.	____	____	____	____

	Strongly agree	*Agree*	*Disagree*	*Strongly disagree*
2. Given enough time and effort, I believe I can solve most problems that confront me.	___	___	___	___
3. Many problems I face are too complex to solve.	___	___	___	___
4. I make decisions and am happy with them later.	___	___	___	___
5. When confronted with a problem, I am unsure of whether I can handle the situation.	___	___	___	___
6. I have the ability to solve most problems even though no solution is immediately available.	___	___	___	___

The above statements come from the Problem Solving Inventory (Heppner & Peterson, 1982). If you agreed with statements 1, 2, 4, and 6 and disagreed with statements 3 and 5, you have relatively high confidence in your problem-solving ability. But, no matter how high your problem-solving confidence is at the present time, there is a good chance you will raise it after reading this chapter.

Problem solving is the procedure we follow when developing plans for respond-ing to life challenges. It is a practical coping skill, but it is also useful psychologically. The practice of good problem solving is a confidence builder. Our sense of com-petence and mastery is bolstered when we know we have problem-solving skills at our disposal. Research studies have found that good problem solvers accept the fact that overcoming life challenges requires personal effort (Baumgardner, Heppner, & Arkin, 1986).

There are five stages of problem solving: self-perception, defining the problem, listing options, decision making, and testing (D'Zurilla & Nezu, 1982; Goldfried & Davison, 1976):

1. *Self-perception.* The first step in successful problem solving is developing the self-perception that we are a problem solver. Problem solvers realize that problem situations are part of life, and they are in touch with the fact that it is important to face such challenges calmly and rationally and not impulsively. To develop a problem-solving orientation, we have to be able to say to ourselves: "Part of life involves facing problems and hardships. When I'm in trouble I know that I have to remain calm and rely on my problem-solving skills to decide on the best possible course of action."

2. *Defining the problem.* The first thing to do when faced with a threat or challenge is to understand exactly what is happening. Take some time to figure out the critical issues and conflicts. Then make a list of goals. This is a stage in problem solving when support people can be helpful by encouraging us to take an objective view and see all sides of the problem.

3. *Listing options.* This is the stage where we define plan A, plan B, and plan C. To develop good plans we have to remain open-minded. Before deciding on a

course of action, so it is important to consider *all* alternatives. Write down every possible plan—the more the better. Be creative. We need to come up with as many plans as possible so we will have plenty of ideas to work with. Again, support people can help us brainstorm and avoid getting stuck on one track.

4. *Decision making.* If we have taken sufficient time to define the problem and generate many alternatives, we are ready to decide on a course of action. The decision-making stage is much easier when we have a full grasp on the issues facing us and a flexible list of options. Run through the possible responses. Which are the most feasible? Which are most likely to get us what we want without causing other problems? After choosing the most appropriate response it is always good to anticipate the possible outcomes. Remember, in most situations there is not one "correct" course of action. Responses to life challenges have drawbacks as well as advantages. We have to be flexible and have alternative plans if our first decision does not work out.

5. *Testing.* If our first course of action achieves success, great! If not, it is time to work through the stages of problem solving again. Have we defined the problem correctly? Did we consider all possible alternatives? We need to open ourselves to all options—always keeping in mind that we are a problem solver.

SELF-RELAXATION

Since prehistoric times, humans have learned to face threats and challenges with the *fight-or-flight* response. The fight-or-flight response was described in the early twentieth century by a famous physiologist of that time, Walter B. Cannon (1929). Cannon explained how humans learned to protect themselves by reacting with increased adrenalin, muscle tension, and blood flow so they could more energetically battle their adversaries or more quickly flee when faced with overwhelming danger. The fight-or-flight response was very useful during early human history because fighting or fleeing were the most adaptive responses to the kinds of threats people faced. In modern times the fight-or-flight response has lost much of its utility because the hassles and challenges that confront us now are often psychological. For example, while the fight-or-flight response might be adaptive for hunting and physical survival, it is not an appropriate method for coping with traffic jams, pollution, and interpersonal conflicts. If humans still inhabit the earth a million years from now, they very well may develop a natural relaxation response to daily frustrations and hassles. In the meantime, it is well worth our time to master the relaxation response. Fortunately, this response is not difficult to learn. It mainly requires patience and practice. Begin mastering self-relaxation as a coping skill by following the instructions suggested below. As you go along, you may wish to modify these statements to fit your individual tastes and needs.

Instructions for Self-Relaxation

Find a comfortable sitting or lying position. Take several slow, deep breaths. Feel the oxygen as it fills your lungs. Make your breathing slow and relaxed. Deep, slow breaths. Say to yourself, "Breathe deeply . . . hold . . . exhale." Let your mind rest. Put all of your thoughts and worries aside. There is plenty of time to attend to them later. This time is for you. If any distractions occur, let them pass. Just breathe deeply and slowly. As you continue to take slow, deep breaths, concentrate on your legs. Stiffen the muscles in your legs, either separately or one at a time. Hold the tenseness for several seconds, and then relax. Let all the tension out of your muscles. As your leg muscles loosen you will feel warmth as the blood in your legs flows more freely. As you alternate tensing and relaxing your leg muscles you will learn to appreciate the difference between muscles that are tense and those that are relaxed. We all spend much of our days with tense muscles without even realizing it. This exercise will help you get in touch with your body so you can learn how to control it better. After tensing and relaxing your leg muscles several times, let your legs completely relax. Allow all of the tension to go out of your muscles. Let the blood in your legs flow freely. Feel your legs as they get warmer and very comfortable. Imagine that your legs are floating in some nice warm water. You can hardly feel them because they are so comfortable and light.

Now focus on your arms and hands. Tense your hands, either together or one at a time. Then let them relax. Do the same with your arms. Learn to recognize the difference between tense and relaxed muscles in your arms and hands. After tensing and relaxing your hands and arms several times, let all the tenseness go out of them. Allow your hands and arms to get loose. As you release all of the tension in your arm and hand muscles you will feel the blood flow more freely. Your hands and arms will feel warmer, relaxed, and comfortable, like they are floating, weightless, in nice warm water.

Focus now on your neck and shoulders. Lift your shoulders and make your shoulder and neck muscles tense. You can see that if you did this for very long you would end up with a stiff neck and backache. This is what happens sometimes when we spend the day tense and uptight without even realizing it. Relax the muscles in your shoulders and neck to become aware of the difference between tense and relaxed muscles. Try tensing and relaxing several times so you can learn how to recognize tenseness. Learning how to recognize tenseness is a valuable skill because it tells us when to put our relaxation exercise into effect. Now let all of the tension out of your neck and shoulder muscles. Say to yourself, "Relax . . . relax." Feel the muscles in your neck and shoulders get looser and looser and appreciate the warm and relaxed sensation as the blood flows freely. Your neck and shoulders are getting more and more relaxed. You are floating on a cloud through the sky. There is no pressure on your neck and shoulders. Only a feeling of pure comfort.

Continue breathing deeply and slowly. Take slow, deep breaths. Let the oxygen flow into your body, replenishing your blood cells as you practice your self-relaxation exercise. Continue your slow, deep breathing. Now focus on the muscles in your face. Tighten your jaw muscles. You may be surprised to feel how strong these muscles are. Learn to recognize the difference between tight and loose jaw muscles. Close your eyes tightly and make a strong grimace. Compare the tension when you do this with your facial muscles when they are relaxed. You can easily tell that if you went through your day with tenseness in your facial muscles you would end up with a tension headache. Now let the muscles in your face get completely relaxed. Feel the blood flow into your face as it begins to get warm and comfortable.

Continue breathing deeply and slowly. While you were concentrating on your neck and shoulder muscles and facial muscles you probably forgot completely about your legs and arms. Your legs and arms are now so relaxed they hardly feel like part of your body. You know they exist, but you are allowing them to be so relaxed that you barely feel them. You are floating on a cloud through the sky. You are lying on a beautiful beach in the warm sun. You are relaxing in the mountains by a refreshing waterfall. Self-relaxation is a skill to use to do something good for yourself. It is your time to take a break from life's hassles. It is your time to find peace within yourself, to let your body do its miraculous work. As you breathe deeply and slowly, you are helping oxygen come into your blood. Your heart is working at a relaxed pace, pumping the enriched blood through your body. You can take time in your relaxed state to appreciate the inner workings of your body and the value of your relaxation skill for helping you put yourself in a positive state of being. Breathe slowly and deeply. Let all of your muscles get more and more relaxed as you float on a cloud to your favorite place and take some time to be alone with yourself, far away from everything else in the world.

The relaxation response is made up of three components: environment, body, and mind (Benson, 1976; Jacobson, E., 1938; Wolpe, 1969):

1. *Environment.* The relaxation response is easiest to learn in a quiet environment. You want to place yourself in a comfortable posture in a place where there aren't too many distractions. As you improve your relaxation skills though, you will find that you can relax even in distracting places.

2. *Body.* When we practice relaxation, our bodies slow down. Our breathing and blood pressure decrease, our heart beats more slowly, and our muscles are less tense. How can you get your body to respond this way? A good place to start is by slowing your breathing. Breathe deeply and slowly, hold, and exhale. Repeat this process for 5 minutes. Breathing deeply and slowly gets oxygen into your body with greater efficiency. When we are anxious and under stress we tend to take quick, shallow breaths. Breathing is a crucial part of living. Yet we pay little attention to how efficiently we are breathing most of the time. After a few moments of slow, deep breathing, you will begin to feel more relaxed.

A second way to teach your body to relax is to get in touch with your muscles as in the self-relaxation procedure described above.

3. *Mind.* We can apply our mind power to relaxation in several ways. The relaxation response is enhanced when we distract ourselves from daily thoughts and move into a relaxing frame of mind. One aid to distraction is repeating a word or phrase as we relax. In Transcendental Meditation this is called a mantra. Herbert Benson (1976) suggests repeating the word "one" to yourself as you go through your relaxation exercise. I often like to say to myself, "Relax . . . relax." You can also use your mind creatively by practicing relaxing imagery. As you work on deep breathing and muscle relaxation, imagine you are in a special place, such as by a cool waterfall, on a warm beach near the ocean, or in a peaceful meadow. Use your mind power to enhance your feelings of peacefulness. Take your thoughts far away from your daily world.

Another way to apply your thinking process to relaxation is to suspend all judgment about how well you are doing. As you relax you are bound to be distracted from time to time by outside sounds or unpleasant thoughts. Be easy on yourself when this happens. Just let the distracting sounds or thoughts pass and allow yourself to fall back into relaxation. The relaxation response requires an accepting attitude. Remind yourself to breath deeply and slowly, to relax your muscles, and see yourself again floating on a cloud to your special place, far removed from the activities of the world around you.

Even though the relaxation response is not automatic like the fight-or-flight response, it has been practiced by people for thousands of years. The important thing to remember is that relaxation is a skill that is learned through patience and practice.

MAINTAINING INTERNAL CONTROL

Check whether you agree or disagree with the following statements:

	Strongly agree	Agree	Disagree	Strongly disagree
1. I have little control over the things that happen to me.	____	____	____	____
2. There is really no way I can solve some of the problems I have.	____	____	____	____
3. There is little I can do to change many of the important things in my life.	____	____	____	____
4. I often feel helpless in dealing with the problems of life.	____	____	____	____
5. What happens to me mostly depends on me.	____	____	____	____
6. I can do just about anything I really set my mind to do.	____	____	____	____

If you disagreed with statements 1, 2, 3, and 4 and agreed with statements 5 and 6, you have a sense of mastery and control over your life. Researchers have found that people with strong feelings of mastery suffer fewer symptoms of physical and psychological stress than those who feel much of their life is beyond their control (Folkman, Lazarus, Gruen, & DeLongis, 1986; Pearlin & Schooler, 1978).

The observation that people differ in their perceptions of how much control they have over their lives has been of interest to psychologists for many years. People who take responsibility for things that happen to them are called "internals" because they have an internal locus of control. Those who believe that most of what happens to them is beyond their control are called "externals" because they have an external locus of control. It is important to point out that we are not born as internals or externals. Our locus of control develops according to our learning and experiences as we grow up. Even more important is the fact that because locus of control is based on life perceptions it can be reevaluated and changed.

There are many areas in life where it is adaptive to have an internal locus of control. For example, internals often achieve more than externals because they react less negatively to failure and derive more personal satisfaction from success. Internals are also more independent. Internals take more responsibility for events in their lives and for their mental and physical health (Lefcourt, 1976; Phares, 1976). Internals tend to hold the following beliefs (Rotter, 1966):

> In the long run people get the respect they deserve in this world.
> Becoming a success is a matter of hard work, luck has little to do with it.
> People's misfortunes result from the mistakes they make.
> People who can't get others to like them don't understand how to get along with others.
> People are lonely because they don't try to be friendly.
> There is a direct connection between how hard I study and the grades I get.

Externals tend to hold the following beliefs (Rotter, 1966):

> Unfortunately, an individual's worth often passes unrecognized no matter how hard he or she tries.
> Getting a good job depends mainly on being in the right place at the right time.
> Many of the unhappy things in people's lives are partly due to bad luck.
> No matter how hard you try some people just don't like you.
> There's not much use in trying too hard to please people, if they like you, they like you.
> Sometimes I can't understand how teachers arrive at the grades they give.

If you look back at the definition of coping in Chapter 1, you can appreciate the value of an internal locus of control. Coping involves planning, problem solving, and learning and practicing new skills. It is based on an attitude of self-responsibility and active mastery over one's life.

Although developing an internal locus of control is a useful goal, we don't want to push ourselves past reality. There are many events in the world we can't control and it would be foolish to think otherwise. It doesn't serve a useful purpose to blame ourselves for accidents, disasters, or even minor frustrations for which we are not responsible. We often have to live with life events we would like to control but can't. When this happens our best course of action is to accept these life events as reality and use our internal locus of control to come up with the most adaptive ways to adjust to them.

TALKING OURSELVES THROUGH CHALLENGES

As human beings, we all have a special ability to talk to ourselves. Whether we talk to ourself out loud or silently, we can use this ability to coach ourself through difficult challenges. Although you probably talk to yourself during difficult situations already, there are three techniques that will help you do this more effectively. These techniques include preparing for the challenge, confronting the challenge, and reflecting on what you learned (Meichenbaum, 1977, 1985).

Preparing for the Challenge

We can prepare for a challenge by talking to ourself in a way that will increase our feelings of control over the situation. We can use our problem-solving skills to plan how we will get through this challenge. We need to think in terms of how we will cope and what we will gain from this experience, even though it may be stressful. We can plan effective ways to utilize our support systems. And we need to stop ourselves from blowing things out of proportion and suffering before the challenge really happens. It helps to make a list of coping statements such as the ones below:

It won't help to sit and worry about it.
I will not upset myself.
I will use my problem-solving skills to make a plan.
It might not be fun, but I can handle it.
It will be a good learning experience.
I'm feeling anxious, but that is natural.
I can use my self-relaxation skills while I plan my strategy.

We can also prepare for a challenge by going over what it will be like in our minds. Picture yourself going through the situation as you use your problem-solving skills to cope when things become stressful. If you feel anxious or angry while rehearsing this challenge, use your self-relaxation skills to calm yourself down. Practice coping with the challenge over and over until you can get through the whole situation and still feel in control.

Confronting the Challenge

When the challenge is happening we can give ourselves a psychological boost so we will feel satisfied about our performance. Tell yourself you are a coper who knows how to use the coping skills described in this chapter. Learn how to talk yourself through the challenge by telling yourself:

"I'm a coper and I know I can handle this."
"This is tough, but I will survive."
"I'm getting uptight. It's time to relax."
"Stick to my plan. Don't let negative thoughts get me off track."
"Relax. I must concentrate on what I have to do."
"I won't let anxiety and anger get the best of me."
"If I act like I'm in control, I'll feel that way."

Use your creativity to think of things you can say to yourself when you are confronting challenges. Sometimes it helps to see the humor in difficult situations. Be easy on yourself. Use challenges as opportunities to test your coping skills. Be willing to make mistakes. Don't force yourself to be perfect.

Reflecting on What You've Learned

When the challenge is over we should take some time to reflect on what we've learned. It's OK to notice our mistakes and ask ourselves how we can improve as long as we're not too critical. We need to be willing to look at ourselves as fallible human beings who are always open to learning new things. But we also must be sure to look at what we did right. Take some time to visualize yourself as you were coping and getting through the situation. People often make the mistake of focusing on the negative side of their performance without taking credit for their successes. Our learning experiences are built up by appreciating what we did right as well as by correcting what we did wrong. Take some time to reflect on your performance by saying the following kinds of things to yourself.

"I survived and that's what counts."
"It wasn't as bad as I expected."
"I did pretty well and I can do even better next time."
"Life is full of difficult challenges. I might as well learn how to cope with them."
"It's gratifying to see myself as a coper."
"Life challenges give me an opportunity to practice my coping skills."

USING OUR SENSE OF HUMOR

Which of the following statements describe your way of responding to challenges?

	Strongly agree	Agree	Disagree	Strongly disagree
1. I usually look for something comical to say when I am in tense situations.	____	____	____	____
2. I have often felt that if I am in a situation where I either have to cry or laugh, it's better to laugh.	____	____	____	____
3. I often lose my sense of humor when I'm having problems.	____	____	____	____
4. I must admit my life would be easier if I had more of a sense of humor.	____	____	____	____
5. I can usually find something to laugh or joke about even in trying situations.	____	____	____	____
6. It has been my experience that humor is often a very effective way of coping with problems.	____	____	____	____

The above statements come from the Coping Humor Scale (Martin & Lefcourt, 1983). People who use humor as a coping skill tend to agree with statements 1, 2, 5, and 6 and to disagree with statements 3 and 4. Research studies have found that humor can be an effective strategy for coping with stressful life events (Martin & Lefcourt, 1983; Nezu, Nezu, & Blissett, 1988). Humor helps us avoid jumping to negative conclusions and blowing things out of proportion when faced with problems. A sense of humor allows us to make more balanced and objective primary appraisals. A good sense of humor also has a favorable impact on the people around us. We receive a lot more cooperation and support from others when we're perceived as pleasant instead of as a grouch. Developing a sense of humor also boosts feelings of self-efficacy. A sense of humor encourages a creative rather than passive attitude toward life challenges.

EXERCISING

Exercising is a coping skill that is being practiced by an increasing number of people. Exercising regularly improves health (see Chapter 13) and has a beneficial effect on aging (see Chapter 11) (Pollock, Wilmore, & Fox, 1978).

Exercise is a useful skill for coping with stress (Brown, J. D., & Siegel, 1988). In addition to increasing our feelings of psychological control, an active exercise program enhances the body's ability to utilize oxygen and to recover physiologically when we are under psychological stress (Keller & Seraganian, 1984; King, Taylor, Haskell, & DeBusk, 1989).

Research studies have shown that an exercise program is a good method for reducing anxiety, while at the same time enhancing physical fitness (Long, 1984; Long & Haney, 1988).

An exercise program can have a positive effect on people's self-concept and mood. These benefits come from the knowledge that we are doing good things to take care of ourselves and from the benefits of feeling better physically and developing an attractive and well-functioning body (Folkins & Sime, 1981; King et al., 1989).

Exercise programs seem to also enhance our sense of internal control and self-efficacy (see Chapter 2; Jasnoski, Holmes, Solomon, & Aguiar, 1981; Long & Haney, 1988). The immediate psychological benefits of an exercise program are most apparent for those with poor fitness who are under high stress (Wilfley & Kunce, 1986). However, no matter what kind of shape we are in, maintaining a regular exercise program gives us a reason to feel good about ourselves and provides an opportunity for supportive interactions with other people. As with all of the coping skills outlined in this chapter, exercise must be practiced on a regular basis.

Motivating Ourselves

One of the most difficult challenges of people wanting to maintain an exercise program is sticking with it. How can we motivate ourselves to exercise regularly? Two general suggestions are to make exercise as pleasant as possible and to follow a daily schedule (Martin, J. E., & Dubbert, 1982).

At first, people not used to exercising may find the experience of a sweaty body, a pounding heart, and shortness of breath unpleasant. However, regular exercisers have learned to associate these physical sensations with good health. Give yourself time to appreciate these sensations as indicating your own good health.

Some people prefer to use exercise as a time to be alone and to engage in their own thoughts. Others have more fun when they share their exercise sessions with friends or in groups and social settings. Develop an exercise program that matches your social preferences.

It is much easier to maintain motivation when we maximize the pleasantness (or at least minimize the unpleasantness) of our exercise program. There are many ways to get exercise, ranging from aerobics to swimming, running, bicycling, and sports. Some people like lots of exercise. Others prefer to keep it to a minimum. Find an exercise program that matches your lifestyle and personality.

Many people find it helpful to use daily logs to make exercise a part of their daily schedule. If you do this, exercise will become a regular part of your life.

And be sure to consult a physician before you start an exercise program.

REWARDING OURSELVES FOR ACCOMPLISHMENTS

One of the most striking experiences I have had as a clinical psychologist is to see how hard people can be on themselves. Check whether you agree or disagree with the following statements:

	Strongly agree	*Agree*	*Disagree*	*Strongly disagree*
1. When I succeed at small things, I am encouraged to go on.	____	____	____	____
2. When I do something right, I take time to enjoy feeling good about it.	____	____	____	____
3. Unless I do something absolutely perfectly, it gives me little satisfaction.	____	____	____	____
4. I don't often think positive thoughts about myself.	____	____	____	____
5. I get through hard times by planning things to enjoy afterwards.	____	____	____	____
6. The way I achieve my goals is by rewarding myself along the way.	____	____	____	____

These statements are adapted from the Frequency of Self-Reinforcement Scale (Heiby, 1983). People who know how to feel good about themselves tend to agree with statements 1, 2, 5, and 6 and to disagree with statements 3 and 4. Who is your best friend? Your answer should be "I am." How do athletes, artists, musicians, writers, and other people who accomplish things find the energy to reach their achievements? They do this to a large degree by setting up their goals in small steps so they can feel good about themselves as they go along. Achievers also understand the value of not being too hard on themselves. Small setbacks don't amount to much if we always have achievable goals that give us a feeling of satisfaction. It is amazing how reluctant many people are to give themselves credit and pat themselves on the back when they do something kind, good, or worthwhile. Of course, it is always nice to be acknowledged by others. Unfortunately, positive strokes from others are not always predictable or reliable. So, if you are going to accomplish anything with consistency, the rewards must come from yourself.

SOME THOUGHTS ABOUT WHAT WE LEARNED IN THIS CHAPTER

An important lesson in this chapter is that being a good coper is a skill. The positive part about this fact is that there is hope for all of us. However, it also means that coping doesn't always come easily. We have to work at it. Practice the eight coping skills described here while you read the rest of this book. Another important point is that emotional reactions are very much influenced by appraisals—and appraisals are subjective. In the following chapters, you will learn how to put your coping skills to work while confronting life challenges that most people, at one time or another, have to face.

SUGGESTIONS FOR FURTHER READING

BENSON, H. (1976). *The relaxation response.* New York: Avon.

GOLDFRIED, M. R., & DAVISON, G. C. (1976). *Clinical behavior therapy.* New York: Holt, Rinehart & Winston.

MEICHENBAUM, D. (1985). *Stress inoculation training.* New York: Pergamon.

SACHS, M. L., & BUFFONE, G. W. (Eds.). (1984). *Running as therapy: An integrated approach.* Lincoln: University of Nebraska Press.

WATSON, D. L., & THARP, R. G. (1989). *Self-directed behavior.* Pacific Grove, Calif.: Brooks/Cole.

4

Coping with Failure

The experience of failure provides a good opportunity for working through the processes of primary and secondary appraisal (Chapter 2). Referring back to Figure 2.1 on page 16, we can identify a failure as a life event that we may or may not perceive as a problem (primary appraisal). Although failure is rarely a positive experience, we can often choose to take it in stride. Primary appraisal allows us to accept many of our failure experiences as part of life and to save our energy for coping with failures that we honestly feel are worth getting upset about.

Coping Skill 1: Saving Energy for Failures Worth Getting Upset About ▲

Think of a time when you failed at something and became upset. What did you tell yourself? Check how much you used each of the following statements to explain your failure.

	Very true	Partly true	Slightly true	Not true
1. I failed because I lacked ability.	____	____	____	____
2. I failed because of bad luck.	____	____	____	____
3. I failed because I didn't try hard enough.	____	____	____	____
4. I failed because the challenge was too difficult.	____	____	____	____
5. I failed because of someone else.	____	____	____	____

You may recognize that these explanations for failure are secondary appraisals that have a strong influence on your response to the failure experience. Secondary appraisals determine what we do after failing. They also have a bearing on how we feel. Researchers have identified feelings that commonly occur as a result of how you explain successes and failures (Russell, D., & McAuley, 1986; Weiner, 1979, 1985; Weiner, Russell, & Lerman, 1979). Table 4.1 gives some examples of feelings associated with explanations for success and failure that will most likely match your experiences. These examples should remind you of the discussion in Chapter 2 about how much feelings are influenced by what you tell yourself. This fact has important implications for coping with failure that will be outlined in this chapter.

MAKING RATIONAL APPRAISALS

The first thing you want to ask yourself after deciding that a failure is worth getting upset about is, "How can I understand the reason for this failure in a rational way?" You might be surprised to know that you make appraisals, judgments, and decisions every day without really thinking about them. This is a good thing because we would exhaust ourselves if we tried to stop and carefully weigh all options every time we moved. However, the ability we have to make quick appraisals can serve us wrong if these appraisals are not in our best interest. For example, most of us need to be realistic and accept the fact that we are not world-class athletes or geniuses. We would not be very happy if we went around being grandiose and expecting far more

TABLE 4.1   Feelings Associated with Explanations for Success and Failure

Secondary Appraisal	Resulting Feeling
I failed because I lack ability.	Incompetence, resignation
I succeeded because of my ability.	Competence, confidence
I failed because of bad luck.	Sadness, surprise
I succeeded because of good luck.	Surprise, thanks
I failed because I didn't try hard enough.	Guilt, shame
I succeeded because I tried hard.	Satisfaction, pride
I failed because the challenge was too difficult.	Inadequacy, anger
I succeeded because the challenge was easy.	Security, modesty
I failed because of someone else.	Anger, bitterness
I succeeded because of someone else.	Gratitude, appreciation

From "The Cognition-Emotion Process in Achievement-Related Contexts" by B. Weiner, D. Russell, and D. Lerman, 1979, *Journal of Personality and Social Psychology, 37,* pp. 1211–1220. Copyright 1979 by the American Psychological Association. Adapted with permission.

of ourselves than we could possibly deliver. On the other hand, how often do you sell yourself short and write off a failure to bad luck or lack of ability when you could most likely succeed if you sacrificed the necessary time and effort?

An important part of coping with failure is developing the kind of coping attitude toward life that was discussed in Chapter 1. When we fail at something worth getting upset about, we need to stop and make a rational appraisal. If our failure resulted because the challenge was beyond our *ability,* we might wish to reach our goal through a different route. If failure resulted because we didn't devote sufficient *effort,* or because we underestimated the *difficulty* of the task, we might wish to take the time to develop our skills and to learn new strategies. If we failed because of *bad luck,* we might want to try again. And if we failed because of *someone else,* we might wish to practice assertiveness and negotiation. Realistic appraisals help us feel less stuck after experiencing failure because they suggest a positive course of action.

Coping Skill 2: Using Rational Appraisals to Seek a Positive Course of Action ▲

BEING PERSISTENT

It is apparent from the above discussion on making rational appraisals that we are most likely to persist and not give up after failing if we view our failure as resulting from lack of effort. This way of appraising failure allows us to use the problem-solving skills described in Chapter 3. When adopting a problem-solving attitude it is up to us to take responsibility for our failure, to perfect our skills, and to expend greater effort next time. Persistence also involves focusing on achieving success rather than worrying about avoiding failure (Atkinson, 1957, 1964; Weiner et al., 1971).

It may help you appreciate the value of persistence by considering the experiences of some of the world's most famous and productive people (Bandura, 1989; White, J., 1982):

Gertrude Stein continued to submit poems to editors for 20 years before one was finally accepted.

James Joyce's book *The Dubliners* was rejected by 22 publishers.

Van Gogh only sold one painting during his lifetime.

Rodin's sculptures were not accepted by major gallerys.

Stravinsky was run out of Paris when he first presented the *Rite of Spring*.

The architecture of Frank Lloyd Wright was widely rejected during his career.

Hollywood originally responded to Fred Astaire as a "balding skinny actor who can dance a little."

Decca Records turned down a recording contract with the Beatles by saying, "We don't like their sound. Groups with guitars are on their way out."

Coping Skill 3: Being Persistent and
Using Problem-Solving Skills to Seek Success ▲

MAINTAINING PRIDE

What kind of self-concept would you have if you explained all of your successes as resulting from good luck and help from others? You might feel thankful, but it would be hard to experience much sense of pride. Pride comes from the feeling that you took time to develop your skills and that you devoted the effort necessary for achieving success.

Coping Skill 4: Maintaining Pride by Applying Effort and Talent ▲

After considering how we can feel good about ourselves when we succeed, we might want to ask how we maintain pride when we fail. One way to protect self-esteem after failing is to practice the kinds of adaptive appraisals discussed later in this chapter. Instead of blaming our failure on our "incompetence," we can use our problem-solving skills to figure out a strategy for doing better in the future. A second way to maintain self-esteem after failing is to follow the suggestions in this chapter for living with realistic expectations and seeking meaningful challenges. We can also maintain our self-esteem after failing by giving ourselves a break and not being too hard on ourselves. For example, if your hobby is playing the piano, remind yourself that you do not have to play as well as Horowitz. Or, if you are sick or under a lot of stress, remind yourself that your performance will be affected. That is, we should be fair with ourselves when things beyond our control are preventing us from reaching ordinarily realistic goals. On the other hand, we want to take responsibility when our performance could honestly be better. When people avoid responsibility for their performance they are engaging in a *self-handicapping* strategy that is not always in their best interest.

SELF-HANDICAPPING

Check how much you agree or disagree with the following statements.

	Strongly agree	Agree	Disagree	Strongly disagree
1. When I do something wrong, my first impulse is to blame the circumstances.	____	____	____	____
2. I suppose I feel "under the weather" more often than most people.	____	____	____	____
3. Someday I might "get it all together."	____	____	____	____
4. Sometimes I get so depressed that even easy tasks become difficult.	____	____	____	____
5. I would do a lot better if I tried harder.	____	____	____	____
6. I never let emotional problems in one part of my life interfere with other things in my life.	____	____	____	____
7. I tend to put things off until the last moment.	____	____	____	____
8. I always try to do my best, no matter what.	____	____	____	____

These statements come from the Self-Handicapping Scale (Jones, E. E., & Rhodewalt, 1982). Self-handicappers tend to agree with statements 1, 2, 3, 4, 5, and 7 and to disagree with statements 6 and 8.

One example of self-handicapping, with which you are most likely familiar, is the use of drugs or alcohol as an excuse for poor performance and undesirable behavior ("I can't be blamed because I was drunk"; Tucker, Vuchinich, & Sobell, 1981). The use of drugs for self-handicapping was examined in a study where participants worked on an intellectual task (Berglas & Jones, 1978). Some participants succeeded because of their efforts. They were confident about their success. Other participants succeeded, but weren't sure why. They were not confident about their success. Before working on a second test the participants were asked to choose between one of two drugs that were supposedly under investigation in the study. One drug was expected to help people perform better and the other drug was expected to make them do worse. Which drug did participants choose? The majority of those who were confident about their previous success preferred the perfor-mance-enhancing drug. They wanted to see if they could do even better. In contrast, participants who were not confident about their previous success chose the drug that would hurt their performance. Because these participants were unsure about themselves they handicapped themselves by taking a drug that they could blame for their future performance.

Another self-handicapping strategy is the exaggeration of psychological or phys-ical symptoms. Studies of psychiatric patients have shown how they use psychiatric symptoms to obtain privileges and to maintain control over their protected environment (Braginsky, Braginsky, & Ring, 1969; Braginsky, Grosse, & Ring, 1966; Fontana, Klein, Lewis, & Levine, 1968). Other people have aches and pains and other ailments that "prevent" them from being able to do their best (Smith, Snyder, & Perkins, 1983).

An example of symptom exaggeration by college students is seen in a study where students took an intellectual test and then rated the level of their anxiety (Smith, Snyder, & Handlesman, 1982). Students who were generally fearful of tests said they were more anxious than students who did not fear tests. This difference in self-reported anxiety was greatest when it was acceptable for students to use anxiety as an excuse for poor performance. When anxiety is not an acceptable excuse, students handicapped themselves by saying that they didn't take the tests very seriously and that they hadn't bothered to prepare (Harris, R. N., & Snyder, 1986).

In Chapter 6 you will discover that most of us have experienced feelings of shyness. However, some people are "shy like a fox." They use shyness as an excuse for not putting themselves out in certain social situations (Snyder & Smith, 1986; Snyder, Smith, Augelli, & Ingram, 1985). Other self-handicapping strategies include blaming one's traumatic past experiences (DeGree & Snyder, 1985) and the insanity plea (Szasz, 1987).

An example of blaming one's traumatic experience is seen in the following case (Szasz, 1987):

> In 1980, Michael Tindall, who had served as a helicopter pilot in Vietnam, was charged with taking part in smuggling hashish from Morocco to Gloucester, Massachusetts. He insisted that he did it "because of a need to relive the excitement he experienced in combat," and that this need was a symptom of his illness, the "Vietman Syndrome." In September, 1980, a federal court jury in Boston acquitted Tindall of the charges against him (p. 287).

One of the most famous uses of the insanity plea is found in the trial of John Hinckley, Jr., who shot President Reagan and three others. Hinckley's parents offered the following explanation for his act: "How could anybody do such a horrible thing? The answer is schizophrenia, an overpowering mental illness that robbed John of his ability to control his thoughts and actions. . . . The disease is the culprit, not the person" (Szasz, 1987, p. 255).

A self-handicapping strategy that has hidden costs is that of setting goals below our capabilities (Arkin & Baumgardner, 1985). Being an underachiever may give a feeling of security because people will never expect much from us. By sticking with simple goals we can protect ourselves from coming face to face with the limits of our competence. But there is a hidden cost in being an underachiever since it undermines self-esteem. It's hard to feel a sense of pride when we withhold our best talents. We can overcome the urge to be an underachiever by practicing the following skills:

1. Set goals that are stimulating.
2. Don't allow your goals to be compromised by a desire to please others.
3. Don't let fear of failing interfere with the pleasure of taking on challenges.
4. Remember that the efforts put into a challenge are as important as the outcome.

In summing up the research findings on self-handicapping, we can see that it is important to find the right balance between not being too hard on ourselves and taking honest responsibility for our performance. We can keep this balance by making rational appraisals and living with realistic expectations.

***Coping Skill 5: Finding the Right Balance
between Self-Handicapping and Self-Responsibility***   ▲
••

SEEKING CHALLENGES

Seeking challenges has a lot to do with *self-efficacy*. Self-efficacy is developed by living a life of goals, seeking out good role models, and exerting enough energy to experience meaningful accomplishments. What happens to people who don't cope well with failure? Researchers have found that they cop out by either sticking with simple challenges on which they are bound to succeed or by choosing impossible goals on which they are certain to fail (Atkinson, 1957, 1964; Weiner et al., 1971). Obviously there is no reason to worry about failing when we stick with simple goals. And if we choose impossible goals and fail, nobody can blame us. But how much self-efficacy can we enjoy by achieving guaranteed success or by failing on an impossible task? We develop self-efficacy by seeking goals that challenge us to develop our skills and problem-solving abilities. When we do this, we will sometimes succeed and we will sometimes fail. We therefore have to learn how to savor successes and to cope adaptively with failures. When it comes to savoring successes, we will want to practice the skill of rewarding ourselves (Chapter 3). Research has shown that people who are "achievers" know how to feel pride and take credit for their accomplishments. Achievers seek challenges because they are not preoccupied with protecting themselves from failure (Weiner et al., 1971).

***Coping Skill 6: Developing Self-Efficacy
by Seeking Meaningful Challenges***   ▲
••

DEVELOPING COMPETENCIES

The concepts of self-efficacy and internal control are related to the desire to learn new things, to master challenges, and to develop competencies. This kind of life attitude is very useful for helping us cope with failure. There are two different orientations people can have when they are faced with problems: *performance-oriented* or *mastery-oriented* (Dweck & Leggett, 1988; Elliott & Dweck, 1988; Nicholls, 1984). These orientations are not fixed at birth. They are developed as a way of seeking the best method for coping with challenging situations.

Being Performance-Oriented

When we are performance-oriented, our focus is on proving our talents to others. We want to gain their approval and to avoid any possibility of being evaluated in a negative light. Performance-oriented people get frustrated and feel stuck when things don't come easily. When people take this attitude toward challenges, they become preoccupied with avoiding failure. We learned earlier in this chapter how the motivation to avoid failure often leads people to set goals that are either too high or too low. Performance-oriented people tend to say the following kinds of things:

"What will people think of me?"
"Making a good impression is more important than enjoying myself or improving my skills."
"There is nothing to be gained from failure."
"Don't take risks. I should stay within my proven abilities."

Being performance-oriented is OK when we face simple challenges. However, when challenges become difficult, a performance orientation will hinder our problem-solving skills and prevent us from turning them into a useful learning experience. When faced with tough problems, people who are performance-oriented tend to feel helpless and give up.

Being Mastery-Oriented

People who are mastery-oriented focus on turning challenges into useful learning experiences. They don't demand that things come easily. It doesn't matter so much whether they succeed or fail as long as they feel they gain something from their efforts. Rather than being concerned about what others think of them, they are motivated by the chance to develop their skills and competencies. Mastery-oriented people tend to say the following kinds of things to themselves:

"What can I learn from this challenge?"
"People's judgments of me should not prevent me from having fun and improving my skills."
"Even if I fail, it can be a useful learning experience."
"It's OK to take risks and try new solutions."

Being mastery-oriented is adaptive for easy as well as difficult problems. Mastery-oriented people don't feel helpless when faced with tough challenges because their goal is to make the most of the experience and they know they can learn from their failures.

Appreciating Our Ability to Learn

It is a valuable experience to be exposed to talented people. We sometimes assume that great athletes, musicians, artists, and writers were born with their skills and we overlook their long hours of practice and self-discipline. One of the most serious mistakes we can make is to believe that our talents, intelligence, and abilities are fixed at birth and cannot be developed (Dweck & Leggett, 1988). If we take this kind of "fixed" position, we are bound to react to failure by saying the following kinds of things to ourselves: "My failure proves that I'm not capable of solving this problem. I guess I'd better stick with easier challenges that I know I can handle."

On the other hand, if we appreciate our ability to develop our skills and to learn new problem-solving strategies, we are more likely to react to failure by thinking: "My failure shows that I used the wrong approach. My challenge is to figure out how to do better next time."

Appreciating our capacity to learn does not mean that we can all be geniuses if we work at it. It is true that we must be realistic about the limits of our abilities. However, we won't know our limits until we test ourselves. Think about how much more interesting your life will be if you view it as an opportunity to learn new things as opposed to playing it safe.

Coping Skill 7: Using Failure as an
Opportunity to Develop Competencies ▲

We now have a good idea how appraisals about failure can affect our moods and our decision to either persist or give up. We have also gained an understanding that coping successfully with failure involves making appraisals that are in our best interest. Psychologists have conducted a large amount of research on how people learn to practice adaptive appraisals for successes and failures. We will turn now to discoveries and conclusions in the remainder of this chapter.

TEACHING EFFECTIVE COPING

One important challenge for psychologists has been to teach people how to cope more effectively with failure. From what we have learned, it will not come as a surprise that children and adults who are low achievers often don't make adaptive appraisals of their successes and failures. Low achievers have not learned to savor their successes. They also tend to falsely blame many failures on lack of ability (Diener & Dweck, 1978; Dweck, 1975; Dweck & Gilliard, 1975).

How can we teach others (as well as ourselves) to seek challenges and to persist after experiencing failure? One important objective for low achievers is to stop blaming their failures on things beyond their control. It is important to recognize when failures can be avoided by expending more energy or by trying a different strategy or approach. We all need to set specific goals and ask for help with tough hurdles. Overcoming failure often means taking the responsibility to persist until we find the best solution. When we adopt such an attitude, our motivation increases, our expectations for success are greater, and we are more likely to succeed (Anderson, 1983; Peterson & Barrett, 1987).

Avoiding Self-Defeating Conclusions

Teaching programs have been developed where low achievers learn to stop after they fail and ask themselves the following questions before jumping to self-defeating conclusions (Chapin & Dyck, 1976; Dweck, 1975; Dweck & Reppucci, 1973): "Did I honestly fail because I lack ability? If not, what do I need to do to improve my performance? Do I need to try harder? Do I need to improve my skills and learn new strategies? Should I give up or can I succeed by being persistent?" As a result of learning how to talk to themselves adaptively, low achievers began to set higher goals and to expend greater effort toward achieving success.

First-year college students often suffer self-doubts when they find themselves not doing as well as they did in high school. A self-defeating conclusion for this experience is: "I'm not as smart as I thought. Maybe I'm not cut out for college." As you can appreciate, a more realistic conclusion is: "The study skills I need for college are different from those I used in high school. If I give myself a year to master them, my grades will get better."

Research was conducted in which first-year college students were instructed that it is normal to experience a drop in grades during the first year in college and that grades improve as students adjust to the new style of learning (Wilson & Linville, 1982, 1985). As a result of these simple instructions, the students did significantly better during the following semester than a similar group of first-year students who weren't instructed to understand their first semester "setback" in a realistic way.

Enhancing Our Sense of Ability

Coping with failure is developed through experiencing success and learning to attribute success to our effort and ability. We can encourage ourselves by saying, "I worked really hard. I didn't give up. I'm really good at this. I'm smart." When we appreciate our efforts, we are encouraged not to give up on a problem until we have explored all possible solutions. The appreciation of ability helps us realize that while some problems require a lot of work, many can be solved (Schunk, 1982, 1983, 1984).

Coping with failure is often learned from good role models. Children learn coping skills by observing how others talk themselves through problems. A good role model is a person with whom we can identify. We're not going to learn much from someone whose skills are far better or worse than our own. We get our best lessons by watching people similar to us take on a problem, work it through without giving up, and take satisfaction for their success (Schunk & Hanson, 1985; Schunk, Hanson, & Cox, 1987).

Comparing Boys and Girls

Another insight about how people appraise failure comes from research showing that girls are more likely than boys to explain their experiences of failure in school as caused by lack of ability (Dweck & Gilliard, 1975). Girls suffer when they falsely blame their failure on lack of ability and become discouraged and give up. Boys, in contrast, explain their failures as caused by problems they can overcome. They say things such as: "Maybe I didn't try hard enough. Or maybe the teacher was being really hard. But I'm not dumb and I can do better next time."

Why should boys and girls react to experiences of failure so differently? This question was explored by observing the responses of teachers to their students. The researchers found that teachers focus their criticisms of girls on poor intellectual performance. When teachers criticize boys, it is often for "goofing off" or breaking rules. Boys, therefore, learn to take teachers' criticisms with a grain of salt. They don't personalize a teacher's negative remarks as a reflection on their abilities. Even though teachers criticize girls less often than they criticize boys, girls suffer because they take the criticism to heart (Dweck & Bush, 1976; Dweck, Davidson, Nelson, & Enna, 1978; Dweck, Goetz, & Strauss, 1980).

Coping Skill 8: Taking Credit for Our Effort and Ability ▲
• •

LIVING WITH REALISTIC EXPECTATIONS

Coping successfully with failure means living a life of realistic expectations. If we set our goals too high we will always fail, and that is discouraging. If we set our goals too low we will never fail, but life will be boring. To live an interesting and challenging life we must set our goals at a level where we sometimes succeed and sometimes fail. Disadvantaged children grow up with very few experiences of success. Since these children have not learned to savor success, they have no reason to set challenging goals for themselves. Advantaged children who grow up with nothing but success also suffer because they never learn how to cope with inevitable failures (Chapin & Dyck, 1976; Dweck, 1975).

Coping Skill 9: Setting Goals That Will
Make Our Lives Interesting and Rewarding   ▲
● ●

In addition to making our lives more interesting, there is another reason for living with realistic expectations. The goals we seek and the explanations we give for success and failure have a strong impact on our attitude toward the future. If we convince ourselves that we have no ability, that the world is against us, and that we are doomed to bad luck, we are in danger of falling victim to a self-fulfilling prophecy. People who *expect* to do poorly end up *doing* poorly. People who expect to do better than they possibly can also end up doing poorly. It is important to size up each challenge in a realistic way so we can prepare ourselves to use the skill and effort required for success (Brickman & Hendricks, 1975; Sherman, Skov, Hervitz, & Stock, 1981). Here are some suggestions:

1. When faced with a simple task that verges on boredom, you have several options. You might appreciate having a chance to take it easy for awhile. Or you can use your creativity to give this task a personal touch, or even to have some fun with it.
2. When pursuing challenges that are tough, but within your grasp, "go for it." This is your chance to enjoy a feeling of accomplishment.
3. When faced with problems that appear unsurmountable, you have two choices. You can protect yourself from failure by declining the challenge. Or you can decide that failure is not an issue and take on the problem as a learning experience. Instead of being performance-oriented, you want to take a mastery-oriented attitude. The goal is not a perfect outcome, but rather an opportunity to practice your skills.

Coping Skill 10: Matching Expectations
to the Difficulty of the Challenge   ▲
● ●

COPING WITH FAILURE AS A MENTAL HEALTH SKILL

In Chapter 5 you will learn some techniques for coping when you are feeling down. As a way of leading into that chapter, let's explore how feeling down is related to experiences of failure. Earlier in this chapter you read about how explanations for successes and failures can influence people's moods. Therefore, it will not come as a surprise to learn that depressed people are especially likely to perceive their failures as beyond their control. Depressives usually explain their failures as caused by bad luck and poor ability. Because they underestimate the power of problem-solving skills for coping with failure, they often feel helpless and give up. Depressed people spend an inordinate amount of time focusing on their failures. They are so preoccupied with their failures that they have little energy left for maintaining their self-esteem (Pyszczynski & Greenberg, 1987a, 1987b).

We all know that it is hard to motivate ourselves and to expend a lot of effort when we're feeling down. Feeling down makes us feel less ambitious. However, it is also important to understand that forcing ourselves to be ambitious and energetic will make us feel less down. Depressives feel better and start to accomplish things when they are taught to make realistic appraisals for their failures ("Failing doesn't prove I'm dumb or worthless," "Failing once doesn't mean I'll always fail," "I can tolerate failures because that's how I learn"); and to take appropriate credit for their successes ("I don't have to be perfect to feel good about my accomplishments," "Even if I fail, I can take pride in my efforts," "The challenge is as important to me as the outcome") (Klein, Fencil-Morse, & Seligman, 1976; Klein & Seligman, 1976; Sweeney, Anderson, & Bailey, 1986). What they found in these treatment studies is relevant for everyone. In order to lead a challenging and productive life, we have to learn how to fail.

Coping Skill 11: Learning How to Fail ▲
••

▲ LIST OF SKILLS FOR COPING WITH FAILURE

Coping Skill 1: Saving Our Energy for Failures Worth Getting Upset About

Coping Skill 2: Using Rational Appraisals to Seek a Positive Course of Action

Coping Skill 3: Being Persistent and Using Problem-Solving Skills to Seek Success

Coping Skill 4: Maintaining Pride by Applying Effort and Talent

Coping Skill 5: Finding the Right Balance Between Self-Handicapping and Self-Responsibility

Coping Skill 6: Developing Self-Efficacy by Seeking Meaningful Challenges

Coping Skill 7: Using Failure as an Opportunity to Develop Competencies

Coping Skill 8: Taking Credit for Our Effort and Ability

Coping Skill 9: Setting Goals That Will Make Our Lives Interesting and Rewarding

Coping Skill 10: Matching Expectations to the Difficulty of the Challenge

Coping Skill 11: Learning How To Fail

SUGGESTIONS FOR FURTHER READING

ELLIS, A., & KNAUS, W. (1977). *Overcoming proscratination.* New York: New American Library.
SNYDER, C. R., HIGGINS, R. L., & STUCKY, R. J. (1983). *Excuses: Masquerades in search of grace.* New York: Wiley.

SZASZ, T. S. (1987). *Insanity: The idea and its consequences.* New York: Wiley.

WEINER, B. (1972). *Theories of motivation: From mechanism to cognition.* Chicago: Rand McNally.

WHITE, J. (1982). *Rejection.* Reading, Mass.: Addison-Wesley.

5

Coping When
We're Down

Everyone has ups and downs. As long as they are not too extreme, our ups and downs make life interesting and challenging. But when we feel exceptionally low, or in the dumps for a long period of time, it is time to appraise the situation and look for suitable coping responses.

SYMPTOMS OF DEPRESSION

To put this chapter into perspective, we should look at the clinical term *depression,* and understand how a diagnosis of depression is used by professional psychother-apists. The American Psychiatric Association (1986) outlines the following list of symptoms that are experienced by people when they are clinically depressed over a period of two or more weeks:

1. Change in appetite. Either poor appetite and weight loss or increased appetite and weight gain.
2. Inability to sleep or sleeping more than usual.
3. Low energy and fatigue.
4. Loss of interest or pleasure in previously enjoyed activities.
5. Feelings of worthlessness, self-reproach, or excessive guilt.
6. Diminished ability to think or concentrate.
7. Recurrent thoughts of death. Suicidal thoughts.

Although the coping skills discussed in this chapter are useful for clinically depressed people, they are not enough. Those people who are *clinically* depressed should seek professional help. The purpose of this chapter is to offer some tips for pulling ourselves up when we're feeling sad, blue, low, or down.

FACTORS UNDERLYING DEPRESSION

The following factors have been identified among people who are most likely to get depressed (Barnett & Gotlib, 1988; Pyszczynski & Greenberg, 1987a, 1987b).

Unrealistic dependency on others: There is a tendency to tie one's self-esteem too strongly to someone else's approval.

Lack of a social support system: People prone to depression tend to be intro-verted and withdrawn. They don't exert the social skills required to sustain supportive relationships.

Stress in close relationships: Depression is often exacerbated when there is disharmony in close relationships.

Depressive self-focusing style: Depressed people are preoccupied with nega-tives. They spend too much time ruminating on the bad things in their lives and never get around to implementing their coping strategies.

When we feel down it is usually because something has happened (an activating event) that we feel is unacceptable or intolerable (belief system). In terms of the appraisal model described in Chapter 2 (see Figure 2.2, p. 17), feeling down is the consequence of how we interpret the life event. One possible response is to alter the situation. A second response is to ask whether our primary appraisal is accurate. A third response is to ask whether our primary appraisal is rational. A fourth response is to use good coping skills. You will learn how to use each of these responses in this chapter.

ALTERING THE SITUATION

The most important rule about altering an unhappy situation is to be realistic. We must face the fact that many life events that lead us to feel down are beyond our control. It is not adaptive to burden ourselves with the following kinds of unrealistic thoughts:

"Why did it have to happen?"
"If only I had done things differently."
"It isn't fair."
"If only I had another chance."

When an unhappy life event is beyond our control, it is in our best interest to acknowledge this fact (as unpleasant as it might be) and to focus our energies on our appraisals and coping responses. No purpose is served in brooding about life events we can't change. Reinhold Niebuhr summed up our first coping skill in his Serenity Prayer (Bartlett, 1982): "God, give us grace to accept with serenity the things that cannot be changed, courage to change the things which should be changed, and the wisdom to distinguish the one from the other."

Coping Skill 1: Acknowledging When
Unpleasant Situations Are Beyond Our Control   ▲
••

Life events we sometimes can influence are those involving relations with other people. If we are feeling down because someone is not treating us right or is not meeting our needs, we may be able to alter the situation by negotiating, using social skills, and being assertive. A number of suggestions for using good social skills are given in Chapter 6. One important point made in Chapter 6 is that we will usually get more favorable reactions from others if we are *responsive*. A natural reaction when other people don't meet our needs is to withdraw, get angry, and pout. The concept of responsiveness suggests that when we want something from others, we often have to be the first to give. Getting our needs met is a matter of pragmatics over pride. It is better to be assertive and ask directly for what we want than to seek attention "symptomatically" by trying to make others feel guilty. It is true that asking for something and being denied is not pleasant. However, when we are direct, others at least know where we stand. Even if we are denied, we can still control our life by making adaptive appraisals and using our coping skills. When taking a responsive and assertive approach toward others it is important to recognize the value of negotiation (see Chapter 8). It is a fact of life that if we want good treatment from others, we have to give something in return.

Coping Skill 2: Enhancing Personal Relations with
Social Skills, Assertiveness, and Negotiation   ▲
••

MAKING ACCURATE PRIMARY APPRAISALS

Which of the following statements do you make to yourself when you try to accomplish a task and don't succeed?

"I failed and this means I'm dumb."

"I failed because I didn't try hard enough, because I didn't approach the task
correctly, or because I'm not good at that task, but not because I'm dumb."

It is obvious that the second statement is more accurate than the first. However,
when we are feeling down we tend to make inaccurate appraisals by overgeneralizing and looking at unhappy life events as absolute and unchangeable (Coyne &
Gotlib, 1983). When this happens, we must force ourselves to question our faulty
appraisals and to change them into appraisals that are reasonable and accurate. For
example, assume that your best friend is abrupt with you. How would you feel if
you made the following appraisal? "My friend doesn't like me any more." This
appraisal would most likely cause you to feel hurt, sad, or angry.

To pull yourself out of the dumps you would have to argue with yourself in the
following manner:

"That abrupt treatment means A doesn't like me anymore."

"How often is A abrupt with me?"

"Hardly ever."

"How often is A nice to me?"

"Most of the time."

"Is it possible that A's abruptness had nothing to do with me?"

"I guess so."

"Now let's assume that A was mad at me. Does that mean A dislikes me?"

"Not really."

"Friends can be abrupt with each other at times and still be friends, can't they?"

A valuable skill for coping with inaccurate primary appraisals is to listen to our
accurate self. We have to train ourselves to question and revise inaccurate primary
appraisals that cause us to feel low. Here are some examples of common inaccurate
primary appraisals and accurate revisions (Beck, Rush, Shaw, & Emery, 1979).

Self-blame:
> Inaccurate self: Because I forgot my mother's birthday I'm a bad person.
> Accurate self: Making a mistake is unfortunate, but it does not mean I am a
> bad person.

Irreversibility:
> Inaccurate self: I am lonely and shy and will always be this way.
> Accurate self: I can learn how to overcome my loneliness and shyness.

Overgeneralization:
> Inaccurate self: Person A was mean to me. Nobody likes me.
> Accurate self: Person A was mean to me, but there are many people who
> like me.

Absolutism:
> Inaccurate self: My life is worthless without my lost love.
> Accurate self: My lost love doesn't constitute my whole life.

Personalization:
> Inaccurate self: The boss is mad because my productivity is low.
> Accurate self: The boss is mad because our department's productivity is low.

Overreacting:

> Inaccurate self: We had an argument and our friendship is over.
>
> Accurate self: One argument does not end a friendship.

Another way to compare appraisals made by depressed and nondepressed people is by looking at their perceptions of *stability*, *globality*, and *internality* (Peterson & Seligman, 1984).

Stability: Depressed people see negative events in their lives as stable, that is, as unlikely to change. Nondepressed people view negative experiences as temporary setbacks that won't last forever.

Globality: Depressed people are overwhelmed by their problems. Nondepressed people can put things into perspective. They balance the positives against the negatives in their lives.

Internality: Depressed people blame themselves for their problems. Nondepressed people take responsibility for things they can change, but don't put themselves down for not being perfect.

Coping Skill 3: Questioning and Revising Inaccurate Primary Appraisals ▲

MAINTAINING A SENSE OF CONTROL

Jerome Frank (1973) points out that one of the most important things psychotherapists can do for their clients is to help them overcome their feelings of hopelessness and demoralization. This is especially true for people who are depressed. When we are feeling down, we don't see any way to improve the situation and we engage in many of the negative patterns of thinking described in this chapter.

As you might expect, maintaining a sense of control over our lives is an important skill when we are down (Anderson & Arnoult, 1985; Brown & Siegel, 1988). Granted, it isn't always easy to be hopeful when all the odds appear to be against us. It is important to remember, however, that optimism comes from within and not from events in the outside world. We need to practice our skills for maintaining internal control (Chapter 3) and to follow the philosophy of self-efficacy discussed in Chapter 2. A sense of control reinforces our commitment to take responsibility for our problems and to use our problem-solving skills to find solutions for life challenges.

Coping Skill 4: Maintaining a Sense of Control ▲

MAKING RATIONAL PRIMARY APPRAISALS

Sometimes we don't make the kinds of inaccurate primary appraisals described in the previous section, but a life event still brings us down. What are we saying to ourselves when this happens? Are our appraisals accurate and *rational*? For example, assume that someone is unfriendly to you. How would you feel if you made the following appraisal? "There must be something wrong with me." This appraisal would most likely cause you to feel down in the dumps because you are basing your self-worth on how others treat you. What if, however, you appraised the person's unfriendliness in a more rational manner? For example: "It's too bad that person was unfriendly, but my self-worth is not determined by how someone treats me." This appraisal would cause you to feel sorry or disappointed, but wouldn't leave you in the dumps. When we are feeling too low for too long about something that happened, we have to question, and possibly revise, what we are saying to ourselves about this life event. We can gain a useful perspective on how irrational appraisals bring us down by looking at findings from research studies comparing appraisals made by depressed and nondepressed people (Eaves & Rush, 1984; Hammen & Cochran, 1981; Kanfer & Zeiss, 1983; Pietromonaco & Markus, 1985; Tabachnik, Crocker, & Alloy, 1983). For example:

> *Depressed people* are preoccupied with sad thoughts about themselves.
> *Nondepressed people* know how to get their minds off their sadness.
> *Depressed people* don't give themselves the benefit of doubt.
> *Nondepressed people* give themselves a break when judging themselves.
> *Depressed people* make unrealistic demands about what they need to be happy.
> *Nondepressed people* have realistic expectations about what they need to be happy.
> *Depressed people* allow unhappy life events to get the best of them.
> *Nondepressed people* balance happy life events against unhappy life events.
> *Depressed people* feel incapable.
> *Nondepressed people* feel capable.

Coping Skill 5: Questioning and Revising Irrational Primary Appraisals ▲

USING ADAPTIVE COPING SKILLS

Check how often you do each of the following things when you are feeling down:

	Never	Rarely	Sometimes	Often
1. I seek out friends for support.	___	___	___	___
2. I blame myself.	___	___	___	___
3. I watch TV.	___	___	___	___
4. I work out a plan to make myself feel better.	___	___	___	___
5. I take tranquilizers.	___	___	___	___
6. I sleep, daydream, or try to escape.	___	___	___	___
7. I engage in some sort of activity, such as reading, music, art, or sports.	___	___	___	___

The above list of coping responses is adapted from the Depression Coping Questionnaire (Kleinke, 1984a, 1988a; Kleinke, Staneski, & Mason, 1982). This questionnaire was administered to hundreds of people from a wide range of backgrounds and ages. Respondents included people who were clinically depressed, moderately depressed, and nondepressed. It was of particular interest to compare the coping responses used by depressed people with the coping responses used by non-depressed people. This comparison yielded some interesting findings. Non-depressed people make an active effort to get busy, to seek support, and to engage in problem solving when they are feeling down. Depressed people, on the other hand, tend to be passive. They withdraw and blame themselves. They often use tranquilizing drugs. This survey indicates that depression, passivity, and self-blame reinforce one another. Depressed people don't seem to have the energy to get out of their rut and engage in active coping responses. On the other hand, if they could force themselves to cope more actively, they would feel better.

Our discussion of adaptive coping skills is divided into three sections. First, we will consider the value of problem solving. Next, we will look at the value of balanced thinking. Finally, we will consider some actions we can take to pull ourselves up when we're down.

PROBLEM SOLVING

A good friend once said when he was having a hard time, "I was down for the count, but not out." Because my friend is a problem solver, he knew he would find a way to pull himself up.

Let's see how we can apply the problem-solving skills outlined in Chapter 3 when we're down. As an example, consider a parent who is overwhelmed with the responsibilities of family, school, and a job. Table 5.1 indicates how the person could divide these problems into manageable parts and make a list of options and possible solutions. When a plan has been formulated, it can be tested to find out which solutions are working and which need to be revised.

There are several things to keep in mind when we use problem solving to pull ourselves out of the dumps. First, it is important to break our problems into manageable parts so they don't seem so overwhelming. Second, we should remember to be creative when considering possible solutions. We shouldn't forget to enlist support people to help us brainstorm and to provide encouragement. We need to combine our energies with the encouragement of our support people to bolster our self-efficacy and feelings of internal control. And, most of all, we should remember that we are a problem solver. Finally, we must be sure to reward ourselves for taking steps to get going.

How well does problem solving work? A study was conducted in which clinically depressed people were given one of two therapy treatments (Nezu, 1986). Some of the depressed people were taught to use a problem-solving strategy similar to the one outlined in Chapter 3. Depressed people in a second group discussed their problems but did not learn about nor practice a problem-solving strategy. Results of this study were very clear. Depressed people who learned and practiced problem solving experienced a significant decrease in their depression that was still present 6 months after the study was completed. In contrast, depressed people who discussed their problems without practicing problem solving experienced only a slight decrease in depression.

TABLE 5.1   Problem Solving for Parents
• •

Problem	Possible Solutions
Family	
1. Taking care of children	Enlist help of in-laws
	Trade baby-sitting time with friends who have children
	Find a reputable day-care program
	Share child-care responsibilities with spouse
	Arrange schedule to allow meaningful time with children
2. Having meaningful time with spouse	Set up regular schedule with spouse for meaningful time together
School	
1. Finding time to study	Schedule study time when others are available to care for children
2. Needing support	Contract with spouse to give encouragement about school work, progress
3. Guilt	Schedule meaningful time with spouse and children
Job	
1. Fatigue	Enlist spouse's help with housework
	Hire part-time housekeeper

Two important conclusions are apparent. First, problem solving is an effective skill for coping when we are down. Second, it is necessary to push ourselves into activity when we are feeling low.

Coping Skill 6: Making Active Use of Problem Solving   ▲
• •

THINKING ADAPTIVE THOUGHTS

A number of years ago, E. Velten (1968) was conducting research on the effects of positive and negative moods. To instill negative moods in his research participants, he instructed them to repeat the following kinds of statements to themselves:

"I feel worn out."
"No matter how hard I try, things don't go my way."
"Sometimes I feel so alone that I could cry."
"Life often doesn't seem worth living."

As a result of making these statements, the participants' moods became more negative and their performance on various tests of concentration deteriorated. Most likely, you can see the connection between this study and your thoughts when you are feeling low. We perpetuate our blue moods by getting stuck on negative thoughts. When you catch yourself doing this, stop the negative thoughts and shift to thoughts that will make you feel better. For example, participants in the above study experienced more positive moods, and their performance on tests of concentration was enhanced, when they repeated the following kinds of statements to themselves:

"I feel great!"
"I'm pleased that most people are so nice to me."
"There are so many things in life I enjoy."
"I feel energetic and happy."

Let's consider some steps we can take to bolster our adaptive thinking.

Stopping Negative Thoughts

Depressed people are more likely than nondepressed people to occupy themselves with the following kinds of negative thoughts: *personal dissatisfaction, negative expectations, low self-esteem,* and *helplessness* (Hollon & Kendall, 1980):

Personal dissatisfaction. "Something has to change." "What's the matter with me?" "I wish I were a better person."
Negative expectations. "My future is bleak." "I'll never make it." "I'm a failure."
Low self-esteem. "I'm worthless." "I hate myself."
Helplessness. "I can't finish anything." "It's just not worth it."

We often go through the day bringing ourselves down with negative thoughts without paying attention to what we are doing. To stop this from happening, we have to train ourselves to pay attention to what we are thinking. When you get stuck on negative thoughts, yell "Stop!" (If there are people around, you can "yell" to yourself.) Wear a rubber band on your wrist and snap it when you think negative thoughts. Don't allow yourself to get in the dumps with your thinking.

If you find it important to have some time each day to focus on "how awful things are," set up a schedule. Allow yourself to think negative thoughts during certain prearranged times (but *not* during any other time). Set aside a special chair or a place where you can make yourself feel blue. During your scheduled negative thinking times, try to exaggerate your negative thoughts to extremes. Maybe you can find humor in your propensity to make yourself miserable.

Practicing Positive Thoughts

It's helpful to keep track of what we tell ourselves during the day. We should try to balance thoughts that bring us down with thoughts that bring hope and satisfaction. For example, make a list of your accomplishments and of positive things in your life. Don't overlook small accomplishments like getting to work on time, reading a book, doing something healthy, or helping someone else. Value the people close to you and things in your life (nature, art, music) you enjoy. Don't hold unrealistically high expectations for what must happen before you allow yourself to experience pleasure.

There are four kinds of positive thoughts that nondepressed people think more often than those who are depressed: *life satisfaction, positive self-concept, acceptance by others,* and *positive expectations* (Ingram & Wisnicki, 1988).

Life satisfaction.: "I am comfortable with life." "My life is running smoothly." "Life is exciting." "I am a lucky person."

Positive self-concept. "I have many good qualities." "I take good care of myself." "I deserve good things in life." "I have many useful qualities."

Acceptance by others. "I am respected by my peers." "I have a good sense of humor." "I'm fun to be with." "I have a good way with others."

Positive expectations. "My future looks bright." "I will be successful."

When we are feeling down, we may not feel like thinking these positive thoughts. However, the more we focus on them, the more automatic they become.

Taking Charge of Our Thinking

We can't just wait around passively for negative thoughts to go away and for positive thoughts to happen. We need to reinforce our feelings of self-efficacy and internal control by taking the initiative to balance our thoughts.

Coping Skill 7: Taking the Initiative to Think Positive Thoughts   ▲
••

GETTING BUSY

There are three good reasons why it is important to get busy when we are down. First, in order to change how we're feeling, we have to change what we're doing. Second, getting busy is a useful way to bolster our feelings of self-efficacy. Third, getting busy when we're down encourages positive responses from others.

Actions Change Feelings

Often when we're in the dumps we say to ourselves, "I feel too low to do anything. I'll get busy when I feel better." It is truly more difficult to be active when we're feeling low than when we're feeling great. However, if we insist on feeling better before we get busy, we'll waste a lot of time. Psychologists have verified through research and clinical practice something we all know from our life experiences: *Actions change feelings* (Kleinke, 1984b, 1986).

Psychological research has indicated that depressed people engage in fewer pleasant activities than nondepressed people. Research has also indicated that depressed people feel better when they are taught to bring more pleasant activities into their lives. For this reason, an important component in the psychotherapy of depression is the *daily activity schedule.* The purpose of this schedule is to help depressives get busy with activities that will provide a sense of mastery and pleasure. To make an activity schedule we write down all hours of a given day and fill in these time slots with activities we promise to accomplish during that day. At the end of the day we record the activities we actually accomplished and rate them from 0 (low) to 5 (high) on how much mastery and pleasure they helped us experience (Beck, Rush, Shaw, & Emery, 1979; Brown, R. A., & Lewinsohn, 1984; Lewinsohn, 1975).

Table 5.2 is an example of a daily activity schedule for a weekend or holiday. A daily activity schedule such as this serves three purposes. First, it commits us to being active. Second, it helps us see which activities are boring and nonfulfilling and which provide a sense of mastery and pleasure. We can use our activity schedule to plan more meaningful activities in the future. Third, the daily activity schedule provides an opportunity to reward ourselves for our accomplishments.

The Value of Self-Efficacy

The value of self-efficacy in pulling ourselves up when we're down is demonstrated in a study that looked at factors related to successful therapy for depression (Steinmetz, Lewinsohn, & Antonuccio, 1983). The most important characteristic of people who got over their depression was how depressed they were in the first place. Not surprisingly, very depressed people did not pull themselves up as easily as moderately depressed people did. Two other factors related to improvement were people's expectations of success and their feelings of internal control. In other words, it was much easier for people to overcome depression when they were determined to feel better and when they took the responsibility to make this happen.

Another research study demonstrating the value of self-efficacy involved a program where depressed people were divided into three therapy groups (Zeiss, Lewinsohn, & Munoz, 1979). Each therapy group emphasized a different coping skill: interpersonal relations, balanced thinking, or activities. The most interesting result of this study was that the *kind* of coping skill people learned was not as important as the fact that, as a result of their therapy, they felt a greater sense of self-efficacy and control over their lives. Even though the three therapy groups differed in content, they all provided the same message: *You can learn coping skills that will help you take control of your life.*

Encouraging Positive Responses from Others

One good reason for getting busy when we are down is to encourage positive responses from others. Research has demonstrated that people get turned off by someone who is depressed because low moods are contagious. A depressed person also rubs others the wrong way because he or she doesn't engage in appropriate social interactions. Research comparing conversational responses of depressed and nondepressed people found that depressed people were weak in the following areas (Blumberg & Hokanson, 1983):

> Depressed people did not maintain the conversation.
> Depressed people put themselves down.
> Depressed people communicated too many negative feelings.
> Depressed people acted helpless.

Depressed people come across more negatively than nondepressed people in communicating interest, pleasantness, and responsiveness. Because depressed people are not much fun to be around, it is not surprising that they are avoided and

TABLE 5.2   Daily Activity Schedule for Weekend or Holiday

Time	Activity	Accomplished?	Mastery	Pleasure
8–9	Eat breakfast	Yes	2	4
9–10	Listen to music	Yes	2	4
10–11	Do laundry	Yes	3	2
11–12	Write letter	No—sat around	0	0
12–1	Meet friend for lunch	Yes	3	5
1–2	Relax with friend	Yes	3	5
2–4	Physical exercise	Yes	5	4
4–5	Relax at home–read newspaper	Yes	2	3
5–6	Housework	1/2	4	3
6–7	Cook special dinner	Yes	5	4
7–8	Eat dinner with friends or family	Yes	3	5
8–10	Watch TV	Yes	2	3
10–11	Read book	Sat around from 10–10:30	0	1
		Read from 10:30–11:30	4	4

rejected. Depressives are a burden and a strain on others. And to make matters worse, depressed people feel even more depressed because others avoid them (Blumberg & Hokanson, 1983; Coyne et al., 1987; Gotlib & Robinson, 1982; Strack & Coyne, 1983).

The message from this research is loud and clear. If we want others to support us when we're down, we have to give something in return. This does not mean that we should never share our blue moods. In order to have close relationships it is necessary to communicate feelings. The point is that we have to balance the amount of time we lean on others against the time they can lean on us. Depressed people are inordinately dependent and self-critical (Blatt, Quinlan, Chevron, & McDonald, 1982). Nobody likes being around someone like this for too long. So, let others know when you are down. It is valuable to have support people to lean on. But make an effort to be responsive so your support people can also lean on you.

Coping Skill 8: Being Responsive ▲

HOPELESSNESS AND DESPAIR

This chapter has taken an upbeat tone in order to emphasize the value of taking charge when we are down. However, our discussion would not be complete if we did not acknowledge the fact that people can have feelings of hopelessness and despair. Check whether the following statements are true or false descriptions of your current life:

	True	False
1. I look forward to the future with hope and enthusiasm.	____	____
2. I expect to get more of the good things in life than the average person.	____	____
3. I might as well give up because I can't make things better for myself.	____	____
4. All I can see ahead of me is unpleasantness rather than pleasantness.	____	____
5. My future seems dark to me.	____	____
6. I can look forward to more good times than bad times.	____	____
7. I never get what I want, so it's foolish to want anything.	____	____
8. My past experiences have prepared me well for my future.	____	____

These statements come from the Hopelessness Scale (Beck, Weissman, Lester, & Trexler, 1974). When people are feeling hopeless, they agree with statements 3, 4, 5, and 7 and disagree with statements 1, 2, 6, and 8. When people feel hopeless and suicidal, they have no positive expectations about the future. They have lost faith that things will get better and they are ready to give up. Some warning signs of suicide are: suicide threats, previous suicide attempts, sudden changes in behavior (withdrawal, apathy, moodiness), symptoms of depression (crying, sleeplessness, loss of appetite, hopelessness), and final arrangements (saying good-bye, giving away personal possessions). It is important to be aware of suicide signs so we can direct people at risk toward professional help.

Coping Skill 9: Recognizing Hopelessness and Signs of Suicide Risk   ▲

● ●

A CONCLUDING THOUGHT

When we're feeling down, the last thing we need to do is engage in self-blame. Life is full of ups and downs and we wouldn't be normal if we didn't experience both. It is challenging enough to cope with the downs of life without making things harder by expecting perfection and putting ourselves down.

▲ LIST OF SKILLS FOR COPING WHEN YOU'RE DOWN

Coping Skill 1: Acknowledging When Unpleasant Life Events Are Beyond Our Control

Coping Skill 2: Enhancing Personal Relations with Social Skills, Assertiveness, and Negotiation

Coping Skill 3: Questioning and Revising Inaccurate Primary Appraisals

Coping Skill 4: Maintaining a Sense of Control

Coping Skill 5: Questioning and Revising Irrational Primary Appraisals

Coping Skill 6: Making Active Use of Problem Solving

Coping Skill 7: Taking the Initiative to Think Positive Thoughts

Coping Skill 8: Being Responsive

Coping Skill 9: Recognizing Hopelessness and Signs of Suicide Risk

SUGGESTIONS FOR FURTHER READING

BURNS, D. D. (1980). *Feeling good: The new mood therapy.* New York: Signet/New American Library.

EMERY, G. (1987). *Getting undepressed: How a woman can change her life through cognitive therapy.* New York: Touchstone Books.

GORDON, S. (1988). *When living hurts.* New York: Dell.

GREIST, J. H., & JEFFERSON, J. W. (1985). *Depression and its treatment.* New York: Warner Books.

LaHAYE, T. (1985). *How to win over depression.* New York: Bantam.

LEWINSOHN, P. M. (1984). *The coping with depression course: A psychoeducational intervention for unipolar depression.* Eugene, Ore.: Castalia.

LEWINSOHN, P. M. (1985). *Control your depression.* Englewood Cliffs, N.J.: Prentice-Hall.

PAPOLOS, D. F., & PAPOLOS, J. (1986). *Overcoming depression.* New York: Harper & Row.

WRIGHT, H. N. (1988). *Beating the blues: Overcoming depression and stress.* Ventura, Calif.: Regal.

6

....

Coping with Loneliness, Shyness, and Rejection

THE EXPERIENCE OF LONELINESS

How often do you have the following feelings?

	Never	Rarely	Sometimes	Often
1. I lack companionship.	____	____	____	____
2. There is no one I can turn to.	____	____	____	____
3. I feel in tune with the people around me.	____	____	____	____
4. There are people I feel close to.	____	____	____	____
5. No one really knows me well.	____	____	____	____
6. I do not feel alone.	____	____	____	____

These statements come from the revised UCLA Loneliness Scale (Russell, Peplau, & Cutrona, 1980). People who feel lonely tend to agree with statements 1, 2, and 5 and to disagree with statements 3, 4, and 6. Loneliness is viewed by most people as a negative experience. A survey by a university student health service determined that college students ranked loneliness as one of their most common health problems (Bradburn, 1969). In a national health survey, 26% of U.S. respondents said they recently felt "very lonely and remote from other people" (Peplau, Russell, & Heim, 1979). Two influential books by sociologists David Riesman (*The Lonely Crowd,* 1953) and Philip Slater (*The Pursuit of Loneliness,* 1970) describe how U.S. values of competition, independence, and individuality result in feelings of loneliness and alienation. Loneliness is an experience with which most of us can identify and one that is detrimental for many people (Jones, W. H., 1982).

Researchers have defined two kinds of loneliness: *social loneliness* and *emotional loneliness* (Russell, Cutrona, Rose, & Yurko, 1984; Weiss, 1973). As indicated in Table 6.1, social loneliness is caused by not feeling part of a group and not having people with whom to share activities. Social loneliness occurs when we are dissatisfied with our friendships and when we need reassurance about our worth. Emotional loneliness is caused by estrangement and rejection. Emotional loneliness occurs when we are not satisfied with our personal attachments and when we don't have anyone to lean on for nurturance.

Although social loneliness and emotional loneliness result from different needs, they are both associated with feelings of depression. Whether their loneliness is social or emotional, lonely people are unhappy and they suffer from low self-esteem (Russell et al., 1984; Perlman & Peplau, 1981; Peplau et al., 1979).

Loneliness occurs when there is a discrepancy between a person's desired and achieved social relations (Peplau et al., 1979). Loneliness is a subjective experience because it is governed by the appraisals we make when our social relations do not meet our expectations. The subjectivity of loneliness can be appreciated by looking at people's interpretations of this experience.

EXPLANATIONS FOR LONELINESS

Psychologists have conducted a large amount of research on people's explanations for life events. This research is called *attribution research* because it focuses on the

TABLE 6.1   Social and Emotional Loneliness

Social Loneliness	Emotional Loneliness
Common experiences	
Not feeling "in tune" with others	Having no one to turn to
Not having things in common with others	Not feeling close to anyone
Not feeling part of a group of friends	Not being understood as a person
Major need	
Reassurance of worth	Attachment and nurturance
Resulting emotions	
Depression	Depression, anxiety

From "Social and Emotional Lonelienss: An Examination of Weiss's Typology of Loneliness" by D. Russell, C. E. Cutrona, J. Rose and K. Yurko, 1984, *Journal of Personality and Social Psychology, 46,* 1313–1321. Copyright 1984 by the American Psychological Association. Adapted with permission.

causes and meanings we attribute to things that happen to us (Kleinke, 1978, 1986). Table 6.2 demonstrates how attributions can influence our emotional and coping responses to loneliness (Michela, Peplau, & Weeks, 1982; Peplau et al., 1979; Rubenstein & Shaver, 1980, 1982; Shaver & Rubenstein, 1980). According to the table, we explain loneliness on the basis of two factors. First, we ask whether our loneliness is caused by something about ourselves (personal cause) or whether our loneliness is due to our life situation (external cause). Second, we judge whether there is anything we can do to change the cause of our loneliness. Table 6.2 makes two very important points:

1. The explanations we give for our loneliness have a strong influence on our emotional reactions and coping responses.
2. The explanations we give for our loneliness are largely subjective.

Table 6.2 suggests that it is advantageous to confront loneliness with self-responsibility rather than self-blame. Lonely people often suffer because they believe their loneliness is due to a shortcoming within themselves that they can't control (Anderson & Arnoult, 1985; Anderson, Horowitz, & French, 1983). Table 6.2 helps us appreciate that it is useful to understand loneliness as a condition we can change. A good way to outline the skills for coping with loneliness is to follow the experience of loneliness through the appraisal process described in Chapters 1 and 2.

Coping Skill 1: Interpreting Loneliness as Changeable   ▲

PRIMARY APPRAISAL OF ALONENESS

In Chapter 2 we learned that our primary appraisal of a life event can affect our resulting emotions. Let's take the life event of "aloneness" and look at the various

TABLE 6.2   Influence of Attributions about Loneliness on Emotions and Coping Responses

• •

Attribution about Cause and Changeability	*Probable Emotions*	*Probable Response*
Personal: unchangeable	Depression, shame, self-depreciation	Passivity: cry, sleep, eat, take drugs, drink, watch TV
I am lonely because I'm unattractive and there's nothing I can do about it.		
I am lonely because I don't have an outgoing personality.		
I am lonely because people just don't seem to like me.		
Personal: changeable	Dissatisfaction, impatience	Active coping: self-mastery, self-motivation
I am lonely because I'm shy, but this is something I can work on.		
I am lonely because I haven't put enough energy into developing relationships.		
I am lonely because I haven't spent enough time learning how to get along with people.		
External: unchangeable	Anger, hostility	Solitude: walk, go to movie, exercise, read, listen to music
I am lonely because other people don't ever try to get to know me.		
I am lonely because people where I live are too tied up with their own lives.		
I am lonely because I live in a place where it is impossible to meet people.		
External: changeable	Dissatisfaction, impatience	Active coping: call or visit people, attend groups, attend social events
I am lonely because I haven't taken the time to find out where I can meet people.		
I am lonely because I haven't asked enough people to do things with me.		
I am lonely because I don't belong to any social groups.		

ways we can appraise this experience. The example on the next page is based on Figure 2.2 from Chapter 2.

What kinds of primary appraisals of being alone might lead to feelings of depression? Probably saying things to ourselves like: "I'm all alone. Nobody cares about me. My life is worthless because I don't have anyone close to me." What kinds

of appraisals might make us feel *anxious?* Probably saying things to ourselves like: "I'm all alone and I can't stand it. I can't bear living without someone close to me." What kind of appraisals might cause feelings of *dissatisfaction?* Probably saying things to yourself like: "I'm all alone and I'm not satisfied with my relationships. I have to look at what I need to do to improve this situation." What kind of appraisals might engender feelings of *solitude?* Probably saying things to ourselves like: "I'm all alone. This is a good time for me to do something for myself."

You may remember from Chapter 2 that Albert Ellis's rational-emotive therapy is deceptively simple. It's easy to see how emotional reactions to aloneness are affected by primary appraisals. However, teaching ourselves to reconsider primary appraisals takes time and effort. You would probably agree that dissatisfaction and solitude are more desirable responses to the experience of being alone than anxiety and depression. How can we learn to achieve these appraisals?

Appraising Aloneness as Solitude

Philosopher Tom Wenzel has pointed out that creative people have learned to cherish times of aloneness as "solitude" where they work on self-fulfilling activities (Wenzel, personal communication, 1984). Of course, people differ in how much time they spend with others and how much time they spend alone (Jones, W. H., Carpenter, & Quintana, 1985). However, it seems fair to say that everyone could benefit from learning to allow some solitary time for pursuing hobbies, interests, and other activities devoted to personal growth. It is unfortunate that many people are afraid of being alone and view aloneness as a stigma and a negative experience. The fact is that we are each our own best friend. It is important to appreciate solitude as an opportunity to learn to like ourselves. One of the best favors we can do for children is to help them develop creative ways for being alone (Rook, 1984; Young, 1982). We live in a fast-food society that encourages passivity and lack of initiative. When we're bored we flip on the TV to be entertained by others rather than taking the effort to engage in a creative activity. When people get too used to seeking external sources of entertainment they become helpless when they have to entertain themselves (Skinner, 1986). Consider the following quotations from writers who understood solitude as an opportunity for self-fulfillment (Henry, 1959): "In solitude, when we are *least* alone" (Byron). "Solitude is as needful to the imagination as society is wholesome for the character" (James Russell Lowell). "I never found the companion that was so companionable as solitude" (Thoreau).

Coping Skill 2: Learning to Like Ourselves
by Using Solitude for Pursuing Self-Fulfilling Activities   ▲
• •

Appraising Aloneness as Dissatisfaction

Even people who are very good at using solitude have times when they say to themselves, "I've spent enough time right now doing things by myself. I'd like some closeness with others." When we appraise aloneness as dissatisfaction, it is time to make a *secondary appraisal* to settle on a course of action.

Secondary appraisal is when we recognize a problem and ask what, if anything, we can do about it. When we are dissatisfied with being alone there are three issues to be considered. First, it is important to take a serious look at our social skills. Second, we want to overcome shyness and initiate personal contacts. Third, it is in our best interest to increase our tolerance for rejection. We will consider all of these issues in this chapter.

SOCIAL SKILLS DEFICITS OF LONELY PEOPLE

Lonely people are often deficient in social skills. Researchers have found that lonely people are hard to get to know because they don't disclose things about themselves in an appropriate manner. Lonely people are too cautious about revealing themselves to members of the opposite sex. On the other hand, they sometimes make people of the same sex uncomfortable because their "need for a friend" causes them to share intimate details about themselves too soon (Jones, W. H., 1982; Solano, Batten, & Parish, 1982).

Another example of social skills deficits is seen in a study where college students were introduced to someone of the opposite sex with whom they could talk for 15 minutes (Jones, W. H., Hobbs, & Hockenbury, 1982). The conversations were video-taped, and each student was rated on social skills. Results showed that students with high scores on the UCLA Loneliness Scale had poorer social skills than students with low scores. Poor social skills were characterized by not showing interest in what the other person was saying and not following up the other person's statements with relevant questions and responses. A second phase of this study was especially interesting because it demonstrated that lonely students could be taught to increase their attention-showing skills by observing videotapes of successful conversations and by practicing their own skills by role-playing. As a result of this training, lonely students demonstrated significant improvement in their conversational skills, and they experienced decreased feelings of loneliness.

Shy people have poor social skills because they are preoccupied with making a good impression and are doubtful about their ability to do so (Arkin, Lake, & Baumgardner, 1986; Carver & Scheier, 1986). Because they feel vulnerable, they take a cautious and retiring approach toward others. They "play it safe" by sitting back, staying uninvolved, and remaining anonymous. Shy people are reluctant to take the initiative in social interactions. They let others do the work. And because they are nonresponsive and socially reticent, it is understandable that they don't make a particularly good impression on others (Gough & Thorne, 1986).

THE COSTS OF PLAYING IT SAFE

Playing it safe as a way of relating to others has all of the disadvantages of avoidance that were discussed in Chapter 1. People who avoid taking the initiative in social interactions (*avoiders*) differ from those who are willing to put themselves out and take chances (*initiators*) in their perceptions, self-statements, actions, and internal control (Langston & Cantor, 1989). For example, avoiders have low expectations for experiencing success and pleasure. They tend to perceive social interactions as stressful and don't look forward to the possibility of positive outcomes. On the other hand, initiators view social interactions as interesting and absorbing. They aren't preoccupied with negative thoughts, and they don't let themselves become overwhelmed. Avoiders tend to make self-depreciating statements. They feel others are more appealing than they are. And they blame themselves for unsuccessful social interactions. On the other hand, initiators are satisfied with their efforts in social interactions. They don't ruminate about unsuccessful social interactions; they move on to new challenges. They accept their strengths and weaknesses.

In terms of actions, avoiders are indecisive—they are too worried about failing. They don't effectively seek social support, and they feel like outsiders who don't fit in. Initiators, in contrast, focus on effective courses of action. They align themselves with others who can help them. And they put themselves out to become part of a group.

Avoiders are passive and follow the lead of others. They try to please others. In general, avoiders get lost in the crowd. Initiators, on the other hand, are active and don't passively follow others. They gain self-worth from their own standards. They are willing to assert their individuality.

Because of their style, avoiders are anxious. They suffer from stress and dissatisfaction about their social interactions. However, there is hope. By practicing good social skills and learning to tolerate rejection, avoiders can turn themselves into initiators.

Coping Skill 3: Being an Initiator ▲

SOCIAL SKILLS TRAINING

In recognition of the value of social skills, psychologists have developed training programs that teach people to improve their skills in social interactions. Participants in these programs usually sign a contract outlining their goals and their commitment to the program. Training groups are then set up. The group leader usually begins by describing effective social skills for various situations. He or she then models these behaviors in such a way that participants can adapt them to their personal styles and practice them in the group with the benefit of group feedback. Video recordings are often used. Group participants are also taught to use their imagination to prepare themselves for situations in which effective social skills are required. After sufficient practice and feedback, participants are given homework assignments for practicing effective social skills in their daily lives. Participants receive continued feedback from the group and are encouraged to enlist friends and family members for support. Participants are taught to work gradually from easy to more difficult social interactions, to monitor their progress, and to reward themselves for success. When the training group ends, group members might agree to meet at a later date for a follow-up or "booster" session (Eisler & Frederiksen, 1980; L'Abate & Milan, 1985).

LEARNING TO BE RESPONSIVE

Of all the social skills taught in social skills training groups, probably the most important overall skill is that of being *responsive* (Davis, D., & Perkowitz, 1979). The power of responsiveness was demonstrated in a study where college men were introduced to an attractive woman with whom they chatted for 5 minutes (Gold, Ryckman, & Mosley, 1984). For one group of men, the woman made a special effort to show interest, maintain eye contact, and hold up her end of the conversation. A second group of men met the same woman but were not given the opportunity to chat with her and receive her interest and attention. Since the woman was attractive, all the men liked her. However, the men who had received her attention were attracted to her even more. In fact, the 5 minutes of attention were enough to outweigh any disagreements that existed between the men and the woman about personal opinions and attitudes. Thus, by being responsive, we can encourage others to like us and also help them to like themselves. It makes people feel good when we are able to provide them with the experience of a positive interaction (Haemmerlie & Montgomery, 1984).

Responsiveness means being "with" another person by showing attention, maintaining eye contact, and hearing what he or she is saying. Carl Rogers (1961) has pointed out that we often respond to others by stating our own opinion without acknowledging their feelings. For example, assume someone says, "I liked that movie," or "I felt bad about what happened to so-and-so." A responsive reply would be, "What did you like in the movie?" or "I'm sorry you felt bad. Tell me about it." However, most of us would be more likely to simply state our own opinions by saying things like, "I didn't like the movie either," "I thought the movie was pretty good," "I felt bad, too, but in many ways what happened was to be expected." A responsive reply is empathetic. It communicates an understanding of the other person's feelings (Davis, D., & Holtgraves, 1984).

Research on social skills has identified the following factors that are associated with successful social interactions (Conger & Farrell, 1981; Greenwald, 1977; Kupke, Calhoun, & Hobbs, 1979; Kupke & Hobbs, 1979):

1. Personal attention to what the other person is saying.
2. Encouraging the other person to express his or her opinions.
3. Holding up your end of the conversation, but balancing interest in the other person's statements against talking about yourself.
4. Maintaining sufficient eye contact.
5. Looking your best.

We can all understand why people like others who are responsive. Responsiveness communicates personal interest and positive feelings. Responsiveness also reinforces certainty and self-confidence. People like to know we are paying attention and taking them seriously.

What does it take to be responsive? Here are some suggestions (Davis, D., & Perkowitz, 1979):

Motivation: Instead of simply expressing our own opinions, we have to be willing to expend the energy to hear what the other person is saying.
Attentiveness: We need to maintain eye contact and to listen carefully. What are the issues, feelings, and problems to which he or she desires a response?
Empathy: How is the other person feeling? If we are not sure, we need to ask.
Skill: Social skills should be practiced so we can respond in an appropriate manner.

It also helps to take care of your clothes and grooming.

There is one last point about responsiveness that has a lot to do with the issue of internal versus external control discussed in Chapter 3. To be responsive, *we* have to take the initiative in social interactions. We can't just say, "That person didn't seem very interested in me so I didn't respond." Instead, we should take the attitude that if we are responsive, the other person will probably reciprocate. Research shows that people who are skillful at initiating interactions are willing to take the responsibility for getting a conversation started (Lefcourt, Martin, Fick, & Saleh, 1985). People who are good at getting others to "open up" have practiced their social skills to the point where they can answer yes to the following questions (Miller, L. C, Berg, & Archer, 1983):

1. Are you a good listener?
2. Are you accepting of others?
3. Do you help people feel relaxed?
4. Do you encourage people to tell you how they are feeling?
5. Are you sympathetic to people's problems.

Of course, when we take the initiative to be responsive, there are times when we will be rejected. Some tips for tolerating rejection are presented later in this chapter.

Coping Skill 4: Practicing the Social Skill of Being Responsive   ▲
•••

OVERCOMING SHYNESS

Shyness can be defined as being fearful about meeting people and suffering discomfort in their presence. An important thing to know about shyness is that it is an experience shared by most people. It may surprise you to learn that over 80% of Americans in a recent survey cited by Philip Zimbardo (1977) in his book, *Shyness,* said they knew what it means to feel shy. Only 7% claimed that they had never experienced shyness. Shy people describe themselves as having trouble making conversation and maintaining eye contact and as experiencing discomfort when attempting to initiate interactions with others. Shy people experience the following symptoms (Cheek, Melchior, & Carpentieri, 1986):

Physical discomfort: Upset stomach, pounding heart, sweating, and blushing
Self-consciousness: Self-depreciating thoughts, worries about being negatively evaluated by others
Poor social skills: Awkwardness, social inhibition

People say they feel shy primarily when they are with strangers, members of the opposite sex, and authority figures. Zimbardo reports that feelings of shyness are common among some of the most seemingly outgoing television and movie personalities. To feel shy inside and still push yourself to be outgoing takes special coping skills. Let's look at what they are.

Adaptive Explanations for Shyness

Earlier in this chapter we learned the value of understanding loneliness as personal and changeable. An adaptive way to explain shyness is to say something like: "It is natural to feel shy at times, but I can learn how to be outgoing in spite of these feelings." It is not adaptive to explain shyness with the following kinds of statements: "Being shy is part of my personality and I'm not likely to change." "The reason I am shy is because other people don't understand me." Shy people take a pessimistic attitude by assuming they will always be shy and that their social life depends on the initiative of others (Teglasi & Hoffman, 1982).

The value of rational explanations for shyness was demonstrated in the following research study (Hoffman & Teglasi, 1982). People suffering from shyness were assigned to one of three different therapy groups. Shy people in one group were helped to understand their shyness as an outcome of their childhood experiences. Those in a second group learned to understand their shyness as a product of their thinking styles and self-perceptions. The third group of shy people received counseling that did not focus on finding explanations for shyness. Which therapy group was most successful? In general, the first two approaches, which helped the shy people find an explanation for their shyness, were more effective than the third approach, which did not. However, there is reason to argue that the approach taken in the second therapy group was most advantageous because it encouraged shy people to take responsibility for their shyness and to commit themselves to reevaluating their thinking styles and self-perceptions. Shy people in the first group might be tempted to cop out by "blaming" their shyness on their childhood experiences.

To have satisfactory interpersonal relations it is useful to work on our social skills. It is also important to take control of our thinking style and the interpretations we make about our social situation (Glass & Shea, 1986).

Coping Skill 5: Taking Control of Our Thinking Style   ▲

Opening Lines

You are probably aware that marriages in many societies are arranged by family elders. Sons and daughters have nothing to say about their future spouses. Although you probably prefer to choose your own romantic partners, you can appreciate the fact that arranged marriages avoid all the hassles of meeting people and the discomforts of dating until you find Mr. or Ms. "Right." On the other hand, meeting people can be an adventure if we have the proper attitude.

My interest in opening lines began with the realization of their potential for expanding one's social networks. Most of the time our social contacts are limited to people we meet at work, school, or through family members and friends. Although we may see people walking down the street, and in stores, parks, buses, and numerous other places, whom we would *like* to meet, it might not occur to us that it is actually possible. In theory, our social marketplace is wherever we happen to be at a given time. How can we put this theory into practice? When we run across a person we would like to meet, we have to initiate social contact. To initiate contact, we have to start a conversation, and to start a conversation, we have to say something—an opening line. An opening line is a negotiation. It is a way of expressing interest in another person in a nonthreatening way. The other person then has the opportunity to communicate whether she or he is willing to reciprocate. When using opening lines as a process of negotiation, we are faced with two challenges. First, we have to take a risk and say something. Second, we have to learn to tolerate rejection. The remainder of this chapter considers both of these challenges.

Preferred and Nonpreferred Opening Lines

Frederick Meeker, Richard Staneski, and I surveyed more than a thousand people about their attitudes toward opening lines for men meeting women and for women meeting men (Kleinke, Meeker, & Staneski, 1986). When we analyzed our data we found that our opening lines could be separated into three categories: innocuous, direct, and cute/flippant. Some of the opening lines that were most preferred and least preferred are listed below:

Most Preferred Opening Lines	*Type of Approach*
"Hi."	Innocuous
"Can you give me directions to ———?"	Innocuous
"Can you help me with ———?"	Innocuous
"Did you see (a particular movie) or read (a particular book)?"	Innocuous
"I feel a little embarrassed about this, but I'd like to meet you."	Direct
"That's a very pretty (sweater, shirt, etc.) you have on."	Direct
"You have really nice (hair, eyes, etc.)."	Direct
"Since we're both sitting alone, would you care to join me?"	Direct
"Is it OK if I sit with you?"	Direct

Least Preferred Opening Lines	
"I'm easy. Are you?"	Cute/flippant
"I've got an offer you can't refuse."	Cute/flippant
"What's your sign?"	Cute/flippant
"Didn't we meet in a previous life?"	Cute/flippant
"Your place or mine?"	Cute/flippant
"Is that really your hair?"	Cute/flippant
"You remind me of a woman (man) I used to date."	Cute/flippant
"Isn't it cold? Let's make some body heat."	Cute/flippant

When we look at these opening lines, two things become clear. First, the respondents did not like opening lines that were cute/flippant. Second, innocuous and direct opening lines were both viewed as acceptable. However, two additional points must be considered. Although our respondents did not like cute/flippant opening lines, we found that women disliked cute/flippant lines even more than men did. In other words, men underestimated how much women dislike cute/flippant opening lines. Also, although innocuous opening lines were generally viewed as acceptable, women liked this kind of approach more than men. Direct lines were equally liked by men and women.

Results from research on opening lines offer the following advice for men and women (Cunningham, 1988; Kleinke & Dean, 1990; Kleinke et al., 1986).

Advice for Men

Men should be aware that most women prefer a soft, nonthreatening approach and that it is risky to come on too strongly. They should realize that although the macho approach may work in the movies or on TV, this has little to do with real life. Men should also be aware of the fact that most stories about successful pickups they hear from friends or read about in magazines exist more in the realm of fantasy than reality. Cute/flippant opening lines may help protect the user from admitting lone-liness and the desire for a personal relationship. But they are likely to lose the woman. Men who have difficulty tolerating rejection are advised to stick with innocuous lines. Innocuous lines minimize vulnerability and give the woman an opportunity to respond without being turned off or driven away. For men who are willing to admit vulnerability, direct opening lines should be considered.

Advice for Women

The people we surveyed said they felt it is equally appropriate for women to approach men as it is for men to approach women. My first advice to women is to recognize this fact. Women don't need to sit and wait for a man to get up the nerve to approach them. After all, the man with the nerve might not be the right man. Women should seriously consider taking control of their social contacts. Of course, in taking the initiative for meeting men, women face some challenges. Many men are not used to being approached by women and don't know how to respond in a gracious manner. Women learn from a young age how to be polite and yet get away from men they don't like. Most men have not developed this skill. It is important for women to approach men in a nonthreatening manner. To do this takes sensitivity. The woman wants the man to know she is interested in him, but she does not want to come across as overbearing. Another challenge facing women is that men tend to interpret any interest shown by a woman as sexual (Abbey, 1982, 1987; Shotland & Craig, 1988). Women are advised to develop their self-esteem and confidence so they can deal with the discomfort experienced by some of the men they want to meet.

Coping Skill 6: Recognizing the Value of Opening Lines ▲

MAKING CONVERSATION

Margi Lenga Kahn, Tracy Beach Tully, and I conducted a series of studies to find out how people are evaluated when they talk a small amount, a medium amount, or a large amount in a conversation with someone they have just met (Kleinke, Kahn, & Tully, 1979). We made up a series of taped conversations between men and women and systematically varied the amount of time each person spoke. In some of the tapes the man talked 80% of the time, the woman 20% of the time. In other tapes the woman talked 80% of the time and the man 20%. In a third series of tapes the man and woman each talked 50% of the time. We asked research participants to listen to these tapes and evaluate the speakers on a rating form. Although we did not tell our raters what we were studying, the amount of talking had a strong effect on how the talkers were evaluated. Two of our findings were especially interesting. First, people talking 50% of the time were liked more than people who talked 20% or 80% of the time. Second, the 20% talkers were evaluated as being exceptionally submissive and introverted. The negative ratings given to men and women who spoke 20% of the time were surprising and suggested that people in first meetings are expected to hold up their end of the conversation. It seems that a good listener is not necessarily a person who is quiet but rather one who is responsive and adds to the other's statements.

We thought that men who talked 80% of the time might not be evaluated as unfavorably as women doing so because men are stereotyped as being more domineering than women, and a high amount of talking by men might be expected and taken for granted. This was not so. Our research participants did not favor 80% talkers whether they were men or women.

The results of our study reinforce advice about being responsive. Getting along with others requires good conversational skills. Research has found that conversational skills of shy people are seriously lacking (Pilkonis, 1977). Shy people are reluctant to initiate conversations, they don't break silences, and they don't respond with enthusiasm to other people's statements.

Conversational Styles of Introverts and Extraverts

A study comparing conversational styles of extraverted and introverted women found very different styles when the women were getting acquainted with a new person (Thorne, 1987). Extraverted women came across as cheerful, enthusiastic, and sociable. They talked about activities and interests that were fun. Introverted women were more reserved. They asked questions and acted more as interviewers. When they did volunteer information, they tended to focus on their problems. Conversations between two introverts were the most uncomfortable because both people held back and waited for the other to take the initiative. Although such a study has not been conducted with men, the results would probably be similar. When meeting new people, we want to match our conversation to their style. When talking with introverts, we have to draw them out and not be put off by their reticence. With extraverts, we can spend more time being a good listener. But we still have to hold up our end of the conversation, make the effort to be responsive, and share things about ourself so the other people get to know us.

IMPROVING CONVERSATIONAL SKILLS

Fortunately, conversational skills can be learned and improved. People who have trouble making conversations often complain that it is hard to think of anything to say. There are two solutions to this problem. First, it is important to have realistic expectations. People who are "talkers" have learned not to censor many of their thoughts before they speak. They have also learned to reduce their expectations for "meaningful" conversations and to be satisfied with small talk. The purpose of small talk is to communicate to others that we are interested in them. When we first meet somebody, it is not so important *what* we say as long as we demonstrate our willingness to carry on a conversation. A deeper and more meaningful relationship will come later.

The second solution for those with conversational difficulties is to *practice* talking with others. Here are some ideas for practicing talking skills (Zimbardo, 1977).

Use the telephone: Call the public library and ask the reference librarian for some information you would like to have. Call a theater and ask for show times. See if you can make the person on the telephone laugh. Call a radio talk show. Express an opinion and notice the announcer's reaction.

Say "hello": Say "hi" or "good morning" to people you see at work or school. Smile and say "hi" to people you pass on the street. Notice their reaction. If they don't respond, that's OK. It's still fun to see that you can do it.

Give compliments: Compliment someone standing in line in a bank or grocery store. Maybe the person is wearing some unusual jewelry or attractive clothing. Ask where it came from.

Ask questions: Ask questions about a person's dog, running shoes, bicycle, or portable radio. Be open to learning new things. People love to talk about their activities and hobbies. Ask questions that require explanations rather than simple yes or no answers.

Share a common experience: Look for something you can share with a person you want to meet. Perhaps there is something unusual about the weather or the experience of standing in a long line or being in a crowd that you can talk about.

Read, ask, and tell: Read the newspaper, read movie and book reviews, learn about political situations in the world and events in your community. Ask people for their opinions on these issues and share your knowledge with them.

Coping Skill 7: Developing the Ability to Make Conversation   ▲

LEARNING TO TOLERATE REJECTION

Lonely and shy people have difficulty tolerating rejection. One reason for this difficulty is that shy and lonely people take a different view of personal interactions than nonlonely people do. Research indicates that people who can handle rejection tend to look at social interactions as an opportunity to develop closeness with others and to share pleasant feelings (Goldfried, Padawer, & Robins, 1984). Shy and lonely people are more likely to view social interactions as a threatening experience where they are being judged and evaluated. This kind of attitude causes anxiety and defensiveness. Instead of relaxing and having fun with others, shy and lonely people tend to be uptight and negative (Goswick & Jones, W. H., 1981; Hansson & Jones, 1981; Jones, W. H., Sansone, & Helm, 1983). It is important for us to avoid being preoccupied with our own feelings of wanting acceptance and approval. We need to focus our attention on the people with whom we are interacting and to ask ourselves what we can do to help them feel comfortable (Alden & Cappe, 1986).

Another reason why shy and lonely people can't tolerate rejection is because they make negative primary appraisals. Referring back to Figure 2.2 on page 17, in Chapter 2, we can define the life event as an experience of rejection. What are some of the worst things we can say to ourselves when we are rejected? Some possible examples are: "If I'm rejected it's just awful." "I can't stand it unless everyone likes me." "If I'm rejected it means I'm unattractive, unlikable, and no good." Obviously, these kinds of appraisals are likely to result in depression, anger, anxiety, and low self-esteem, which are exactly the kinds of feelings lonely people suffer. Weigh those unadaptive thoughts against the following, more adaptive beliefs: "Even if I'm rejected I can be proud for trying." "The more I can tolerate rejection, the more people I can meet." "Some people will like me and some people won't like me, but I feel I am accomplishing something when I can get out there and try."

How rational are the following expectations? "I can't be happy unless everyone I meet is responsive to me." "If every conversation I attempt doesn't lead to a good relationship it is a failure." Can you substitute the following, more realistic expectations? "If I just say 'hi' to someone, I am achieving a goal." "I have to play the odds. The more people I talk to, the more people I will meet." "Some conversations go further than others. I must be patient and find satisfaction in making the attempt."

You can practice coping with rejection by using the self-relaxation skills described in Chapter 3. Sit down in a quiet, relaxing place, close your eyes, and imagine that you are approaching someone you would like to meet and are being rejected. What does it feel like? Start with mild thoughts of rejection and counteract them with relaxation. Work your way up slowly until you can imagine harder rejections while still remaining relaxed. Remember what it feels like to be relaxed when you are trying to meet people. Keep in touch with your feelings of self-doubt and anxiety and use them as cues to put your relaxation skills to work. Relaxation skills will help you realize that although being rejected is not fun, you can stand it. Teach yourself that the mild inconvenience of being rejected is a worthwhile price to pay for the opportunity to meet many special and interesting people.

Coping Skill 8: Learning to Tolerate Rejection   ▲

▲ LIST OF SKILLS FOR COPING WITH LONELINESS AND SHYNESS

Coping Skill 1: Interpreting Loneliness as Changeable

Coping Skill 2: Learning to Like Ourselves by Using Solitude for Pursuing Self-Fulfilling Activities

Coping Skill 3: Becoming an Initiator

Coping Skill 4: Practicing the Social Skill of Being Responsive

Coping Skill 5: Taking Control of Our Thinking Style

Coping Skill 6: Recognizing the Value of Opening Lines

Coping Skill 7: Developing the Ability to Make Conversation

Coping Skill 8: Learning to Tolerate Rejection

SUGGESTIONS FOR FURTHER READING

GAMBRILL, E., & RICHEY, C. (1985). *Taking charge of your social life.* Belmont, Calif.: Wadsworth.

JONES, W. H., CHEEK, J. M., & BRIGGS, S. R. (Eds.). (1986). *Shyness: Perspectives on research and treatment.* New York: Plenum.

KLEINKE, C. L. (1986). *Meeting and understanding people.* New York: W. H.. Freeman.

PEPLAU, L. A., & PERLMAN, D. (Eds.). (1982). *Loneliness: A sourcebook of current theory, research, and therapy.* New York: Wiley-Interscience.

ZIMBARDO, P. G. (1977). *Shyness: What it is, what to do about it.* Reading, Mass.: Addison-Wesley.

7

Coping
with Anxiety

We all feel anxious at various times in our lives. Because anxiety can be both objective and subjective, it is an interesting experience to understand in terms of the process of primary appraisal discussed in Chapter 2. Some life events give us good reason to believe we are in jeopardy. Anxiety under these circumstances is a normal response. It works to mobilize the body for defense and signals us to pay attention and protect ourself. When our primary appraisal of impending danger is realistic and accurate, our challenge is to come up with a suitable coping response. Anxiety here is helping to energize us during the coping process. It is when our primary appraisal of a life event is not accurate or realistic that anxiety can be undesirable. Anxiety causes trouble when we are tense and stressed for no good reason. We then suffer needlessly because our mind and body are keyed up to ward off a threat or danger we have falsely created.

SOME DEFINITIONS OF ANXIETY

It will be useful to begin our discussion of anxiety with some definitions. The terms *fear* and *anxiety* are often used interchangeably. One distinction that can be made between these terms is that fear usually refers to the primary appraisal of actual peril or danger. Anxiety is related more to the resulting emotional state of tenseness and distress. *Phobias* are exaggerated and often disabling fears of specific events or objects. Phobias are characterized by the urge to avoid these fear-provoking experiences. *Panic* is a sudden overpowering fright accompanied by frantic attempts to find safety (Beck & Emery, 1985; Greist, Jefferson, & Marks, 1986).

In this chapter we will learn how to analyze our appraisals of life events so we can ask ourselves whether our feelings of anxiety are adaptive and self-protective or whether they are unnecessary and needlessly stressful. People whose lives are *seriously* debilitated by anxiety, phobias, and/or panic, however, will find it useful to seek professional help.

THE EXPERIENCE OF ANXIETY

The first step in coping with anxiety is learning to recognize the symptoms of anxiety and how they affect us. As noted above, anxiety can energize and prepare us to meet a challenge. Anxiety can also be a distraction that gets in the way of our normal functioning. We know when we're anxious by a combination of symptoms in our body, our thinking, and our sense of well-being (Beck & Emery, 1985).

The body: When we're anxious, our body reacts by heart palpitations, rapid breathing, shortness of breath, lump in throat, loss of appetite, nausea, insomnia, pressure to urinate, flushed face, sweating, trouble with speech, and/or restlessness.

Thinking: Anxiety causes the following problems in thinking: confusion, impaired memory, difficulty concentrating, distractability, fear of losing control, self-consciousness, hypervigilance, and/or repetitive thoughts.

Well-Being: When we're anxious we might feel edgy, impatient, nervous, alarmed, terrified, jittery, jumpy, frightful, depressed, tense, and/or wound-up.

It is important to be aware of these reactions so we can recognize when we are anxious. The question we want to ask when we recognize these symptoms of anxiety is whether they represent a natural reaction to a real threat or whether they are causing needless stress. How can we learn to do this? The first step is to look carefully at our primary appraisals.

Coping Skill 1: Recognizing Symptoms of Anxiety ▲

You can get a measure of your anxiety by checking how much you are bothered by the following symptoms:

	Not at all	Moderately	Severely
1. Feeling hot	___	___	___
2. Feeling dizzy or light-headed	___	___	___
3. Feeling unsteady	___	___	___
4. Having trembling hands	___	___	___
5. Having a flushed face	___	___	___
6. Fearing the worst happening	___	___	___
7. Being terrified	___	___	___
8. Feeling nervous	___	___	___
9. Fearing losing control	___	___	___
10. Being unable to relax	___	___	___

The above items come from the Beck Anxiety Inventory (Beck, Epstein, Brown, & Steer, 1988). Items 1 through 5 measure somatic symptoms and items 6 through 10 measure subjective anxiety. This inventory was developed as an index of anxiety independent of feelings of depression.

Accepting Anxiety as Part of Life

It is challenging enough to suffer anxiety that interferes with life functioning. We don't need to compound our problems by derogating ourselves (see Chapter 1) *because* we are anxious! If we do that, we will not only suffer from anxiety but also from self-imposed low self-esteem. If we find ourselves thinking such irrational thoughts as: "I'm weak." "I'm neurotic." "No one else gets anxious like I do," we must remember to yell "Stop!" Anxiety is part of life. Everyone knows what it is like to be anxious. We are not weak, foolish, or neurotic because we are anxious—we are human. We have enough work to do to master the coping skills. We shouldn't waste precious energy on self-imposed blame and punishment.

Coping Skill 2: Avoiding Self-Imposed Blame and Punishment ▲

PRIMARY APPRAISALS

When faced with a problem or challenge, our primary appraisal determines whether we are in jeopardy or danger. If we determine that we have good reason to be anxious, we should remember not to punish ourselves for being anxious and to use the techniques for living with anxiety outlined later in this chapter.

If we determine that our anxiety is unnecessary and is causing needless suffering, we need to practice rational thinking (see Chapter 2). Aaron Beck has studied how faulty thinking patterns can cause people to feel miserable. Here are some examples of how we sometimes make ourselves suffer from anxiety (Beck, 1979; Beck & Emery, 1985).

Automatic thinking: When we are preoccupied with something we are trying to avoid, we lose objectivity. We can't get this feared object or event out of our mind. Our preoccupation becomes involuntary and automatic and starts to consume our life.

Overgeneralization: We see danger in things that only remotely resemble the object or event we are avoiding. We get anxious about sounds, sights, smells, and people's actions that remind us of these things we fear. We have fantasies about how a perfectly normal event could harm us.

Catastrophizing: We blow things out of proportion, always thinking of the worst possible outcome. Everything seems terrible, awful, or horrible. We are beyond any possibility of reassurance because we have convinced ourselves that the only possible outcome is disastrous.

Selective perception: We have an aptitude for picking out the negatives. There may be three positive aspects and one negative aspect of an event, and we'll focus on the one negative. If we are feeling really anxious, we may even search for negative facts just to prove to ourselves that it's right to be anxious.

Rigidity: We see things only in black and white. We can't tolerate uncertainty or ambiguity. Things are either good or bad, and because of our overgeneralization, selective perception, and lack of proportion, most things end up looking bad.

Circular reasoning: We say to ourselves, "The fact that I'm not handling this proves that I can't handle it." We use our anxiety as evidence that something is wrong with us.

Unrealistic expectations: We demand perfection. We insist on a life free of challenges, tests, and traumas.

Coping Skill 3: Making Rational Primary Appraisals   ▲

UNDERSTANDING HOW ANXIETY CAN GET THE BEST OF US

Anxiety is compounded by the kinds of irrational thinking outlined above. It is easy to get caught up in the kind of vicious cycle indicated in Figure 7.1. An irrational appraisal of a life event makes us feel needlessly anxious. This anxiety then begins to "prove" to us that something must be wrong and it reinforces our irrational appraisal. It can get to the point where the anxiety we are perpetuating with irrational thinking becomes an overriding problem that has nothing to do with reality. Anxiety gets the best of us when we blow things so far out of proportion that *fear of anxiety* is more debilitating than any realistic fear we could possibly have about the actual life event (Chambless & Gracely, 1989). An important skill for coping with anxiety is not getting caught up in this vicious cycle.

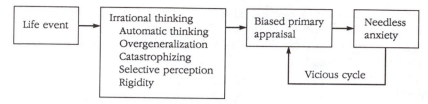

FIGURE 7.1   Vicious cycle where needless anxiety resulting from inaccurate primary appraisal provides "proof" for biased appraisal.

Coping Skill 4: Preventing Anxiety from Getting the Best of Us   ▲

FIVE RULES FOR COPING WITH ANXIETY

Before looking at techniques that can help us live with anxiety it will be worthwhile to learn five basic rules. These include not being an avoider, using positive confrontation, being mastery-oriented, keeping records, and being willing to work.

Don't Be an Avoider

In Chapter 1 we were advised about the ineffectiveness of avoidance. Avoidance is a particularly problematic coping style when it comes to anxiety. It does alleviate anxiety in the short run, but since it does not address the problem or issue, we end up paying a price in the long run. To put it another way, avoidance is a very tempting way of coping with anxiety because it provides immediate relief. It is very reinforcing to hide from people, places, and tasks that make life difficult. Unfortunately, these sources of anxiety will never go away until we confront them. As long as we avoid them, they will haunt us. We won't feel completely relaxed because we are constantly on guard since we never know when a source of anxiety will appear.

Another way to appreciate the disadvantages of being an avoider is by looking at what has been called the *repressive coping style* (Weinberger, Schwartz, & Davidson, 1979). Repressors are people who suffer from anxiety, but deny it. They present themselves as rational, controlled, and undisturbed by stressors in their lives. Unfortunately, while denial might be a useful coping response in the short run, it has negative consequences. Repressors work so hard to convince themselves and others that life problems don't bother them that they don't have much energy left to take pleasure in things they find enjoyable. Their social relationships are often superficial because they don't fully experience and communicate their feelings. Repressors lack flexibility and spontaneity. Their efforts to avoid anxiety prevent them from engaging in creative and stimulating activities. Repressors also pay a price with their health. They are vulnerable to symptoms of stress, such as hypertension, aches and pains, and confusion.

Coping Skill 5: Not Being an Avoider   ▲

Use Positive Confrontation

If avoidance is not a good way of coping with anxiety, what is? You know the answer to this question from your life experience. How did you learn to swim, to give your first speech, and to take risks in front of others? You gritted your teeth, took a deep breath, and did it. And you probably learned that it wasn't as hard as you expected.

A friend was having a hard time with his boss at work. I was struck by his response because instead of avoiding his boss, he used every opportunity to put himself in the boss's presence. As he explained, "I'm going to throw myself into the fire until I master it."

There are two good reasons for using positive confrontation to cope with anxiety. First, confrontation is a way of desensitizing ourselves to people, places, and tasks that make life difficult. Second, positive confrontation affects our self-concept. Think how differently you will feel when you see yourself taking an active response to your anxiety instead of being an avoider. There is plenty of psychological research to document a fact we all know from our own experience (Beck & Emery, 1985; Kleinke, 1978).

> If you want to be,
> Act as if you are,
> And you will become.

Coping Skill 6: Using Positive Confrontation   ▲
· ·

Be Mastery-Oriented

In Chapter 4 we learned that when we are mastery-oriented, our energies are focused on developing skills and turning challenges into learning experiences. This orientation toward life challenges was contrasted with being performance-oriented, where the primary goal is to avoid making mistakes. Someone who is performance-oriented finds it difficult to bounce back after failure. It is also hard for those people to overcome shyness and to take the initiative in developing personal relationships (see Chapter 6). Another area where a mastery orientation can help is when you are taking tests. Check whether you agree or disagree with the following statements.

	Strongly agree	Agree	Disagree	Strongly disagree
1. I feel distressed and uneasy before tests.	____	____	____	____
2. I feel jittery before tests.	____	____	____	____
3. I find myself becoming anxious the day of a test.	____	____	____	____
4. Before taking a test, I worry about failure.	____	____	____	____
5. During tests, I wonder how the other people are doing.	____	____	____	____
6. Before tests, I feel trouble about what is going to happen.	____	____	____	____
7. During tests, I think about recent past events.	____	____	____	____
8. Irrelevant bits of information pop into my head during a test.	____	____	____	____

	Strongly agree	Agree	Disagree	Strongly disagree
9. During tests, I find myself thinking of things unrelated to the material being tested.	____	____	____	____
10. I get a headache during an important test.	____	____	____	____
11. My stomach gets upset before tests.	____	____	____	____
12. My heart beats faster when the test begins.	____	____	____	____

These statements come from the Test Anxiety Scale (Sarason, I. G., 1984). It measures four kinds of anxious reactions to tests: *tension* (items 1–3), *worry* (items 4–6), *test–irrelevant thinking* (items 7–9), and *bodily symptoms* (items 10–12). When these reactions are severe, a person's test performance can be seriously impaired.

People suffer from test anxiety because they become so preoccupied with avoiding failure that they can't concentrate on the problems they have to solve (Deffenbacher, 1980; Hunsley, 1987; Sarason, I. G., 1984). People who suffer from test anxiety tend to make the following kinds of negative statements to themselves (Blankstein, Toner, & Flett, 1989):

"My skills are not very good."
"I don't think I can do it."
"I'm not smart enough."

Such people don't approach problems with a mastery orientation by taking a problem-solving approach. They don't talk themselves through problems (see Chapter 3). They have not learned to coach themselves by saying such things as:

"Let's see, how should I begin?"
"I want to look for the correct pattern here."
"I'm going to stay open-minded until I find a good strategy."

There are two strategies used by mastery-oriented people to motivate themselves. One is to take a realistic attitude toward strengths and weaknesses. With such a strategy it is usually possible to be optimistic because we are generally clear about surmountable versus insurmountable challenges. When faced with surmountable challenges, we can apply ourselves, be persistent, and usually succeed. When faced with insurmountable challenges, we can give it our best shot, but we shouldn't feel devastated if we fail. With a realistic attitude, there isn't much need to be anxious because we know what we can and cannot accomplish. A second strategy is to take a pessimistic attitude and expect the worst. You are probably familiar with people who do this. They are the ones who always say they're going to blow the test and end up getting A's. This pessimistic strategy serves as a motivator to work hard and overcome the challenge. However, people who use it pay a price by suffering needless anxiety. Although realistic and pessimistic people who are mastery-oriented usually end up being successful, realistic people stand a better chance of feeling relaxed and enjoying the fruits of their labors (Norem & Cantor, 1986a, 1986b).

To be mastery-oriented, we have to do two things. First, we must learn to focus our attention on the task in front of us. We must force ourselves to avoid thinking about self-doubts and other negative ideas that interfere with good performance. Second, we must look at the test as a challenge. We can use the suggestions in Chapter 4 for maintaining a rational attitude toward failure. A combination of self-relaxation and self-talk (Chapter 3) will help us maintain our concentration (Collins, K. W., Dansereau, Garland, Holley, & McDonald, 1981).

Coping Skill 7: Being Mastery-Oriented   ▲
• •

Keep Records

It is a good idea for us to keep records while we are working on our anxiety. The following information should be logged: (1) date, time of day, and situation, (2) a rating of our anxiety on a scale of 1 (moderate) to 5 (severe), (3) our appraisals (what we tell ourselves), (4) the coping skills we employ, (5) a rating of our anxiety on the same 5-point scale. Record keeping serves a number of useful purposes. First, it gives us an accurate idea of *when* and *where* we get anxious. This knowledge will help us plan our use of coping skills. Second, record keeping will help us identify which coping skills are working and which are not. By monitoring our progress we can fine-tune the anxiety reduction techniques we are employing. Finally, if we keep records of our progress we will be able to take pleasure at our improvement. Small improvements aren't always noticeable when we have high expectations. It is important to remember that large goals are reached in short steps.

Coping Skill 8: Keeping Records   ▲
• •

Be Willing to Work

It would be nice (but boring) if everything in life were easy. If we want to live effectively with anxiety, we have to work at it. The skills for coping with anxiety described in this chapter have been found to be effective in scientific research. However, these skills only were effective when the participants in the research studies devoted the time and effort necessary to master them and put them into practice. You must be willing to practice your anxiety coping skills every day.

Coping Skill 9: Being Willing to Work   ▲
• •

HOW TO LIVE WITH ANXIETY

The above rules for coping with anxiety suggest that we must take active responsibility for coping when we are anxious. Coping skills reinforce our feelings of internal control and self-efficacy (see Chapters 2 and 3). When a primary appraisal tells us a life event is worth getting anxious about, we want to know we have good coping skills at our disposal when we make our secondary appraisal and ask, "What can I do about it?" In addition to living by the five rules described above, we can employ two general strategies for living with anxiety. The first strategy focuses on the body and includes the techniques of self-relaxation, flooding, and implosion. The second strategy focuses on brain power and includes testing our thinking, testing our perceptions, and talking ourselves through challenges.

Controlling the Body

Self-Relaxation

Self-relaxation is one of the skills we added to our coping arsenal after reading Chapter 3. Since anxiety causes us to feel tense, uptight, and generally worked up, it stands to reason that we can live more easily with anxiety if we relax. There are two ways to use self-relaxation for coping with anxiety. One generally effective method is to pay attention to our body. We need to pay attention to our breathing, our heart rate, and other signs of bodily arousal such as tense muscles and sweaty palms. We need to listen to our body. When it tells us it is anxious, we know it is time to use our self-relaxation skills. For example, let's say you are performing or giving a speech in front of an audience. Your body tells you it is getting anxious. Instead of going into a panic and losing control, tell yourself, "OK, I need to take a deep breath and relax." The advantage of using our bodily responses as a cue for self-relaxation is that we feel prepared for coping with anxiety in any situation. We are carrying our coping skill with us wherever we happen to be. Psychologists call this practicing self-relaxation *in vivo*—in our everyday life (Deffenbacher & Suinn, 1985; Goldfried, 1971).

Another method for using self-relaxation is to prepare ourselves ahead of time for anxiety-producing situations. Let's say we are planning to ask our boss for a vacation or for a raise. We know we can use our self-relaxation skills to stay on top of our anxiety on the day of the meeting. We can also prepare ourselves for this anxiety-producing event with *systematic desensitization*. This technique, which was pioneered by Joseph Wolpe (1958, 1982), works in the following way. We make a list of the events leading up to the actual meeting with our boss. An example of such a list is shown in Table 7.1. After making the list, we rate each event on a scale from 0 to 100 according to how much anxiety it will cause. We can then use this list to prepare ourself for the meeting. We relax ourself until our anxiety is at a level close to 0. We then imagine riding to work a month before the meeting. We may feel our anxiety go up to 10. As we keep this event in mind, we relax ourself again back down to 0. We then imagine the event again until we can keep our feelings of anxiety about that event close to 0. Then we move on to the next event on our list. In this case we imagine that we are riding to work a week before the meeting. We may feel our anxiety rising up to 20. Again, as we keep this event in mind, we relax ourself back down to 0. We work through our list in this way until we can vividly picture ourself knocking on the boss's door and entering the office while keeping our anxiety level down to 20 or 30. It may take a while until we can work through our entire list of events while keeping our anxiety at a reasonable level. But if we give ourselves enough time and practice we will feel a boost to our self-confidence and sense of preparation.

Flooding and Implosion

Another way to desensitize ourselves from events that make us anxious is to throw ourselves into them until they no longer disturb us. This technique is called *flooding*. The theory behind flooding is that when we force ourselves to confront tasks, people, and places we previously avoided, we discover that they aren't so terrifying. We find

TABLE 7.1   Events Preceding Meeting with Boss

Event (in order of difficulty)	Individual Anxiety Rating (0–100)
Riding to work a month before meeting	10
Riding to work a week before meeting	20
Seeing boss in lunchroom	40
Riding to work day before meeting	45
Passing boss in hallway day before meeting	60
Riding to work day of meeting	80
Ten minutes before meeting	90
Knocking on boss's door	95
Entering boss's office	99

out through direct experience that our reasons for anxiety were exaggerated. However, when we use flooding we must be committed to stick with it and resist our temptation to escape. If we run away before forcing ourselves to become desensitized, our immediate relief will reinforce the urge to be an avoider.

In addition to confronting physical events that cause anxiety, we can practice desensitization through our imagination. We can work through a list of anxiety-producing events such as those in Table 7.1. As we allow ourselves to become anxious, we constantly remind ourselves even though anxiety is not pleasant, it is not fatal. We discover that we can live with it. The technique of desensitizing ourselves with thoughts and imagination is called *implosion*. One advantage of implosion is that we can use this technique anytime to prepare ourselves for the flooding day and to bolster our self-confidence.

If you are a chronic worrier, you should schedule your implosion sessions for specific times and places every day. During your scheduled time you can allow yourself to feel as much anxiety as possible. However, you are not permitted to think anxiety-producing thoughts during any other times of the day. For the rest of the day you must commit yourself to gaining satisfaction through activities that don't involve worrying. The technique of scheduling your worry times is called *stimulus control*. When you catch yourself worrying during nonscheduled times, tell yourself "Stop!" and force yourself to get involved in other activities. This is called *thought-stopping*.

When used together, the techniques described in this section provide an active coping skill that will bolster feelings of internal control and self-confidence (Beck & Emery, 1985; Deffenbacher & Suinn, 1985; Raimy, 1975; Stampfl & Lewis, 1967).

Coping Skill 10: Controlling the Body   ▲

Using Our Brain's Power

As human beings, we are blessed with a powerful brain. We can use our thinking powers to enhance our coping skills in three ways: by testing our thinking, testing our perceptions, and talking ourselves through challenges.

Testing Our Thinking

Earlier in this chapter we learned about faulty thinking patterns that often cause unnecessarily high anxiety—automatic thinking, overgeneralizing, lack of proportion, selective perception, rigid thinking, circular reasoning, and unrealistic expectations. Human beings have a penchant for faulty thinking (Ellis, 1987). It is therefore necessary to make a practice of testing our thinking, particularly when we are dissatisfied or unhappy. We have learned so far in this book how our thoughts can influence our feelings. For this reason, analyzing what we tell ourselves is an important coping skill. A good method for testing our thinking is to keep daily records such as the ones shown in Table 7.2. On the daily log, we record what was going on (the life event), what we were thinking (our primary appraisal), and our resulting feelings. You may recognize that these factors make up the process of primary appraisal outlined in Figure 2.2 (see Chapter 2). We also include a column where we analyze the logic of our thinking. If our thinking is faulty, we fill in a more reasonable way of appraising the life event and conclude the log with the new feelings our corrected thinking will bring.

Coping Skill 11: Testing Our Thinking   ▲

Testing Our Perceptions

At the beginning of this chapter we were advised not to blame ourselves when we feel anxious. In addition to telling ourselves that anxiety is part of life, we can use our thinking powers to look at anxiety in ways that will "psych us up" rather than bring us down. For example, let's say we are preparing to give a speech in class. We can choose to perceive the emotions we are experiencing as panic or as proof of our motivation to do well. If we have to interact with someone who is very intimidating, we can perceive ourself as "freaked out" or we can say that the adrenalin we feel is pumping us up to meet this challenge. Feelings of doom at the prospect of asking someone for a date can be reinterpreted as excitement about the fact that we are finally going to do it (see Table 7.3). That is, we can label the emotions we are experiencing as either negative or positive. Obviously, when we label them as positive it helps us do our best in the anxiety-provoking situation. This procedure of redefining our perceptions is called *adaptive relabeling*. Remember the discussion of rational-emotive therapy in Chapter 2: "There is nothing either good or bad, but thinking makes it so" (Deffenbacher & Suinn, 1985; Goldfried, Decenteceo, & Weinberg, 1974).

Coping Skill 12: Relabeling Perceptions   ▲

Talking Ourselves through Challenges

A good strategy for getting through anxiety-provoking situations is to use the techniques of talking to ourselves in an adaptive manner that were described in Chapter 3. We can use our thinking powers to coach ourselves from the beginning to the end of a challenging life event. For example, before a job interview, we can say to ourselves: "My goal is to have an interesting conversation with the interviewer. I can look at my nervousness as excitement about the challenge of showing my skills. I

TABLE 7.2   Example of a Daily Record

Life Event	Thoughts	Resulting Feelings	Analyzing the Logic	Revised Thinking	New Feeling
Taking an exam	"I'm going to fail."	Panic	Automatic thinking	"I may not do as well as I would like."	Concern
	"My life is ruined."	Desperation	Lack of proportion	"A low grade would be a setback, but it would not ruin my life."	Disappointment
At a job interview	"I can tell the interviewer doesn't like me."	Anxiety	Selective perception	"The interviewer seems to be having a bad day."	Concern
	"They'll never hire me."	Hopelessness	Rigid thinking	"The job market is tight, but I have as good a chance as anyone."	Hope
	"This is too hard. It's not fair."	Anger	Unrealistic expectations	"This interview is tough, but I'll give it my best shot."	Cautious optimism
Giving a speech	"My hands are sweating. I'm falling apart."	Panic	Overgeneralizing, lack of proportion	"I'm a bit nervous, but that is to be expected."	Temporary nervousness
	"That person looks bored. He doesn't like me."	Anxiety	Selective perception, overgeneralizing	"That person has something else on his mind, but most of the audience is with me."	Temporary distraction
	"I'm not relaxed and happy. I'm a failure as a speaker."	Depression	Unrealistic expectations, circular reasoning	"There is always room for improvement, but I'm getting through this satisfactorily."	Satisfaction

TABLE 7.3   Adaptive Relabeling of Perceptions

Live Event	Perception	Revised Perception
Giving a speech	Panic	Motivation to do well
Confrontation	"Freaked out"	"Pumped up"
Asking for a date	Doom	Excitement
Facing uncertainty	Terror	Nervousness, caution
Taking an exam	Panic	Challenge
Job interview	Anxiety	Enthusiasm

must remember to keep my expectations realistic. I am prepared to use my coping skills when I feel anxious." Then, during the interview, we can remind ourselves:

"Don't think about being afraid, just focus on making clear statements."
"This is a good opportunity to sell myself."
"Take a deep breath now and relax."

And, after the interview, we need to take credit for our success by telling ourselves: "That wasn't so bad after all. I was able to enjoy myself and that's what counts. It was good for me to get this practice. My goal was realistic and I met it—I can be proud of myself."

This technique of coaching ourselves through stressful experiences was developed by Donald Meichenbaum (1977, 1985). It is called *stress inoculation* because it is designed to provide a sense of readiness and preparation. Stress inoculation statements such as those above can be used in two ways. We can employ stress inoculation to coach ourselves as we go through a challenging life event. We can also practice ahead of time for the life event by relaxing and talking ourselves through the experience in our imagination. The more we practice, the more prepared we will be to cope with the challenge when it happens.

Coping Skill 13: Talking Ourselves through Challenges   ▲

SELF-MEDICATION

If anxiety is a problem that interferes with a major part of our life functioning, it is possible to receive medication from a qualified physician. However, we need to think very seriously about medicating ourselves with drugs and alcohol. Sometimes a quick drink or drug dose will help numb us during a stressful life event. But often this self-medication reduces our mental powers and undermines our functioning. It's not going to help much to get stoned before an exam if we're not able to think clearly and work out coherent answers. And even though it may be less scary to interact with others while drunk, our social skills are severely diminished by alcohol. And our sense of self-efficacy is undermined when we are psychologically addicted to drugs in order to get through tough situations. Self-medication is tempting because it is much easier than learning, practicing, and working at the coping skills suggested in this chapter. But in the long run, enduring and mastering these coping skills will do more for our self-esteem than any quick fix from alcohol and drugs.

Coping Skill 14: Avoiding Self-Medication ▲

▲ **LIST OF SKILLS FOR COPING WITH ANXIETY**

Coping Skill 1: Recognizing Symptoms of Anxiety

Coping Skill 2: Avoiding Self-Imposed Blame and Punishment

Coping Skill 3: Analyzing the Rationality of Your Primary Appraisals

Coping Skill 4: Preventing Anxiety from Getting the Best of Us

Coping Skill 5: Not Being an Avoider

Coping Skill 6: Using Positive Confrontation

Coping Skill 7: Being Mastery-Oriented

Coping Skill 8: Keeping Records

Coping Skill 9: Being Willing to Work

Coping Skill 10: Controlling the Body

Coping Skill 11: Testing Our Thinking

Coping Skill 12: Relabeling Perceptions

Coping Skill 13: Talking Ourselves Through Challenges

Coping Skill 14: Avoiding Self-Medication

SUGGESTIONS FOR FURTHER READING

BECK, A. T., & EMERY, G. (1985). *Anxiety disorders and phobias.* New York: Basic Books.

EMERY, G., & CAMPBELL, J. (1987). *Rapid relief from emotional distress.* New York: Fawcett.

GRIEST, J. H., JEFFERSON, J. W., & Marks, I. M. (1986). *Anxiety and its treatment.* New York: Warner Books.

SARASON, I. G. (Ed.). (1980). *Test anxiety: Theory, research and applications.* Hillsdale, N.J.: Erlbaum.

WILSON, E. R. (1985). *Don't panic: Taking control of anxiety attacks.* New York: Harper & Row.

8

Coping with Anger

Anger is one of the most complex human emotions. It is a common reaction to frustration and mistreatment, and we are all destined to face occasions for anger throughout our lives. The problem with anger is that, although it is part of life, it can hinder us from reaching our goals. This is why people have such a conflict about anger. On the one hand, it is a natural human response. On the other hand, it can interfere with interpersonal relationships and keep us from getting what we want.

A HISTORICAL PERSPECTIVE

A good way to appreciate our ambivalence toward anger is to look at how anger has been regarded throughout U.S. history. Carol and Peter Stearns (1986) analyzed Americans' attitudes toward anger in three areas of life: child rearing, work, and marriage.

> *Child rearing:* The prime focus of child rearing in early U.S. history was on obedience and will-breaking. If children felt angry, it was their problem. By the early 1800s, there was a shift in emphasis toward character building, and children were encouraged to manage their anger as a way of showing maturity and self-control. The late 1800s and early 1900s marked a period where anger was disapproved of, and attempts were made to teach children (especially boys) to channel their anger through sports and other activities. The influence of Freud led to an increased permissiveness toward anger in the 1940s, and this more tolerant attitude lasted into the 1960s, when anger was again viewed as a negative emotion that needed to be disciplined and controlled.

> *Work:* Expression of anger in the workplace has become less acceptable in modern times. Companies have adopted psychological testing to screen out "undesirable" workers. Companies have also employed counselors to help workers "manage their feelings" and have set up training groups where workers are taught how to get along better.

> *Marriage:* In early U.S. history, expression of anger was banned in the home. The home was viewed as a sacred retreat, and quarrels between husbands and wives were tantamount to a failed marriage. This restriction of anger changed over time until psychologists in the 1960s were advising husbands and wives to express their anger and to learn how to "fight" with each other in a constructive manner.

Men have generally been permitted more freedom to express anger than women. Women have been urged to take the role of martyrs, never to complain, and to suffer frustrations and mistreatment in silence. Also, Americans have typically viewed anger as something that happens to them rather than as an emotion they choose to experience. While reading this book we have learned that our emotions are determined by our appraisals of life events. We have the power and also the responsibility to react to life events with coping skills that are in our best interests. This chapter will focus on how we can use these coping skills to live effectively with feelings of anger.

A SURVEY OF EXPERIENCES WITH ANGER

Since everyone is confronted at some time with mistreatment and frustration, it is instructive to see how people's experiences with anger compare. Researchers have conducted surveys in which people were asked about their experiences of anger. Here are some of the findings (Averill, 1979, 1983):

1. *Who causes anger?* Most respondents said other people provoked their anger. In a large number of cases, anger was felt toward a loved one. Close friends and acquaintances were also common sources of anger. Disliked people and strangers comprised a relatively small proportion of people who made respondents angry.

2. *What makes people angry?* Since anger is usually experienced toward friends and loved ones, it is not surprising that causes of anger revolve around frustrations of needs and desires. The most commonly reported cause of anger was thwarting or interruption of plans. Other causes of anger were failure by someone to satisfy the respondent's expectations and wishes and actions resulting in loss of pride or self-esteem. Respondents also reported feelings of anger toward others who did not act in a socially appropriate manner.

3. *Why do people get angry?* The most commonly reported reason for getting angry was to assert one's authority and independence. The second and third most commonly reported motives for anger were to strengthen the relationship with the anger-provoking person and to influence that person to change "for his or her own good." Getting revenge and "letting off steam" were also reported as reasons for getting angry.

4. *How do others react to expressions of anger?* Most respondents reported that they experienced negative consequences for their anger. The most commonly reported reactions to anger were: indifference or lack of concern, defiance, apology or other signs of contrition, anger or hostility, denial of responsibility, hurt feelings, surprise, rejection, jokes, frivolity, or silliness. It is striking that these responses to anger are largely not in the angry person's best interest.

5. *How do angry people react to their own expressions of anger?* After recognizing that others generally respond negatively to expressions of anger, it is not surprising to learn that people often experience their own expression of anger in an unpleasant manner. The most commonly reported reactions to one's own expression of anger were: feeling irritable, hostile, and aggravated; feeling depressed, unhappy, and gloomy; feeling ashamed, embarrassed, and guilty; feeling relieved, calm, and satisfied; feeling good, pleased, and glad; and feeling triumphant, confident, and dominant.

There are several important conclusions we can reach from surveys of people's anger:

1. Anger is a common emotion that is often felt toward friends and loved ones who fail to live up to our wishes and desires.
2. Anger is often motivated by the desire to get what we want.
3. People's reactions to expressions of anger are often negative.
4. Although we sometimes feel satisfaction after expressing anger, we don't necessarily achieve our goals in the long run.

These conclusions strongly suggest that we have to use other skills in addition to anger for getting our needs met. That's what this chapter is about. How can we constructively live with anger?

ASSESSING ANGER

Before looking at ways to cope with anger, it might be useful to measure your feelings of anger. Check how much you agree or disagree with the following statements.

	Strongly agree	Agree	Disagree	Strongly disagree
1. I tend to get angry more frequently than most people.	____	____	____	____
2. It is easy to make me angry.	____	____	____	____
3. I am surprised at how often I feel angry.	____	____	____	____
4. I get angry when something blocks my plans.	____	____	____	____
5. I get angry when I am delayed.	____	____	____	____
6. I get angry when people are unfair.	____	____	____	____
7. People can bother me just by being around.	____	____	____	____
8. When I get angry, I stay angry for hours.	____	____	____	____
9. I get angry when I have to work with incompetent people.	____	____	____	____

These statements come from the Multidimensional Anger Inventory (Siegel, 1986). Statements 1, 2, and 3 measure *anger arousal*. Anger arousal refers to the intensity, duration, and frequency of your anger. Statements 4, 5, and 6 measure the *range* of things you get angry about. Statements 7, 8, and 9 measure your tendency to have a *hostile outlook*. Another dimension measured by the inventory is the ease with which you express your anger. People who express their anger very readily tend to agree with these statements:

When I am angry with someone, I let that person know.
It is not difficult for me to let people know I'm angry.

Those who keep their feelings of anger to themselves tend to agree with these statements:

I feel guilty about expressing my anger.
I harbor grudges that I don't tell anyone about.

Later in this chapter we will learn about the virtues of communicating our feelings of anger in a way that is assertive but not aggressive. First, it will be useful to consider the kinds of appraisals we make when faced with anger-provoking situations.

MAKING RATIONAL PRIMARY APPRAISALS

A good place to start learning how to cope with anger is by analyzing our primary appraisals. When we make a primary appraisal of a frustrating or difficult life event, we must decide whether it is something worth getting angry about. This is a time when we want to put our rational thinking skills (Chapter 2) into practice. If we find ourselves suffering from needless anger, we are probably making the following kinds of irrational demands:

> Because I strongly desire people to treat me considerately and fairly, they *absolutely must* do so, and they are evil, damnable people who deserve to be severely condemned and punished if they don't.
> Because I strongly desire people to treat me considerately and fairly, and BECAUSE I AM A SPECIAL KIND OF PERSON, they *absolutely must* treat me well.
> Because I strongly desire people to treat me considerately and fairly, they *absolutely must* AT ALL TIMES AND UNDER ALL CONDITIONS DO SO.

These examples of irrational beliefs were collected by Albert Ellis (1987) during his psychotherapeutic work with thousands of people. Although these statements might strike us as unrealistic, the fact is that we all make unrealistic demands of life. Because it is a natural human tendency to want the best out of life, we are predisposed toward holding expectations and making demands that are not always rational. We have to make it a habit to test the rationality of our appraisals. If we insist that things should *always* go our way, that others must *always* treat us right, and that we should *never* suffer frustration, we are certain to become angry. A useful coping skill is to catch ourselves and change our demands to ones that are more realistic. For example, instead of insisting on beliefs such as those outlined above, we can talk to ourselves in a more rational manner: "I strongly desire people to treat me considerately and fairly. When they do it makes me happy, and when they don't I don't like it. However, since the world does not revolve around my wishes and desires, I have to learn effective skills for coping when I am frustrated and mistreated." This kind of appraisal will still lead to feelings of disappointment or frustration when things don't go our way, but it will not result in needless anger.

Coping Skill 1: Testing the Rationality of Our Primary Appraisals   ▲
• •

HOW TO CONTROL ANGER

The general philosophy we want to follow when we experience mistreatment and frustration is that we are copers who know how to use the coping skills outlined in Chapter 3. Because anger gets the best of all of us at various times in our lives, psychologists have developed programs to help people cope with their anger more effectively (Novaco, 1975, 1985). It will be useful to look at these programs to see which skills can be most beneficial for us.

Self-Relaxation

Self-relaxation is a very useful skill to employ when anger gets the best of us. There is truth to the saying that we should count to 10 before making a response when we are provoked. This gives us time to use our problem-solving skills to decide on the best course of action. We can also use our feelings of anger as a cue to tell ourselves to relax. We can use our deep-breathing and muscle-relaxation skills right there on the spot to calm ourselves down. We will then be in a better condition to weigh our options. If we feel that shouting or being aggressive is in our best interest, we can do so. We will then be acting *out of choice* and not as a result of uncontrolled anger.

Self-relaxation can also be used to prepare ourselves for an anger-provoking situation. We can desensitize (see Chapter 7) ourselves by rehearsing how we will respond when this situation occurs. We relax and imagine that we are confronted with frustration and mistreatment. When we feel our blood pressure rise, we score our anger on a scale of 0 to 100. Then we relax until our anger level is back down to a lower level. Now we imagine that the frustration and mistreatment is even worse. Again, we score our anger and bring it under control with self-relaxation. If we give ourselves enough practice, we will feel prepared to cope successfully when the frustration and mistreatment actually occur (Deffenbacher, Demm, & Brandon, 1986; Hazaleus & Deffenbacher, 1986; Novaco, 1976).

Coping Skill 2: Using Self-Relaxation to
Maintain Control When We Are Frustrated and Mistreated   ▲
. . . .

Stress Inoculation

In Chapter 7, we learned how to use stress inoculation as a skill for coping with anxiety. Stress inoculation is designed to give people a sense of readiness and preparation for difficult life events. This is done by learning how to coach ourselves through challenges. We can prepare ourselves to maintain self-control and efficacy during an anger-provoking situation by making a list of adaptive self-statements like those below (Meichenbaum, 1985). For example, before the event, we can say to ourselves:

> "This is going to upset me, but I know how to handle it."
> "It's not going to be fun, so I have to be prepared."
> "I can use my coping skills to maintain control."
> "Take it easy. This can be a good learning experience."
> "When I find myself getting angry, I'll relax and calm myself down."
> "I can coach myself through this challenge."

During the event we can remind ourselves:

> "Stay calm. Just continue to relax."
> "As long as I keep cool and use my coping skills, I'm in control."

"Don't blow this out of proportion."

"Think of this as a useful experience."

"It's not fun, but I can roll with the punches."

"Take a deep breath, stay cool, and use your head."

"I have a right to be annoyed, but I need to concentrate on my goals."

"I can gain more by not blowing my top."

"I don't have to let the other person's anger get to me. I have more self-control."

Afterward, we need to remember to give ourselves credit for our success: "I'm not perfect, but I handled it pretty well. It wasn't as hard as I thought. I'm getting better every time. These situations aren't fun, but they are part of life. I feel a lot better about myself when I use good coping skills."

These stress-inoculation statements can be used in two ways. They can be used as we go through the anger-provoking life event. We can also practice ahead of time by relaxing and talking ourselves through the anger-provoking experience in our imagination. We use self-relaxation and adaptive self-statements as we rehearse and practice maintaining our self-control and feelings of self-efficacy (Meichenbaum, 1977, 1985; Novaco, 1980; Schlichter & Horan, 1981).

Coping Skill 3: Using Stress Inoculation
to Coach Ourselves through Anger-Provoking Life Events   ▲
• •

Blowing Off Steam

When anger does get the best of us, it can help to blow off steam by getting busy with a physical or creative activity. The value of "working off" anger is that it will put us in a more relaxed frame of mind to solve the problem that made us angry in the first place. It is important to understand that blowing off steam as a skill for coping with anger is a two-stage process. The first stage involves getting the tenseness and arousal out of our system. The second stage involves working out the problem. Blowing off steam is often misunderstood as a coping skill because people don't recognize the importance of the second stage. Blowing off steam won't make the source of frustration or mistreatment go away. It will just give us more self-control so we can deal with it. We don't want to get in the habit of blowing off steam without taking the second step—solving the problem (Konečni, 1984; Novaco, 1986).

Coping Skill 4: Recognizing that
Blowing Off Steam Is a Two-Stage Process   ▲
• •

Believing in Ourselves as Copers

When we start to believe in ourselves as copers, we no longer ask whether anger is a good or bad emotion. We focus instead on taking care of ourselves and getting our needs met without harming others. At times it may be very useful and appropriate to express anger. On other occasions, expressing anger will only make things worse. As copers, we want to decide when expressing anger is in our best interest or when other tactics will serve us better. Since relating to others with anger is not always an optimal strategy, how else can we protect ourselves? We certainly don't want to be a passive person who is controlled by others. The answer to this question lies in understanding the difference between nonassertiveness, aggression, and assertiveness (Lange & Jakubowski, 1976).

Coping Skill 5: Believing in Ourselves as Copers   ▲

NONASSERTIVENESS

People are nonassertive when they fail to stand up for themselves. To be nonassertive is to be passive, apologetic, diffident, and self-effacing. Nonassertiveness gives the message that our needs are not important and that we are willing to go along with what others want, even when what they want is not in our best interest. Nonassertiveness indicates a lack of respect for our own needs. It also communicates to others that we are not willing to hold up our end of an interpersonal relationship, which, by definition, requires bargaining and negotiation.

One reason we fall into the trap of being nonassertive is that we don't acknowledge our personal rights. We want to be helpful and polite, so we give in to other people's wishes. Sometimes we mistake assertiveness for being pushy and aggressive. We feel that it is inappropriate or impolite to say what's on our mind and to stand up for ourselves. It is also tempting to be nonassertive to avoid negative responses. That is, if we are going to take care of our needs, we are bound to come into conflict with others. We must learn to tolerate the frowns, criticisms, pouts, and other punishments that come when we refuse to be passive. It is often easy to be nonassertive because it is the course of least resistance. But when we get used to being nonassertive, it is difficult to see how we can act any other way. Some hints about how to develop assertiveness are given later in this chapter.

Coping Skill 6: Taking Responsibility to Overcome Nonassertiveness ▲

AGGRESSION

Aggression involves standing up for our rights in a *hostile* manner. Aggression is often directed toward taking advantage of others. When people are aggressive they try to get their needs met by overpowering, belittling, humiliating, and/or degrading others. Aggression communicates that we are concerned only about ourselves. When we are aggressive, other people's rights, needs, and desires don't matter to us.

We often fall into the trap of being aggressive when we feel threatened and vulnerable or mistreated. Our anger then builds up until it is expressed as aggression. Another reason for choosing aggression is that we are bombarded in movies and television with examples of "heroes" who come out on top with aggressive actions. However, in real life these "heroes" would be lonely and isolated people unable to sustain long-term relationships. Aggressive behavior may work successfully within the confines of television and movie scripts that are oriented toward a "quick fix" and immediate gratification. In the long run, aggression alienates us from others and turns us into hostile, fearful, and suspicious people.

Coping Skill 7: Understanding the Limits of Aggression   ▲

ASSERTIVENESS

Assertiveness means standing up for our rights and expressing our thoughts and feelings in a direct, honest, and appropriate manner. When we are being assertive, we show respect for ourselves and for others. On one hand, we are not passive and we don't allow people to take advantage of us. On the other hand, we acknowledge other people's needs and attempt to relate to them in a tactful manner.

There are a number of advantages to being assertive. Assertiveness gives us a feeling of self-efficacy and internal control. This helps boost our self-esteem and confidence when we are interacting with others. Since assertiveness requires tact and negotiation, we have to be flexible and we won't always get everything we want. However, since other people also have needs, wishes, and desires, assertiveness provides the best approach for achieving mutually satisfying interpersonal relationships.

Coping Skill 8: Appreciating the Benefits of Being Assertive ▲

Examples of Assertiveness, Nonassertiveness, and Aggression

A salesman is putting pressure on you to buy something:

> *Salesperson:* "OK, are you ready for me to write up the sale?"
> *Nonassertive response:* "Well, I guess so, if you think it's a good deal."
> *Aggressive response:* "Stop being so pushy! I'm not buying anything from you!"
> *Assertive response:* "I'm sorry, but I'm not ready to make a purchase."

Someone tries to cut in front of you in a supermarket line:

> *Person:* "You don't mind if I cut in here do you? I'm in a hurry."
> *Nonassertive response:* "Well, OK."
> *Aggressive response:* "Hey! What are you trying to do? Get the hell back in line!"
> *Assertive response:* "I'm sorry, but I do mind. I'm in a hurry also."

Your supervisor gives you a questionable evaluation:

> *Supervisor:* "Here is your evaluation. You need to sign it."
> *Nonassertive response:* "There are some things here that I'm not sure about, but I guess I can do better next time."
> *Aggressive response:* "This is a lousy evaluation! If you are not willing to change it, I'm going to the grievance committee."
> *Assertive response:* "I'm having trouble with some of the things you've written here. I'd like to talk with you about them."

A friend asks to borrow your car for the weekend:

> *Friend:* "You don't mind if I borrow your car for the weekend, do you?"
> *Nonassertive response:* "I did have some other plans, but OK. Try to let me know sooner next time."
> *Aggressive response:* "You've got a lot of nerve asking me on such short notice. Forget it!"
> *Assertive response:* "I've already planned to use my car this weekend. I'd be happy to lend it to you in the future if you give me enough notice."

A relative calls and says she wants to visit next weekend:

> *Relative:* "I know this is late notice, but you don't mind if I come visit next weekend, do you?"
>
> *Nonassertive response:* "Well, we did have some plans. But, OK, I guess we can work around them somehow."
>
> *Aggressive response:* "Look, you can't just come and visit whenever you feel like it! We have plans, too, you know."
>
> *Assertive response:* "Next weekend is not a good time for you to visit. We'll have to find another time."

Your neighbors are having a very loud party:

> *Neighbor:* "Don't worry. Everyone will leave in an hour."
>
> *Nonassertive response:* "Well, OK, as long as it's no longer than an hour."
>
> *Aggressive response:* "What right do you think you have to disturb the whole neighborhood! I'll show you! I'm calling the police!"
>
> *Assertive response:* "You are disturbing the whole neighborhood. You have to keep the noise down. Otherwise I have no choice but to call the police."

PERFECTING ASSERTIVENESS

Understanding What It Means to Be Assertive

The first step in perfecting assertiveness is understanding the nature of an assertive response. When we are assertive, we stand up for our rights in an honest and forthright manner, while still showing respect for the other person. Some examples of assertive, nonassertive, and aggressive responses were given above. These examples indicate that when we are assertive we don't let others take advantage of us, but we also acknowledge their needs and desires.

Three Useful Skills

Three skills that help improve assertiveness are owning our feelings, being empathic, and being tactful.

Owning Our Feelings

Owning our feelings means letting others know how we feel about what they are doing. We need to avoid accusing others by saying things like, "You are inconsiderate." "You are pushy." or "You're a slob." Instead, we can communicate how their actions make us feel: "I'm sorry, but I have other plans." "I'm sorry, but I can't oblige you." "It would make me happy if you would take better care of yourself." Owning our feelings will do much to increase our self-respect and the respect others have for us.

Being Empathic

Empathy is powerful medicine for enhancing cordial relationships. Other people will be much more ready to accept our expression of our desires if we are willing to acknowledge theirs. This does not mean that we have to *accept* what others want.

We can disagree with others and still give them the courtesy of letting them know we understand how they feel.

Preferred and Disliked Influence Tactics

T. Falbo (1977) has studied power strategies and found that preferred influence tactics include:

Bargaining: Reciprocating favors and making two-way exchanges
Compromise: Willingness to give up some wishes for sake of agreement
Reason: Being reasonable and rational
Expertise: Relying on knowledge and experience

On the other hand, the following influence tactics were disliked:

Threat: Making threats if person doesn't get his or her way
Deceit: Using false information, flattery, and lies
Ignoring: Doing things own way while ignoring the other person's needs
Evasion: Getting own way secretly without the other person's knowledge

People don't like others who try to influence them with threats, deceit, ignoring, or evasion. Perfecting assertiveness means being tactful and practicing the skills for negotiation outlined later in this chapter.

Accepting Our Rights and Responsibilities

People often get confused about the difference between being selfish and asserting their rights. Aggression is selfish because it is geared toward getting our needs met without regard for others. Assertiveness implies that we are willing to be flexible and to negotiate. However, it also implies that we have a bottom line and are committed to looking out for ourselves. It is hardly selfish to express our beliefs, communicate our feelings, and stand up for our values. People who accuse us of being inconsiderate or selfish when we do this are acting aggressively and trying to make us feel guilty. It is tempting when others accuse us of being inconsiderate and selfish to give in to nonassertiveness. But this is a cop-out because when we are nonassertive we are forsaking our commitment to take responsibility for our lives. As assertive people, we have to be willing to stand up to people's attempts to manipulate us. We have to bear up to their criticisms and rejections. As long as we know we are acting in a fair and mature manner, we have our self-respect. If others choose to be childish and aggressive, that is their problem.

Assertiveness Training Groups

Assertiveness is becoming more recognized as an effective skill for interacting with others. Many books have been written on the topic, and groups have been formed throughout the United States for helping people perfect their assertiveness skills. These groups provide the following experiences (Eisler & Frederiksen, 1980; Lange & Jakubowski, 1976):

1. A description and rationale for new behaviors to be learned
2. A demonstration of new behaviors through modeling
3. A chance to practice new behaviors in role-play situations

4. An opportunity to receive suggestions and support from other group members

Assertiveness training groups give participants the opportunity to practice the coping skills that are outlined in this book within an atmosphere of mutual support.

Coping Skill 9: Perfecting Assertiveness Skills ▲
••

NEGOTIATING

In order to avoid suffering needless anger, we have to recognize that interpersonal relations are founded on negotiation. In some cases we can get our way by bullying others and overpowering them. However, if we always insist on getting our way we will eventually pay a price. We may often win, but we will be lonely and isolated. On the other hand, if we make it a habit of always being passive and giving in to the wishes of others, we can avoid the efforts of negotiation, but we will end up feeling resentful. The best solution is to be a good negotiator. Below are some tips to help improve negotiating skills (Bazerman, 1986):

The Virtue of Compromise
Children are taught from a young age that they can't have everything they want. Ironically, we seem to forget this lesson when we grow up. Compromising is a skill that involves understanding our needs as well as the needs of others. We don't have to accept or agree with someone's desires, but we do need to let the person know that we have understood what they want.

Compromise is also an attitude where we don't look at interpersonal relations as win or lose situations. We have to be flexible enough to give the other person satisfaction. For both of us to get something we want, we both may have to give something to each other.

Be Level-Headed
When we are negotiating, strong feelings are likely to come out. We need to recognize and accept these feelings and try to keep on an even keel. There are several things we can do to prevent emotions from escalating to an unproductive level: (1) We can avoid making rigid demands. Rigid demands rope us into a situation where any compromise seems like a loss. (2) We should not look at negotiations as a competition where one person wins and the other loses. Negotiations are meant to find solutions that will make both parties satisfied. (3) We can use self-relaxation to stay in control of our feelings. (4) We can make the atmosphere cordial by showing empathy. (5) We should be assertive, and not be nonassertive or aggressive.

Be a Coper
We need to see ourselves as copers who know how to be assertive, flexible, and empathic. The outcome of a negotiation is weighed not only in terms of what we get but also in terms of how we conduct ourselves. Circumstances sometimes dictate that we have to give more than we wish. However, if we do this out of choice and with tact, we can take pride in our ability act in a mature and responsible manner.

Coping Skill 10: Being a Good Negotiator ▲
••

A BRIEF SUMMARY

Let's take a moment now and summarize the main points in this chapter about coping with anger. Anger is a natural response to frustration and mistreatment, and we are destined to face occasions for anger throughout our lives. The first question we want to ask ourselves when we are angry is whether we are making a realistic primary appraisal. Some life events give us good cause for feeling angry. Others are not worth getting angry about, and we have to question seriously whether we are making unreasonable demands on life that are causing needless anger. When our primary appraisal tells us that our anger is justified, our secondary appraisal determines what we are going to do about it. Sometimes it is in our best interest to express our anger. On other occasions, we may decide that although we you are justifiably angry, we will be better off controlling our anger with self-relaxation, stress inoculation, and blowing off steam, and confronting the problem with assertiveness and negotiation. We always want to see ourselves as copers who know how to work out strategies for relating with other people that, in the long run, will be in our best interest.

▲   LIST OF SKILLS FOR COPING WITH ANGER

Coping Skill   1: Testing the Rationality of Our Primary Appraisals

Coping Skill   2: Using Self-Relaxation to Maintain Control When We Are Frustrated and Mistreated

Coping Skill   3: Using Stress Inoculation to Coach Ourselves Through Anger-Provoking Life Events

Coping Skill   4: Recognizing That Blowing Off Steam Is a Two-Stage Process

Coping Skill   5: Believing in Ourselves as Copers

Coping Skill   6: Taking Responsibility to Overcome Nonassertiveness

Coping Skill   7: Understanding the Limits of Aggression

Coping Skill   8: Appreciating the Benefits of Being Assertive

Coping Skill   9: Perfecting Assertiveness Skills

Coping Skill 10: Being a Good Negotiator

SUGGESTIONS FOR FURTHER READING

ELLIS, A. (1977). *Anger—How to live with and without it.* Secaucus, N.J.: Citadel Press.

LANGE, A. J., & JAKUBOWSKI, P. (1976). *Responsible assertive behavior.* Champaign, Ill.: Research Press.

NOVACO, R. W. (1975). *Anger control.* Lexington, Mass.: Heath.

STEARNS, C. Z., & STEARNS, P. N. (1986). *Anger: The struggle for emotional control in American history.* Chicago: University of Chicago Press.

9

Coping with Conflicts in Close Relationships

We experience conflicts with people close to us when they do something we dislike or refuse to do something we like. Although this may be obvious, we now know enough to realize that our primary appraisals have a lot to do with what we choose to like and dislike. This chapter will teach us how to cope with conflicts in close relationships by reevaluating and modifying our appraisals. By increasing our flexibility and broadening our options, we can gain a greater sense of effectiveness in our interactions with close others.

TAKING ACTIVE RESPONSIBILITY

When we have interpersonal conflicts, we must take active responsibility for finding a solution. In Chapter 1 we learned about the danger of avoiding problems because they usually catch up with us in the long run. This lesson is reinforced in a study of how people cope with marital conflicts (Menaghan, 1982). A community survey indicated that people generally use one of four different kinds of strategies for dealing with conflicts in their marriage: negotiation, optimistic comparisons, ignoring, and resignation:

> *Negotiation:* Sitting down and talking things out. Working out a fair compromise.
> *Optimistic comparisons:* Appreciating the marriage in comparison with others. Viewing the marriage as improving over time.
> *Ignoring:* Telling self that conflicts don't matter. Underestimating how much the difficulties really bother you.
> *Resignation:* Keeping dissatisfactions to self. Not communicating directly with partner.

The participants were studied for a period of 4 years to learn how these different coping styles influenced their marriage. Not surprisingly, ignoring and resignation were not effective in resolving marital conflicts. Couples who reacted to conflicts with ignoring and resignation suffered the greatest distress and were rarely able to solve their problems. In contrast, the active skills of negotiation and optimistic comparison were both useful for resolving marital conflicts. Because of their effectiveness, negotiation and optimistic comparison are recommended in this chapter. Negotiation requires skills, patience, and cooperation from the other person. Optimistic comparison is an appraisal we can make for ourselves to gain a more objective perspective about our relationships with close others.

Another way to take active responsibility in a relationship is to understand the value of empathy. Three kinds of empathy are important in promoting feelings of closeness in a relationship: *perspective taking, empathic concern,* and *compassion* (Davis & Oathout, 1987). Perspective taking means taking the time to see the issues from your partner's perspective. Emphatic concern is a genuine caring about how your partner is feeling. Compassion means putting yourself in your partner's shoes and experiencing the same feelings and emotions he or she is experiencing. When both partners in a relationship take active responsibility for demonstrating these kinds of empathy, their happiness and satisfaction are likely to increase.

Coping Skill 1: Taking Active Responsibility   ▲
••

REEVALUATING EXPECTATIONS

Figure 9.1 shows that conflicts usually begin when the other person does something negative or neglects to do something positive. Our reaction is colored by our expectations about what we can reasonably ask for. This is a good place to do some serious reality testing and to seek objective feedback. One group of researchers constructed a questionnaire that measures realistic and unrealistic expectations in close relationships (Eidelson & Epstein, 1982). Check whether you agree or disagree with the following statements:

	Strongly agree	Agree	Disagree	Strongly disagree
1. It is destructive when people in close relationships have differences and disagreements.	____	____	____	____
2. My partner should always be aware of how I feel.	____	____	____	____
3. My partner is never going to change.	____	____	____	____
4. My partner should always satisfy me sexually.	____	____	____	____
5. My partner does not have the same needs I do.	____	____	____	____

If you think carefully about these beliefs, you will realize that they sound good but are not very realistic. Not surprisingly, people who hold such unrealistic expectations tend to have less satisfying marriages than people whose expectations are more true to life, like those below (Bradbury & Fincham, 1988):

Disagreements do occur in close relationships.
My partner cannot be a mind reader.
My partner can change if I am willing to negotiate.
Sex is almost always an issue to be worked on in close relationships.
People often have similar needs in a relationship.

In two other studies of realistic and unrealistic expectations, men and women in close relationships were asked to describe their major conflicts (Harvey, Wells, & Alvarez, 1978; Orvis, Kelley, & Butler, 1976). Two interesting results emerged, showing that we are less objective about conflicts with close others than we might believe. First, men and women tended to justify their own negative acts in the relationship as reflecting "good intentions" or as caused by events beyond their control. For example, they explained their aggressive and irresponsible actions as a reaction to something their partner had done. In a similar manner, they claimed their criticisms and demands were a sign of concern and helpfulness. Failure to share feelings and show affection were blamed on external demands and pressures. When explaining the causes of their partner's behaviors, people's perceptions were very different. Men and women felt that negative acts by their partners were intentional and reflected lack of commitment and caring. In short, both men and women found it easy to forgive their own actions and difficult to forgive their partner's actions.

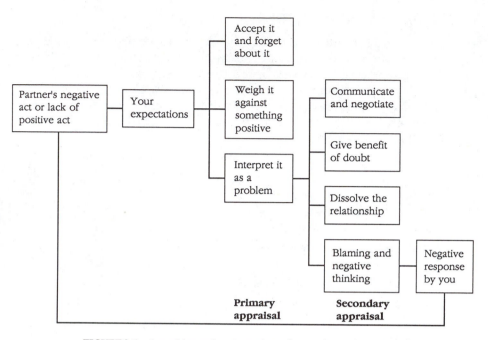

FIGURE 9.1   Appraising and coping with conflicts in close relationships

A second important finding was that men's and women's perceptions about their partner's wishes and desires were not always accurate. For example, sexual relations were seen as a more important source of conflict by men than by women. However, men falsely assumed that their partner felt the same way about sex as they did. Women made a similar error by underestimating men's views of the importance of sexual incompatibility. Women falsely assumed that their partner felt the same about sexual issues as they did. Conflicts related to financial problems and time spent on work and education were rated as more important by women than by men. Women overestimated men's ratings of importance on these issues, assuming that men felt the same way they felt. Men underestimated women's ratings of importance on these issues, assuming that women's feelings were similar to theirs.

It is clear that the demands we make of those close to us are not always realistic. By reevaluating our expectations, we gain a greater sense of flexibility. Our relationships only can improve as we become more willing to appreciate relationship issues from our partner's point of view.

Coping Skill 2: Reevaluating Expectations   ▲

DESIRED AREAS OF CHANGE

Another way to analyze our expectations in close relationships is by looking at what things we would like our partner to change. To clarify this aspect of relationships, researchers developed the Areas of Change Questionnaire, which measures how much people want their partners to change in areas ranging from sex and affection, finances and household matters, friends and relatives, work, and child rearing (Margolin, Talovic, & Weinstein, 1983). When husbands and wives who were getting along fairly well (nondistressed couples) took this questionnaire, they agreed on most areas of desired change, except for sex (see Table 9.1). Husbands ranked improved sexual relations as the most important change they wanted from their wives. Wives wanted many changes from their husbands ahead of sex (thirteenth on their list of desired changes). Not surprisingly, compared with nondistressed couples, distressed couples expressed far more desire for their partners to change. More than half of the distressed couples surveyed wanted their partners to make changes in communicating emotions clearly, not arguing as much, starting conversations, showing appreciation, sexual relations, and spending close time together.

One interesting aspect of the Areas of Change Questionnaire is that it is both objective and subjective. The areas of change we wish from people close to us are real to the extent that they reflect our true desires. Our desired changes are also subjective because they are based on our biased perceptions about what is going on in the relationship. We can do a lot to reduce misunderstandings by being sensitive to changes we desire from others as well as changes others desire from us.

Coping Skill 3: Being Sensitive to Desired Areas of Change ▲

PRIMARY APPRAISAL

When we make a primary appraisal about a negative act (or the lack of a positive act) by someone close, we are asking whether this is something we can accept. For instance, we usually are thinking: "X did something negative or neglected to do something positive. Can I live with it? Or is it unacceptable and therefore a problem?"

Practicing Tolerance

We can save ourselves a lot of grief by accepting the fact that neither we nor those close to us are perfect. Some things are just not worth getting upset about. If we think about it, it's obvious that our relationships with others will be greatly enhanced if we can practice tolerance. Things that bug us and hurt our feelings are a burden. When we can say, "OK, I can accept it and forget about it," we gain a feeling of self-efficacy and control. By being tolerant, we are saying, "I am flexible enough to get along without everything I want."

The value of tolerance was demonstrated in a study comparing reactions of distressed and nondistressed couples to positive and negative behaviors by their spouses (Jacobson, Follette, & McDonald, 1982). Not surprisingly, distressed couples were more likely than nondistressed couples to be upset and bothered when a spouse did something negative. Interestingly, distressed couples were also more pleased when a spouse did something positive. This study demonstrates that distressed husbands and wives are on edge because they take each other's actions too seriously. They are so preoccupied with getting immediate gratification from their partner that they can't flow with the ups and downs that are normal in a close relationship. In contrast, nondistressed husbands and wives are more comfortable

TABLE 9.1 Desired Areas of Change in Nondistressed Couples

Husbands	Wives
Improved sexual relations	Express his emotions clearly
Express her emotions clearly	Start interesting conversations with me
Accept praise	
Start interesting conversations with me	Show appreciation for things I do well
Show appreciation for things I do well	Spend time keeping the house clean
Leave me time to myself	Help in planning our free time
Spend time keeping the house clean	Go out with me
Not letting work interfere with relationship	Help with housework when asked
	Accomplish his responsibilities promptly

From "Areas of Change Questionnaire: A Practical Approach to Marital Assessment" by G. Margolin, S. Talovic, and C. D. Weinstein, 1983, *Journal of Consulting and Clinical Psychology, 51,* 920–931. Copyright 1983 by the American Psychological Asssociation. Adapted with permission.

with each other because they have learned to place each other's positive and negative behaviors into the perspective of a long-term relationship.

Coping Skill 4: Practicing Tolerance   ▲

Balancing the Negatives and Positives

Another way to live with the imperfections of close others is by balancing their negative and positive actions. Even though people close to us are not perfect, they usually do more things we like than dislike. Reminding ourselves of their good deeds will often help us accept their not-so-good deeds. Of course, this would be easier to do if we were perfect and completely objective. Research has shown, however, that human beings are rarely objective, especially when judging the actions of others. Our perceptions of someone's behaviors are very naturally affected by our expectations, needs, and values (Baron & Byrne, 1987, chap. 3).

A good example of people's subjectivity in reading each other's actions is shown in a study where men and women in close relationships talked together about their conflicts (Gaelick, Bodenhausen, & Wyer, 1985). The couples consented to have their conversations videotaped. The videotapes were later analyzed by researchers who carefully coded the couple's communication patterns. One important finding was that men and women were much more sensitive to each other's negative messages than they were to each other's positive messages. In other words, both men and women were quick to reciprocate their partner's hostility. It was much more difficult for them to return their partner's expressions of love.

There are three possible reasons why couples have a hard time reciprocating expressions of love. First, we often do not communicate feelings of love very clearly.

Second, we probably have a tendency to be more "on the lookout" for hostility than for love. Finally, when we do recognize expressions of love, it is sometimes difficult to open ourselves up and communicate love in return. Balancing the positives and negatives requires us to be aware of how those close to us are expressing their positive feelings.

Balancing the positives and negatives also means that we must give others credit for their attempts to do nice things for us. We have a tendency to react very personally to negative actions by those close to us. On the other hand, we often take their positive actions for granted. Distressed couples have a particular problem giving fair weight to each other's positives and negatives. Distressed couples blame their partner's negative behaviors on unacceptable motives and bad intentions. Non-distressed couples have learned to give each other the benefit of the doubt. Non-distressed couples are also able to give their partners credit and appreciation for positive actions. Because distressed couples don't recognize the good intentions behind their partner's positive behaviors, they aren't able to fully appreciate these positives in their relationship (Jacobson, McDonald, Follette, & Berley, 1985).

Coping Skill 5: Balancing the Negatives and Positives ▲

Deciding There Is a Problem

The above discussion on practicing tolerance and balancing the negatives and positives does not imply that we have no right to decide what is acceptable and unacceptable in a close relationship. The discussion is intended to help us to be more objective. It is in our best interest to reevaluate our expectations and to place other people's negative and positive actions and words into their proper perspective. It is also in our best interest to be aware of our needs and to acknowledge our bottom line for what we can and cannot live with in a close relationship. We have every right to decide which positives we want from others and which negatives we are not willing to tolerate.

Coping Skill 6: Acknowledging Our Right
to Determine Our Needs in a Relationship ▲

OVERCOMING JEALOUSY

Check how often you have the following feelings or reactions toward your current romantic partner:

	Never	*Rarely*	*Sometimes*	*Often*
1. I suspect he/she is attracted to someone else.	___	___	___	___
2. I am worried that someone else is trying to seduce him/her.	___	___	___	___
3. I suspect he/she is secretly seeing someone else.	___	___	___	___

	Never	Rarely	Sometimes	Often
4. I think that others may be romantically interested in him/her.	___	___	___	___
5. I question my partner about his/her whereabouts.	___	___	___	___
6. I join in whenever I see him/her talking to a potential rival.	___	___	___	___
7. I call unexpectedly, just to see if he/she is home.	___	___	___	___
8. I question him/her about previous or present romantic relationships.	___	___	___	___

Now check how the following events make you feel.

	Very pleased	Pleased	Upset	Very upset
9. He/she is flirting with someone.	___	___	___	___
10. He/she smiles in a very friendly manner at a potential rival.	___	___	___	___
11. He/she comments on how good-looking someone else is.	___	___	___	___
12. Someone else is trying to spend time alone with him/her.	___	___	___	___

These experiences are adapted from the Multidimensional Jealousy Scale (Pfeiffer & Wong, 1989). *Cognitive jealousy* is measured by items 1 through 4, *behavioral jealousy* is measured by items 5 through 8, and *emotional jealousy* is measured by items 9 through 12. Emotional and behavioral jealousy are related to feelings of unhappiness, and cognitive jealousy can be the root of considerable anxiety.

Jealousy can have a negative impact on our lives if we allow it to get the best of us. By gaining a clearer understanding of this complex emotion, we will be able to cope with jealousy-provoking situations in a more effective manner. The first thing to recognize is that we do not have an inborn need to be jealous. While people in some cultures are fiercely jealous, there are other cultures where jealousy is unknown (Mead, 1986). Jealousy is inevitably related to the desire to control someone else who is important to us (Davis, K., 1986). When we are jealous, we are dependent on another person and also insecure (Berscheid & Fei, 1986). It is as if we demand a guarantee that this person will always be available to please us. Obviously, this isn't very realistic. Looking back at Figure 2.2 in Chapter 2, we can define a jealousy-provoking situation as a life event. What kinds of appraisals are likely to result in feelings of jealousy? Probably demands such as:

"I demand that X be available whenever I need him/her."
"X isn't treating me right unless he/she caters to my needs."
"X is a bad person because he/she is not giving me what I want."
"X owes it to me to treat me the way I desire."

These are the kinds of beliefs that put us in a no-win situation because they are unrealistic and bound to make us miserable (Ellis, 1987). Margaret Mead (1986) explains the experience of jealousy in the following way: "It is a negative, miserable state of feeling, having its origin in a sense of insecurity and inferiority" (p. 121).

We can use our powers of rational thinking to talk ourselves through jealousy-provoking situations by saying things to ourselves such as:

"I truly desire X's affection, but I know it is not in my power to demand things I don't own."

"Sometimes I get what I want from X and sometimes I don't. I have to balance the positives and negatives."

"The more I demand things from others, the more I set myself up for frustration. I have to rely on my own resources to get my needs met."

"It's a pain and a disappointment when others don't give me what I want, but it is a fact of life I must learn to accept."

Peter Salovey and Judith Rodin (1988) asked people how they coped when they experienced jealousy at school or work, in their family, and in friendships and romantic relationships. The most successful copers were men and women who took an attitude of self-reliance. Instead of upsetting themselves or the people about whom they felt jealous, they got busy with other activities in their lives. Successful copers appraised jealousy as an inconvenient hassle. They used the following coping skills to acknowledge their jealousy, and keep it from throwing their life off track:

1. Constructively dealing with anger
2. Not feeling sorry for themselves
3. Not ruminating about the unfairness of the situation
4. Avoiding blaming other people
5. Keeping up their own self-esteem
6. Staying busy with meaningful activities
7. Forcing themselves to let go

Support systems: We should use our support people to lean on for caring when the person we *really* want it from is unwilling or unavailable. Support people may be willing to listen to a limited amount of complaining about the "unfairness of it all" if we promise to reciprocate the favor.

Problem solving: We can use our problem-solving skills to identify realistic strategies for obtaining love and nurturance. We need to remind ourselves that we can't demand that love and nurturance will come from a particular person.

Self-relaxation: We can use our self-relaxation skills to tone down our feelings of insecurity, frustration, and anger. Self-relaxation is also a skill we can use without having to rely on others.

Maintaining internal control: We can remind ourlseves that our worth is based on our personal accomplishments and resources and isn't controlled by another person.

Developing a sense of humor: We need to remind ourselves not to take our-selves so seriously. We should learn how to laugh at our propensity for making ourselves miserable. Sing some of Albert Ellis's rational songs, such as the following one that goes to the tune of "Yankee Doodle":[1]

Love me, love me, only me or I'll die without you!
Make your love a guarantee, so I can never doubt you.
Love me, love me all the time, thoroughly and wholly.
Life turns into slush and slime, 'less you love me solely!

Rewarding ourselves for accomplishments: We must remember not to put ourselves down for feeling jealous. We are fallible human beings and are entitled to imperfections. However, we should give ourselves credit for owning our jealousy and for taking the responsibility to overcome it.

Coping Skill 7: Overcoming Jealousy   ▲
• •

COPING WITH AN UNSATISFACTORY RELATIONSHIP

If we have reevaluated our expectations and balanced the negatives and positives and are still not satisfied with a relationship, it is time to make a secondary appraisal, to say, "My relationship with X has a problem. What am I going to do about it?" Our options will be discussed in the remainder of this chapter.

TAKING POSITIVE ACTION

When a relationship is threatened, both partners must decide together whether they are willing to give what it takes to pull it back together. If they are both motivated to improve the relationship, professional therapists and counselors can be very helpful.

Something partners can do on their own is an exercise developed by R. B. Stuart (1980) to stimulate constructive actions and positive feelings, called *caring days.* The partners make a list of 20 positive actions they would like from each other. The following rules must be followed:

1. The actions must be *positive.* Each person asks the partner to do things the person likes. No one is allowed to ask the partner to stop doing things the person dislikes.
2. The actions must be specific. For example, rather than asking the partner to be more affectionate say, "Hug me three times a day," or "Kiss me more often."
3. The actions must be small behaviors that can be done every day.
4. The actions should not be things the partner is touchy about or that have been the subject of recent conflict.

When the lists are completed, the partners sign a contract agreeing that they both promise to do at least five of the acts on each list every day. Both partners make a daily log on which they record each other's positive actions. This log helps them jointly monitor their progress and reinforces them for their efforts.

[1] Albert Ellis, "Rational Humorous Songs." Copyright 1977–1981 by the Institute for Rational-Emotive Therapy, 45 E. 65th St., New York, NY 10021.

COMMUNICATING AND NEGOTIATING

Another option we have when someone close to us behaves in an unacceptable way is to communicate our dissatisfaction and negotiate a solution. This is where our assertiveness skills (see Chapter 8) can be very useful. Remember that assertiveness means being honest, straightforward, and nonaggressive. To help us appreciate the value of communication and negotiation, let's first look at some less effective methods of getting our needs met by close others.

People in close relationships identified six tactics they most often employ to influence their romantic partners (Buss, Gomes, Higgins, & Lauterbach, 1987):

Charm: "I compliment my partner so he/she will do it." "I try to be loving and romantic when I ask for things." "I act charming so he/she will do it."

Silent treatment: "I ignore my partner until he/she does what I want." "I don't respond to my partner until he/she does what I want." "I am silent until my partner does what I want."

Coercion: "I demand my partner do what I want." "I yell at my partner until he/she does what I want." "I threaten my partner until he/she does what I want."

Logical arguments: "I give my partner reasons why he/she should do what I want." "I ask my partner why he/she doesn't do what I want?" "I explain why I want him/her to do what I want."

Passive-aggressive: "I pout until he/she does what I want." "I sulk until he/she does what I want."

Self-downing: "I put myself down so he/she will do what I want." "I act inadequate so he/she will do what I want." "I act humble so he/she will do what I want."

The striking thing about these influence tactics is that none of them is very adaptive. Couples who engaged in these tactics rated themselves and were rated by people who interviewed them as dissimilar, mismatched, and not likely to stay together. It is instructive that the people sampled in this study did not report much use of communication and negotiation.

A study of communication styles that cause particular problems between husbands and wives found the following three patterns (Epstein, Pretzer, & Fleming, 1987):

1. *Critical and defensive:* Refuses to acknowledge mistakes, refuses to accept criticism, dogmatic and rigid about opinions, inappropriately blames spouse, and/or fails to give compliments

2. *Withdrawn and submissive:* Talks too little, fails to express opinions, is too compliant, fails to express emotions, and/or talks too slowly and quietly

3. *Dominant and controlling:* Talks too much, asks too many questions, interrupts when spouse is talking, changes topics during discussions, and/or talks too loudly

Although all three of these styles end up blocking communication, the one related to the highest level of marital distress was being critical and defensive.

Now that we are familiar with problematic communication styles, let's consider some suggestions for communicating more effectively (Stuart, 1980).

Learning to Listen

Carl Rogers is generally acknowledged as pointing out that we are often so preoccupied with our own thoughts and feelings that we don't really listen to what others are trying to tell us. Consider the following exchange:

Person A: "How was your vacation?"
Person B: "It was great!"
Person A: "My vacation was good too. We went to Hawaii and . . ."

It is clear that person A would rather talk about himself than listen to what person B has to say. Now compare the above conversation with this one:

Person A: "How was your vacation?"
Person B: "It was great!"
Person A: "That sounds exciting. Tell me about it."

Here person A is actually listening to person B. Person A is being responsive (see Chapter 6) and is expressing a personal interest. You can practice listening skills with another person by agreeing to communicate in the following manner. Let's say your partner makes a statement. Before you respond, you have to repeat back the meaning of this statement. Your partner then has a chance to acknowledge that you heard the statement accurately or to correct you. After showing your partner that you really understood the statement, it is your turn to talk. Your partner then repeats back the meaning of your statement and receives feedback from you. For example:

Person A: I'm disappointed because you rarely show me affection.
Person B: You are insecure. You want more from me.
Person A: That's not what I said. Try again.
Person B: You want more affection.
Person A: You didn't say anything about my feelings.
Person B: You want more affection. You're being grouchy.
Person A: No. I'm disappointed because I want more affection from you.
Person B: You're disappointed. You want me to give you more affection.
Person A: Right.

Although it would be cumbersome to carry on all conversations in this manner, you can see how helpful this exercise can be for teaching us to listen to each other.

Owning Your Feelings

Compare the following statements:

A: You never do anything around the house.
B: I want your help with the housecleaning.

A: You never tell me you love me.
B: Once in a while I want you to tell me you love me.

A: Do you want to go to the movies?

B: I would like to go to the movies.

A: Your selfishness and inconsiderateness makes me angry.

B: I am angry because you didn't tell me you would be home late.

In the A statements the speaker is being indirect, and it is not clear what he or she really wants. In the B statements the speaker is owning feelings and saying exactly what he or she wants. When we own our feelings, we say, "*I feel _____ when you do _____.*" Owning statements are *I* statements. *You* statements, such as "*You make me feel _____*" or "*You* are _____" are irresponsible.

Five Rules for Constructive Communication

The following rules for constructive communication will help us make the most of our efforts to be clear and straightforward with others:

Rule 1: Own communications by using the word *I*.

Rule 2: Don't make generalizations about the other person's character. ("You are inconsiderate." "You are lazy.") Focus instead on specific actions. ("I want you to come home on time." "I want you to help with the housework.")

Rule 3: Avoid making things absolute with words like *always* and *never*. ("You are always messy." "You never help.") Instead, try to create a positive attitude. ("Sometimes you're neat. I wish you would be neat more often." "I appreciate it when you help, and it would mean a lot to me if you would help more often.")

Rule 4: Use good timing. Try to respond to the person's actions right after they happen. If you miss the opportunity to respond immediately, be tactful. Wait until an appropriate time to give positive and negative feedback.

Rule 5: Be constructive. When you tell the other person about something you dislike, also tell her or him what you like.

Good communication skills are among the most important predictors of marital satisfaction (Gottman, 1979). Research has demonstrated that when married partners are trained to engage in constructive communication, blood pressure goes down and marital satisfaction increases (Ewart, Taylor, Kraemer, & Agras, 1984; Hahlweg & Markman, 1988; Markman, Floyd, Stanley, & Lewis, 1986; Markman, Floyd, Stanley, & Storaasli, 1988).

Negotiating a Contract

Earlier in this chapter we learned about tactics people in close relationships use to influence each other. What was missing in each of those tactics was honest communication and the willingness to negotiate. We can get an interesting perspective on the process of negotiation by considering a study that was done on conflict resolution between college roommates (Sillars, 1981). Students reported that they used one of three general conflict-resolution strategies:

1. *Avoidance:* Avoiding the person; not talking about the problem; hinting, but not coming out and stating feelings; joking about the problem; denying there is a problem; and/or changing the subject

2. *Influence:* Making demands, faulting the other person, being hostile, making threats, and/or asking the other person to change
3. *Communication:* Saying clearly what is bothering one, asking about the other person's feelings, accepting responsibility, and/or suggesting ideas to solve the problem

Interestingly, the strategy used most often was avoidance (57%). Influence was used 11% of the time, and communication was used 32% of the time. Students were more likely to communicate with their roommate when they accepted responsibility for helping to resolve conflicts in the relationship. Students who blamed their roommate for causing the conflict were more likely to engage in influence and avoidance.

It should be clear by this time that constructive negotiation requires us to take responsibility for helping resolve conflicts we have with close others. In addition, if we want our partner to make changes, it makes sense that we should offer to make changes in return. Negotiation between people in close relationships should be in the spirit of a two-winner approach. This can be accomplished by making a contract that has three columns: My Gain, Your Gain, Our Gain. It is a good idea for both partners to sign this contract to affirm their commitment to carry out the agreement. Negotiation must be a cooperative venture in which each person is willing to give a bit for the sake of the relationship. In this way, even though we end up giving, we are giving for a good cause, and we gain something in return. Negotiations between people in close relationships do not involve one person taking an inflexible position and waiting for the other person to give in. Negotiation between close people is cooperative because both partners accept the following facts of life: We can't have everything our way. It is impossible to find a perfect partner.

Coping Skill 8: Communicating and Negotiating   ▲
● ●

GIVING THE BENEFIT OF DOUBT

One coping skill that is useful in all close relationships is the ability to forgive our partner for doing things we don't like. It is easiest to forgive others when we can give them the benefit of doubt. For instance, we can say to ourselves: "What my partner did (or didn't do) causes a problem for me. However, I know that my partner has good intentions and many positive sides. So, even though I'm not happy about it, I can forgive and give my partner the benefit of doubt."

The value of giving the benefit of doubt was demonstrated in four studies comparing the reactions of distressed and nondistressed couples to positive and negative actions by their partners (Fincham, Beach, & Baucom, 1987; Fincham & O'Leary, 1983; Holtzworth-Munroe & Jacobson, 1985; Thompson & Kelley, 1981). Because nondistressed couples gave their partners credit for positive acts, they found it easier to live with each other's negative acts. Distressed couples were preoccupied with the negatives. They spent a lot of time focusing on dissatisfactions about their partner and had difficulty appreciating their partner's redeeming qualities. The above research demonstrates that people in happy relationships know how to give credit for positives contributed by their partner.

Coping Skill 9: Giving the Benefit of Doubt ▲
· ·

BLAMING AND NEGATIVE THINKING

All of the responses for coping with unsatisfactory relationships described so far involve taking a positive action-oriented approach. The final option, of blaming and negative thinking, is not recommended because it is destructive. Blaming and negative thinking is worth discussing, however, because it is always tempting to avoid responsibility by blaming our partner for relationship problems. Research studies have shown that distressed couples engage in blaming and negative thinking far more often than nondistressed couples do (Fincham, 1985; Fincham, Beach, & Baucom, 1987; Fincham, Beach, & Nelson, 1987; Kyle & Falbo, 1985). People in unhappy relationships feel their partner is more responsible for relationship problems than they are. They view their partner's negative behaviors as resulting from selfishness, an uncaring attitude, and lack of commitment. People who are unhappy with a relationship tend to say the following kinds of things to themselves: "My partner wouldn't act this way if he/she really cared about me." "I refuse to be responsible unless my partner does something nice for me." "I'm going to get even and make my partner suffer for not treating me right."

People in happy relationships are able to put their feelings into perspective: "If I want my partner to respond differently, I have to take the initiative." "I don't always like it, but I know things will work out best if I'm flexible enough to show my partner some affection." "I want to tell my partner I'm angry, but it won't help our relationship to make him/her suffer."

Blaming and negative thinking inevitably lead us to act in a negative way toward our partner. Unless our partner can use some of the coping skills described in this chapter, her or his response is likely to be negative or a refusal to engage in a positive act. We will be caught in a vicious cycle in which negative behaviors, feelings, and thoughts outweigh our ability to make adaptive appraisals (Bradbury & Fincham, 1987; Fincham & Bradbury, 1988).

Coping Skill 10: Avoiding the Temptation to Engage in Blaming and Negative Thinking ▲
· ·

ENDING THE RELATIONSHIP

Close relationships have three active ingredients: *commitment, intimacy,* and *passion* (Sternberg, 1986; Sternberg & Grajeck, 1984). The presence or absence of these components determines the nature of the relationship (see Table 9.2).

Liking requires intimacy, but not commitment or passion.
Infatuation is "love at first sight." There is passion, but the relationship never develops to the depth of commitment and intimacy.

TABLE 9.2   Three Ingredients in Close Relationships

Type of Relationship	Ingredients		
	Commitment	Intimacy	Passion
Liking		X	
Infatuation			X
Empty love	X		
Romantic love		X	X
Fatuous love	X		X
Companionate love	X	X	
Consummate love	X	X	X

From "A Triangular Theory of Love," by R. J. Sternberg, 1986, *Psychological Review, 93,* 119–135. Copyright 1986 by the American Psychological Association. Adapted with permission.

Empty love is commitment without intimacy and passion. It occurs in stagnant relationships where couples stay together out of inertia or because they don't believe in divorce.

Romantic love is a combination of intimacy and passion. It is a "heavy affair" without commitment.

Fatuous love is "Hollywood" love. The man and woman fall madly in love and get married without really knowing each other.

Companionate love is intimacy with commitment but not passion. It is a long-term friendship. It is platonic love or a close marriage lacking in sex.

Consummate love is an ideal relationship that includes passion, commitment, and intimacy.

The kinds of love outlined in Table 9.2 suggest two important conclusions. On the one hand, we must recognize that it is difficult, if not impossible, to maintain a long-term relationship at the level of consummate love. All relationships have their normal ups and downs. On the other hand, we must also realize that we have standards about what is acceptable and unacceptable in a long-term relationship. When we find ourselves in a relationship that is not satisfactory, it is time to make a move. One option is to work with our partner to bring the ingredients that are missing into our relationship. A second option is to end the relationship.

There are three things that generally lead people to dissolve a relationship: dissimilarity, boredom, and negative feelings (Baron & Byrne, 1987, chap. 6).

Dissimilarity: We realize that we and the other person have little in common. There are too many differences in values, interests, and goals for a sustained relationship.

Boredom: The relationship becomes stagnant. We are not growing together or moving with each other in a purposeful direction.

Negative feelings: The negatives outweigh the positives. There is too much criticizing, complaining, and nagging and too little love, support, and affection.

When a relationship is threatened and we and our partner are not motivated to make improvements, it is time seriously to consider going our separate ways. This is where we must take control of our life and assume responsibility for our actions.

Coping Skill 11: Deciding What We Want in a Relationship   ▲

BEING WILLING TO WORK

It is a fact that good relationships don't come easily. They require continuous effort. George Levinger put it very clearly when he said: "What counts in making a happy marriage (or any other satisfactory relationship) is not so much how compatible you are, but how you deal with incompatibility" (Goleman, 1985, p. 19).

Dealing with conflicts in close relationships requires the commitment to practice *consistently* coping skills such as those outlined in this chapter.

Coping Skill 12: Being Willing to Work   ▲

▲ LIST OF SKILLS FOR COPING WITH CONFLICTS IN CLOSE RELATIONSHIPS

Coping Skill 1: Taking Active Responsibility

Coping Skill 2: Reevaluating Expectations

Coping Skill 3: Being Sensitive to Desired Areas of Change.

Coping Skill 4: Practicing Tolerance

Coping Skill 5: Balancing the Negatives and Positives

Coping Skill 6: Acknowledging Our Right to Determine Our Needs in a Relationship

Coping Skill 7: Overcoming Jealousy

Coping Skill 8: Communicating and Negotiating

Coping Skill 9: Giving the Benefit of Doubt

Coping Skill 10: Avoiding the Temptation to Engage in Blaming and Negative Thinking

Coping Skill 11: Deciding What You Want in a Relationship

Coping Skill 12: Being Willing to Work

SUGGESTIONS FOR FURTHER READING

ELLIS, A. (1975). *How to live with a "neurotic"* (rev. ed.). New York: Crown.

ELLIS, A., & HARPER, R. A. (1961). *A guide to successful marriage.* North Hollywood, Calif.: Wilshire Books.

LAZARUS, A. A. (1985). *Marital myths: Two dozen mistaken beliefs that can ruin a marriage (or make a bad one worse).* San Ramon, Calif.: Impact Publishers.

ROGERS, C. R. (1972). *Becoming partners: Marriage and its alternatives.* New York: Dell.

STUART, R. B. (1980). *Helping couples change.* New York: Guilford.

10

Coping with Loss

Loss is an inevitable part of life. Loss encompasses a number of events, ranging from dissolved relationships and separation to death. Different kinds of losses mean different things to different people. However, there are some things about going through a loss that are common for all of us. This chapter will focus on the processes that make loss a human experience. It is helpful to understand these processes and to recognize that loss is a part of life that touches everyone, everywhere. Learning about loss as a human experience helps us gain peace of mind over the losses in our lives. Since this chapter is only an introduction to a deep issue, it cannot provide solutions for all problems. People whose lives are seriously disrupted by a loss will find it beneficial to take advantage of organized groups and professional support.[1]

APPRAISING A LOSS

Our first reaction to a loss is to make a primary appraisal. Because losses are usually traumatic and often unexpected, our primary appraisal is almost automatic. In Chapter 2 we learned that primary appraisals can help free us from life events that are not worth getting upset about. Since most losses are upsetting, it is desirable to accept them as real problems and to go through the appropriate grieving process. When we deny the importance of a loss, we cheat ourselves out of an important experience of mourning and reconciliation.

After accepting a loss as a problem worthy of grief, what kinds of secondary appraisals can we make? It is important to recognize that coping successfully with a loss does not mean fixing it or turning it around. An adaptive secondary appraisal is one where we tell ourselves that we have *grief work* to do (Lindemann, 1944). Grieving is an active process where we are affected by various feelings and need to take time to accomplish certain tasks. We will now look at the experiences and tasks of grief work.

Coping Skill 1: Accepting a Loss as Worthy of Grief Work ▲
• •

THE EXPERIENCE OF MOURNING

Even though the experience of mourning a loss is not pleasant, it is helpful to recognize it as a part of life that is shared by everyone. The experience of mourning a loss affects our feelings, our bodies, our thoughts, and our behaviors (Worden, 1982).

Feelings

Depending on the loss, people usually experience number of different feelings:

> *Sadness:* We may feel empty, dejected, and depressed, and possibly like crying unexpectedly. It is often necessary to allow ourselves to feel the pain of a loss before moving on to the stage of acceptance and reconciliation.

---

[1] Most cities have clearinghouses with lists of support groups. You can also call your local hospital or community mental health center for lists of support groups. Support groups are usually listed each week in a local newspaper.

Anger: We may feel frustrated at the unfairness of the loss and at the fact that we can't control it. We should avoid turning this anger against ourselves and realize that, although we can't control the loss, we do have control of our grief work.

Guilt: We may feel guilty because we weren't "perfect" and because we couldn't prevent the loss. It is important to recognize the fact that we are fallible human beings living in an unpredictable world.

Anxiety: We may wonder, "Can I survive this loss?" We come face-to-face with our vulnerability and mortality. Hopefully, the coping skills we learned in Chapter 3 will help boost our feelings of self-efficacy.

Loneliness: This is an empty feeling that is a combination of sadness and anxiety. We can turn to the information about loneliness discussed in Chapter 6.

Fatigue: We may feel tired and worn out. This is a normal reaction to stress and should not be seen as a deficiency or sign of weakness.

Shock: We may feel shock if the loss is sudden or unexpected. As we will learn later in this chapter, shock, disbelief, and numbness comprise the first stage of grief work.

Relief: It is important to recognize some losses as a mixed blessing that combine sadness and relief. There is no need to feel guilty about having both of these feelings.

Physical Reactions

The feelings experienced after a loss usually affect us physically, and we can expect the following kinds of bodily reactions. If we anticipate these sensations, they won't feel as strange or scary when they happen: hollowness in the stomach, tightness in the chest, tightness in the throat, oversensitivity to noise, shortness of breath, weakness of muscles, dry mouth, and/or lack of energy.

Thoughts

There a number of thoughts we are likely to have after experiencing a loss, and we may be surprised to learn how often these thoughts are experienced by others. These thoughts can involve:

Disbelief: Disbelief occurs during the first stage of grief work. It is hard at first to accept the reality of the loss.

Confusion: We may feel confused and find it difficult to keep our minds on one topic. It is important to give ourselves a break and not expect our performance to be up to its normal level.

Preoccupation: Our thinking may be almost completely focused on the loss and on wishes and desires to return to the past. Preoccupation is common during the second stage of grief work.

Imagination: We may imagine what things were like before the loss and pretend we are back in the past or that the person we have lost is still here.

This kind of thinking is to be expected and is also part of the second stage of grief work.

Behaviors

The experience of loss often affects a number of daily behaviors. As with physical sensations, it can be helpful to anticipate these behavioral changes so they won't appear frightening or abnormal.

Sleeping: It is common after experiencing a loss to have trouble sleeping.

Eating: Eating patterns are often affected. Some people eat more. Others find eating difficult.

Social withdrawal: It may be useful at first to spend time alone with our thoughts and feelings. Later in the grief work we will be ready to push ourselves into resuming social activities.

Dreaming: It is common to dream about the lost person.

Activity: We will probably experience a change in activity. We may feel listless and apathetic, or we may feel restless and have difficulty remaining still. We need to acknowledge this change in activity as a normal part of grief.

Crying: Crying is a normal reaction to a loss. If crying in front of others is uncomfortable, we need to schedule time alone when we can give in to the need to express grief.

Coping Skill 2: Being Open to the Experience of Mourning   ▲

STAGES OF GRIEF WORK

Experts who have studied loss and grief have outlined the following stages that people work through as they attempt to reach a point of reconciliation after experiencing a loss (Rando, 1984; Worden, 1982). As you will learn later in this chapter, the amount of time required to complete these stages of grief work and the degree to which grief is finally resolved is an individual matter (Wortman & Silver, 1987, 1989). We must find a pace and style of working through grief that is best suited to our needs.

Shock, disbelief, and numbness: We feel stunned. It is difficult to accept the loss, and we are tempted to deny that it really happened. Our immediate concern is to block out painful feelings.

Yearning and searching: We ask, "Why did it happen to me?" We feel anger at our inability to reverse the loss. We cling to unrealistic expectations that things will end up as before.

Despair and disorganization: We feel depressed about the reality of the loss and see no hope that things will ever get better.

Acceptance and reorganization: Finally, we give up false hopes and accept the loss as a reality. As a result of this acceptance, we begin to make plans and push ourselves to get on with our lives.

New identity: We adapt to our lives as different from the way they were and recognize how we have grown as a result of our grief work.

It is useful to view the stages of grief work as tasks that we must take the responsibility to solve. This way of looking at grief work reinforces our feelings of internal control and self-efficacy. It is not desirable to interpret stages of grief as phases that *happen* to us because this makes us feel passive and dependent and undermines our identity as a problem solver.

Coping Skill 3: Recognizing the Stages of Grief Work as Tasks for Which We Are Responsible ▲
• •

TASKS OF GRIEF WORK

Now that we have an understanding of the mourning and grief work following a loss, it will be useful to look at these tasks for which we are responsible. J. W. Worden (1982) has outlined four tasks to accomplish when doing grief work after a loss:

Task 1. Accepting the reality of the loss: We have to face the fact that the loss is real and that we can't return to the past. This is a painful and difficult thing to do, and it takes time. We can make it easier for ourselves by looking forward to the freedom and relief we will feel when we are finally able to let go. When working on task 1, we want to avoid getting caught in two undesirable places. First, we don't want to insulate ourselves by downplaying or denying the importance of the loss. Being alive in this world means allowing ourselves the experience of mourning. Second, we need to set a date when we will be completely ready to let go of objects, plans, and desires that reinforce a false hope that the loss can be reversed.

Task 2. Experiencing pain and grief: It is necessary to open ourselves up to the mourning experiences described earlier. It is sometimes difficult to accomplish this task because people around us may be uncomfortable with our need to take time for feeling pain and sadness. This is a period when we need to find a good balance between being alone and taking advantage of support systems.

Task 3. Adjusting to a new life: Our lives are different following a loss. There is no way to get around this. Our lives are made up of chapters, and we never know when one chapter will end and a new one will begin. We must accept the fact that life is a challenge that requires us to learn new skills and to adapt to new experiences.

Task 4. Getting on with life: When we get to task 4 we are ready to accept the fact that it is time to get on with our lives. This does not mean that our loss is forgotten. Our past experiences, both good and bad, are what make us mature. Getting on with our lives doesn't mean forsaking people or events in our past. It simply means we are ready to begin a new chapter.

Coping Skill 4: Taking Time to Accomplish the Four Tasks of Grief Work ▲
• •

UNRESOLVED GRIEF

There are many reasons why people find it difficult to complete grief work after suffering a loss. First, it is tempting to avoid the pain and hard work that grief work requires. In addition, there is often a reluctance to let go of someone who has departed. However, people with unresolved grief often suffer in the long run because they have unfinished business that needs to be taken of before they can get on with their lives. Some symptoms of unresolved grief include (Rando, 1984):

Overactivity without a sense of loss
Development of a psychosomatic or medical illness
Alteration in relationships with friends and relatives
Hostility against people associated with the loss
Social withdrawal
Depression, tension, agitation, insomnia
Poor self-care habits
A feeling that the loss occurred very recently even though it happened years
     ago
Guilt and self-reproach

T. A. Rando (1984) identifies six forms of unresolved grief (abbreviated grief is a shortened form of grief work):

Absent grief: Feelings of grief and mourning are totally absent. It is as if the loss had never occurred. The person is either in a state of shock or complete denial.

Inhibited grief: It is possible for the person to mourn certain aspects of the loss in bits and pieces. However, the mourner is always guarded and never succeeds in completing all of the stages of grief work.

Delayed grief: Grief work is delayed for an extended period of time. Another loss or stressful event in the person's life triggers a delayed grief reaction many years after the loss occurred. At this point, the person can either complete the grief work or avoid it once more and allow it to remain unresolved.

Conflicted grief: This is an uneven response where certain emotions take over a person's life to the point where grief work is never completed. For example, a person may channel all of her or his energy into anger or guilt. The anger and guilt become part of the person's life because they have not been placed in their proper perspective.

Chronic grief: The person freely experiences the loss but never begins grief work. The mourning and grief continue indefinitely to the point where the person may develop pathological reactions such as depression, panic, and total withdrawal.

Unanticipated grief: This reaction may occur when a loss is catastrophic and completely unexpected. The traumatic reaction is so severe that it is difficult for the person to begin the tasks of grief work. A person in this situation needs support. With enough time and encouragement, the grief work will hopefully get started.

Abbreviated grief: Abbreviated grief is a shortened form of grief work. It is sometimes mistaken for unresolved grief because it takes place more quickly than many grief reactions. Abbreviated grief often occurs when a person has had time to get prepared for the loss. Much of the grief work has already been accomplished before the loss occurs.

DISENFRANCHISED GRIEF

Disenfranchised grief is grief experienced by people who suffer a loss that is not or cannot be openly acknowledged, publicly mourned, or socially supported (Doka, 1989). Some examples of disenfranchised grief include the following:

Death of a gay lover: Homosexuals may find it difficult to mourn the death of a lover when they are unaccepted by their own familiy or by the family of their lover. The situation is even more difficult if the lover has died from AIDS, because of the fear and stigma associated with this disease.

Death of a divorced spouse: The death of a divorced spouse is accompanied by many conflicted feelings, often including unresolved anger and hurt, fond memories and love, and lack of reconciliation with the spouse's family. These circumstances can prevent a satisfactory experience of resolving feelings surrounding the spouse's death.

Death of an unborn baby: We are often not prepared to mourn the death of an unborn baby. If the death occurs in a hospital, there is little support from busy nurses and doctors. In addition, friends and family might not identify with the baby as an actual person who requires a formal farewell. If the mother had mixed feelings about having the baby in the first place, she must resolve conflicted feelings of guilt and sadness.

Children who suffer loss: Children are often prevented from resolving losses by being isolated from the rituals appropriate to their culture. Adults may have good intentions in "protecting" children from sadness and grief. However, since losses are unavoidable, it is more helpful to teach children how to deal with them in the first place.

It is important to understand that loss is part of our life experiences and to use whatever rituals are meaningful for finding reconciliation. When it comes to coping with disenfranchised grief, support groups can be very helpful.

THREE FACTORS INFLUENCING THE SUCCESS OF GRIEF WORK

Three factors influencing the success of grief work are the nature of the relationship with the person who is lost, the suddenness of the loss, and the strength of one's social support system (Wortman & Silver, 1987).

1. *The nature of the relationship:* It is more difficult to recover from losing a person when our relationship with that person was ambivalent. Ambivalent relationships are those in which issues of commitment and trust are not resolved. There is "unfinished business" in the relationship causing feelings of hurt, anger, hostility, and guilt. When the person departs, these feelings are often exacerbated. It is also difficult to recover from losing a person on whom we were very dependent. We feel a strong desire to "hang on," and we experience a sense of helplessness because that person fulfilled so many of our needs.

2. *The suddenness of the loss:* It is easier to recover from a loss if we have time to prepare for it. When a loss is expected, a lot of grief work can be accomplished before it occurs. Unexpected losses are traumatic because they remind us of the unpredictable nature of this world.

3. *Support systems:* A good support system does much to help in the recovery from loss. As we learned in Chapter 3, a support system can provide nurturance and bolster our sense of self-worth, trust, and life-direction.

FINDING A MEANING FOR DEATH

It is much easier to cope with death when it has some kind of meaning. Some cultures are *death accepting* (Rando, 1984). They view death as an inevitable and natural part of the life cycle. Death and dying are integrated into the daily patterns of living. Other cultures are *death defying*. They believe in an afterlife and have rituals for preparing people for a new life after they depart from this earth. Still other cultures are *death denying*. In these cultures there is a refusal to confront the reality and inevitability of death. It is probably fair to say that people from death-denying cultures are most vulnerable to unresolved grief about death because they have no answer for death's meaning (Becker, 1973; Schoenberg, 1980). Two important books, by R. Kavanaugh (*Facing Death,* 1974) and E. Kübler-Ross (*On Death and Dying,* 1969), have pointed out the importance of coming to terms with death. Indeed, once we accept the inevitability of death, it is possible to appreciate some of its benefits (Koestenbaum, 1976):

Death helps us savor life

Death provides an opposite by which to judge being alive

Death provides us a sense of a real, individual existence

Death gives meaning to courage and integrity, allowing us to express our convictions effectively

Death provides us with the strength to make major decisions

Death reveals the importance of intimacy in our lives

Death helps us ascribe meaning to our lives retroactively, which is especially useful for older people

Death shows us the importance of ego-transcending achievements

Death allows us to see our achievements as having significance

Whether we rely on our culture, our religion, or our personal philosophy, it is important to make death a meaningful part of our life experience.

Coping Skill 5: Finding a Meaning for Death   ▲

GETTING THROUGH A SEPARATION OR DIVORCE

Almost everyone is touched by divorce, either personally or through close relations and friends. Divorce is an unpleasant experience, and it forces people to make significant adjustments in their lives. The *psychological adjustments* required during a divorce include: coping with loneliness, finding new meaning in life, coping with anger, coping with guilt and low self-esteem, and seeking new sources of love and nurturance. The *tactical adjustments* required by divorce include: finding a new living situation, gaining financial stability, and managing responsibilities of a single parent.

Given the number of major adjustments required by a divorce, it is no wonder that divorce is such a stressful experience.

Four Phases of a Divorce Experience

There are four phases people typically go through from the beginning to the end of a divorce (Kressel, 1986):

1. *Predecision period:* This is the time in a marriage when partners begin to feel dissatisfaction. They know things are not right. The relationship becomes tense. Couples may fight or they may withdraw from each other. Hopefully, they will seek counseling. It becomes clear that the marriage is in trouble and that constructive steps must be taken.

2. *Decision period:* During this phase couples decide whether or not to work through counseling to save their marriage or to call it quits and get a divorce. This is a difficult period because no decision is foolproof and all decisions require significant effort and adjustment. There is a feeling of relief once a decision has been made. There is also anxiety about an uncertain future.

3. *Negotiation:* Negotiations are usually conducted with the aid of therapists and lawyers. Couples who are undertaking counseling to save their marriage make a contract outlining the conditions of their therapeutic work. Couples who have decided on a divorce must achieve an equitable division of financial and child-rearing responsibilities.

4. *Reconciliation:* Reconciliation after a divorce is finalized is difficult. Feelings of guilt, loneliness, and anger place large barriers between the couple. Hopefully, they can learn to cope with these feelings well enough to get on with their lives and to carry on with their financial and child-rearing settlement in a smooth and tactful manner.

The Mourning Process

Mourning a divorce means mourning a loss. Going through this mourning process is necessary for reaching a state of reconciliation.

Using Good Coping Skills

People who are best prepared to cope with a separation or divorce share the following characteristics (Brehm, 1987): they have an independent source of income; they know how to carry out the daily tasks of living (cooking, paying bills, car and household maintenance, etc.); they have a social support system independent of their partner; they know how to enjoy being alone; and they are flexible enough to adapt to new situations.

A good place to begin our discussion of strategies for coping with separation and divorce is with the problem-solving skills outlined in Chapter 3. First, we need to make a list of the challenges facing us so we can work out the best possible course of action. Some of these challenges may be:

Evaluating our satisfaction with the relationship
Deciding on active steps we can take to confront the problem
Recognizing and dealing with feelings of sadness, grief, loneliness, and anger
Working out a plan to support ourselves financially

Learning how to live independently
Finding ways to receive emotional support and nurturance
Maintaining self-esteem and feelings of competence
Finding meaningful activities that will help us get on with our lives.

When we use our problem-solving skills to find a good course of action, it will be helpful to consider again the additional coping skills discussed in Chapter 3. We will also want to practice the skills of rational thinking and self-efficacy described in Chapter 2. Other chapters in this book provide suggestions about how to cope with specific feelings brought forth by divorce, such as loneliness, failure, anxiety, depression, and anger.

LEARNING HOW TO LET GO

One of the most difficult tasks to accomplish when we lose someone is to let that person go. In this section we will consider a number of suggestions about how to let go and get on with our lives after someone has left us.

Accepting the Fact That We Can't Own Others

When we lose someone special, we get angry and frustrated because it doesn't seem fair. After all, nobody asked us if it was all right for that person to be taken out of our life. It is often difficult to accept the fact that relationships are a benefit of life and not a right. Giving up the desire to own people who are close to us is not easy because we truly wish we could dictate the outcome of our relationships. However, when we do relinquish our demand for ownership we will be released of a tremendous burden. It is hard enough in life to manage tasks for which we are responsible. We need to remind ourselves not to put ourselves in the no-win situation of demanding power over events that are not ours to control.

Getting Unhooked from the Addiction

Wanderer and Cabot (1978) describe love relationships as addictions because we often get used to deriving a majority of our gratification from one person. When that person leaves, we are at a loss because we have put all our eggs in one basket. How can all those good things be replaced when that particular person is gone? Here are two steps to follow:

1. *Be philosophical.* Remember, the gratification we received was a *benefit* of life, not a right. Try not to demand instant gratification of all desires. There is no law that says we should have nurturance, caring, and sex whenever we want them. This is a harsh fact, but our primary appraisal of a loss will be more objective if we can put our wants, demands, and expectations into perspective.

2. *Replace the missing nurturance.* We need to find ways to replace the nurturance this person used to provide. We can use our support systems. We can trade hugs and kind words with people we know. We can begin new relationships. We do need to keep in mind though that contracting for nurturance is not guaranteed to make us feel better instantly. It isn't easy to replace a person after we've gotten used

to his or her style and way of doing things. The important thing is to see ourselves as people who understand that overcoming an addiction is hard work. We know we can survive without immediate gratification.

Think Rationally

The experience of loss often triggers unrealistic and irrational thoughts. We feel the loss was unfair. We demand control over everything that happens to us. We feel anger, frustration, and jealousy. We tell ourselves that life is no longer worth living. This is the time to review the information on Albert Ellis's rational-emotive therapy discussed in Chapter 2. We need to analyze the emotions we are choosing to experience as a result of our demands and expectations. If we decide that some of them are not in our best interest, we can get our thinking under control with the following techniques:

Thought Stopping

We can wear a rubber band on a wrist and whenever we start thinking unrealistic, irrational, or maladaptive thoughts snap the rubber band and tell ourselves, "Stop!" Here are some typical irrational things we say to ourselves after a loss: "I will be alone forever." "My life is worthless now." "I'm too old to start again." "It's not fair." "If only I had done things differently."

The goal of thought stopping is to catch ourselves when we start thinking in ways that are sure to bring us down. Learn to substitute the following more realistic and rational thoughts:

"I now feel alone and I don't like it."
"I'm not enjoying my life right now."
"My life is going to be different now. Loss is not fun, but it is part of life."
"I can't control the lives of others."

As we can see, the rational thoughts we want to think after thought stopping are not intended to make everything bright and rosy. It would be ridiculous to tell ourselves after a loss that everything is fine. The purpose of thinking rationally is to use our emotional energy for experiencing legitimately unhappy feelings. That is, we don't want to compound our misery by making demands of life that have no bearing in reality.

Stimulus Control

If we feel we simply must take time for irrational thoughts during our grief work, we can use the technique of *stimulus control.* Find a particular spot and use it only for irrational thinking. We then schedule specific times each day when we go to this location and think irrational thoughts. That is, our assignment is to concentrate only on demands and expectations that make us miserable. We are, however, allowed to think these thoughts only during our scheduled time in our designated spot. During the rest of the day we are bound to strict thought stopping.

Taking a Balanced View

We have a tendency to aggrandize someone we've lost. We focus on all of the good things we miss about the person while forgetting that she or he also had faults. It is touching to remember the best about those close to us. However, we have to be careful not to exaggerate our misery by convincing ourselves that this person was so perfect and absolutely wonderful that we can't survive the loss. Wanderer and Cabot (1978) suggest making a "crime sheet" on which we list the person's faults. We need to bring ourselves to reality and understand that although we legitimately miss this person, our life is still worth living.

Saying Our Final Good-bye

Wanderer and Cabot's (1978) method for saying our final good-bye works as follows. We collect all of the letters, photos, and other articles associated with the person we lost. While we are working through the first stages of grief, we hide these items. At this point it would be too painful to have them in sight. Later, when we are ready to accept the loss and get on with our lives, we get these materials out for a final farewell. This day is called our "implosion day" because these articles are bound to stir up strong feelings. We are at a stage in our grief work where we are ready to handle feelings of legitimate sadness because we have successfully put to rest our unrealistic demands and expectations. When our implosion day is over, we can keep these articles or dispose of them as we see fit. We will always remember the person we lost, but we know it is time to begin a new life chapter.

Coping Skill 6: Learning How to Let Go ▲
....

RECOGNIZING OUR INDIVIDUALITY

Mourning a loss is a personal experience and it is important to recognize the need to cope with losses in our own way. The stages and tasks of grief work outlined earlier in this chapter provide a framework to help understand our personal reactions in times of loss. However, our experiences in coping with loss depend on our individuality. To appreciate this point, it will be useful to look at two myths of coping with loss and put them into perspective (Wortman & Silver, 1987, 1989):

Myth 1: Distress and depression are inevitable
Myth 2: Losses can be completely resolved

Distress and Depression Are Not Inevitable

Although it is certainly common to react to losses with feelings of distress and depression, these reactions are not inevitable. It is possible to face some losses calmly and to maintain positive feelings about ourselves and our lives. We need to remember that failure to experience distress and depression in times of loss does not necessarily indicate something is wrong with us. In addition, we don't always have to experience distress and depression before we can cope with a loss in a satisfactory manner.

Some Losses Are Never Completely Resolved

It is a mistake to assume we can resolve all of our losses completely. While it is important to reconcile losses well enough to get on with our lives, they may still touch us from time to time. It is not uncommon to have dreams, memories, and associations that bring feelings of sadness years after a loss has occurred. These relapses into the past should not be seen as a sign of weakness. To a large degree, mourning a loss means learning to integrate our complex feelings into a life full of challenges and learning experiences.

Coping Skill 7: Recognizing Our Individuality   ▲
••

HOW TO OFFER SUPPORT

Understanding how to offer support allows us to be helpful to others who have suffered a loss. It will also bring us more in touch with our needs from others in times of loss. The following suggestions for offering support come from researchers who interviewed people after they suffered a serious loss (Lehman, Ellard, & Wortman, 1986):

> *Helpful responses:* expressing genuine caring and concern, allowing the griever to express feelings, being available when needed, and offering the opportunity for activities
>
> *Unhelpful responses:* offering advice, encouraging a positive outlook, interfering in the griever's life, and downplaying the griever's loss

Respondents said they derived the greatest comfort from others who were good listeners and who allowed them to express their feelings. It was also helpful to have support people who communicated genuine caring and were available to be leaned on when needed. Grieving respondents also found comfort spending time with others who had suffered similar kinds of losses.

Responses that were not appreciated included statements that downplayed the griever's sense of loss. People who offered advice or encouragement to look at the brighter side of life did more harm than good. Respondents said they needed time to work things out for themselves. They valued concern and support, but resented others who tried to push them to act in ways that denied their feelings.

Why do people trivialize each other's distress (Lazarus, 1984)? Mainly because it is a burden when those close to us are suffering. We'd prefer for them to pull themselves together rather than relying on us for support. The problem with trivializing distress is that it promotes a false expectation that just a little positive thinking will make everything better. It is true that developing self-efficacy and feelings of internal control are valuable coping skills. However, this does not mean that people should deny their suffering. The negative effects of trivializing human distress will come up again in Chapter 13 when we look at helpful and unhelpful responses given to cancer patients. The point is that we value support from others in our efforts to cope with our losses and grief. But, above all, we expect them to take us seriously.

Coping Skill 8: Understanding How to Offer Support   ▲
••

▲ LIST OF SKILLS FOR COPING WITH LOSS

> *Coping Skill 1:* Accepting a Loss as Worthy of Grief Work
>
> *Coping Skill 2:* Being Open to the Experience of Mourning

Coping Skill 3: Recognizing the Stages of Grief Work as Tasks for Which We Are Responsible

Coping Skill 4: Taking Time to Accomplish the Four Tasks of Grief Work

Coping Skill 5: Finding a Meaning for Death

Coping Skill 6: Learning How to Let Go

Coping Skill 7: Recognizing Our Individuality

Coping Skill 8: Understanding How to Offer Support

SUGGESTIONS FOR FURTHER READING

BECKER, E. (1973). *The denial of death.* New York: The Free Press.

FREEMAN, L. (1978). *The sorrow and the fury: Overcoming hurt and loss from childhood to old age.* Englewood Cliffs, N.J.: Prentice-Hall.

KAVANAUGH, R. (1974). *Facing death.* Baltimore: Penguin.

KOESTENBAUM, P. (1976). *Is there an answer to death?* Englewood Cliffs, N.J.: Prentice-Hall.

KÜBLER-ROSS, E. (1969). *On death and dying.* New York: Macmillan.

KUSHNER, H. S. (1983). *When bad things happen to good people.* New York: Avon.

SCHNEIDER, J. (1984). *Stress, loss, and grief: Understanding their origins and growth potential.* Baltimore: University Park Press.

TATELBAUM, J. (1980). *The courage to grieve.* New York: Lippincott & Crowell.

11

Coping with Aging

Aging is a life event that affects everyone. People from all cultures throughout history have had to come to terms with the reality of aging and the inevitability of death. A primary appraisal of aging tells us that it is an experience that we may not always like, but one that we must accept. Given this fact, we want our secondary appraisal to result in coping responses that will help make the most of the aging experience.

This chapter focuses on skills for maintaining self-esteem and self-efficacy during old age. These skills are especially relevant for our society where elderly people often suffer stigma and lack of support.

WHY PSYCHOLOGISTS STUDY AGING

Since aging presents challenges and adjustments for all people, it stands to reason that we would want to understand as much about this process as we could. Interestingly, it has been only within the last 20 years that psychologists have developed gerontology into a major research topic. Psychologists have devoted attention to the study of aging because of a growing consciousness about the lack of preparation for growing old in much of U.S. society. Another reason for the development of this research area is the fact that the elderly population in the United States (and the world) is steadily increasing. In 1900, only 4% of Americans were over 65 years of age, but in 1970, 10% were over 65. By the year 2000, it is estimated that 13% of Americans will be over 65 years, and this percentage is expected to increase to 20% by the year 2030 (Cox, 1988).

Because elderly people are beginning to comprise a larger proportion of the population, they are gaining the power and influence to ensure better care from society.

TWO CHALLENGES OF AGING

Aging brings two major challenges. The first is physical. It comes as a result of the inevitable decline that occurs as our bodies get older. The second challenge is psychological. It results from the need to rise above the stigma of old age and to maintain a sense of self-esteem, mastery, and competence. We will look at both of these challenges in this chapter.

Physical Challenges in Aging

Common medical problems experienced by elderly people are (Libow, 1977):

Arthritis: This is a common ailment with no medical cure.

Bones: Aging bones weaken and break more easily. (See a doctor for a recommended diet and exercise.)

Bowels: Constipation and changes in regularity are common in later life. (See a doctor for a recommended diet, including fruits and other fibrous foods.)

Breast: Breast cancer is a concern for women. (Regular self-examination should be performed.)

Eyes: Cataracts are common but are usually treatable. Farsightedness is experienced by most people.

Heart: Arteriosclerosis, heart attacks, heart failure, and other problems are likely. (It is important at a young age to follow good health care practices such as not smoking, a proper diet, and regular exercise.)

Mobility: There is a decrement in mobility and increased difficulty with walking.

Prostate: Prostate problems common in older men. (Have regular physical checkups.)

Stroke: This is the most common reason for elderly people to be placed in nursing homes. (See a doctor for preventive health practices.)

Although most elderly people experience some of these problems, there are large differences between people in how fast they age.

Other physical challenges experienced in daily living activities by people over age 65 were (Cox, H. G., Sekhon, & Norman, 1978): getting up and down stairs, 40% of the respondents; washing and bathing, 20%; housecleaning, 30%; doing the laundry, 30%; using the telephone, 25%; dressing, 15%; and cooking, 19%.

Although elderly people experience problems with aging, it is worth pointing out that these difficulties are not as bad as younger people believe. A poll by Louis Harris and Associates (1975) compared younger and older Americans' opinions about how much elderly people suffer from problems such as fear of crime, adequate housing and clothing, medical care, and social support. It was interesting to find that younger people's estimates of how much elderly people suffer from these problems were far greater than the elderly people's actual reports. Also worth noting is that in a national survey, people in the 65–85 age bracket rated themselves as being happier than people in any other age group (Russell, C. H., 1989). In the same survey, elderly people said they were less troubled by loneliness and finances than middle-aged and younger people. Elderly people were also generally satisfied with their current state of health. We seem to fear old age and anticipate it to be much worse than it is.

While surveys of elderly people indicate that they often view their lives in a positive manner, the fears and negative perceptions many of us have about growing older can result in a negative self-fulfilling prophecy. If we *expect* aging to be negative and painful, it will surely turn out that way for us. If we *expect* that elderly people are slow, forgetful, and incompetent, we will most likely start acting this way as we grow older. The goal of this chapter is to enhance our options as we grow older. We are not destined to be "over the hill" and in a state of hopeless decline if we remain flexible and realize that aging has constructive possibilities (Langer et al., 1988; Piper & Langer, 1987).

Coping Skill 1: Making Aging a Positive Self-Fulfilling Experience   ▲
• •

THE JOY OF COMPETENCE

It is a refreshing experience to observe children at play. Children love exploring and testing things to learn how they work. They are persistently curious and don't easily give up if their first attempts at creating something are not successful. The sight of children interacting with their world is a poignant example of what Robert W. White (1959) described as the *motivation for competence.* White called attention to people's natural desire to have an effect on their environment, to make things happen, and to achieve "joy in being a cause."

As children grow into adulthood, many of the tasks and skills they practiced and rehearsed when they were younger become automatic. For example, once we have learned to ride a bicycle, to dress ourselves, or to eat by ourselves, we can do these activities without thinking much about them. We go through many of our daily routines with little mental effort. This is quite a change from childhood when we had to consciously attend to everything we did. For adults living in a complex world, there is a real advantage in the automatic performance of routine activities because it reserves one's brain power for mastering new challenges in life. It is the opportunity to master these challenges that satisfies the need for competence and promotes feelings of self-efficacy.

Throughout adulthood, most people are able through work, family, hobbies, and social activities to experience a satisfactory degree of influence on their lives and on the world around them. When people grow older and reach retirement age, a number of things happen that undermine their opportunities to be competent. First, there is the stigma of old age. Elderly people in U.S. society are often stereotyped as being forgetful and less able to do things. A second life change faced by elderly people is retirement, which deprives them of the means for achieving competence they have used all of their lives. Elderly people are also commonly relieved of the gratification they once received from being the head of their family. These life changes can be detrimental because they take away major opportunities for being socially competent. Elderly people have a particular need to maintain personal relationships where their input is valued, or they are likely to become isolated and develop styles of interacting that are seen as odd or idiosyncratic (Hansson, 1989).

A third factor undermining competence in old age is the decrement that occurs in physical ability and in hearing and vision. Because of stigmas and stereotypes, forced retirement, and physical decline, elderly people are often deprived of goals and challenges for achieving feelings of competence and self-efficacy. In many cases, the lives of senior citizens revolve around overlearned, automatic activities that were mastered years ago. While the overlearning of activities served a useful purpose in the past, it is now a detriment because it instills false feelings of incompetence. There is little joy when one's life is made up only of routines.

THE STIGMA OF OLD AGE

In many societies elderly people are held in high esteem. They are respected as family leaders and acknowledged for their wisdom. This is not the case in much of U.S. society. Senior citizens are portrayed in movies and television as foolish, humorous, and forgetful. Children learn to make fun of the elderly and to see them in a negative light. As we grow older (and we *will* grow older), we need to devote our energies toward maintaining our dignity and pride. In working toward this goal, we can offer our services to organizations such as the Gray Panthers, which were founded to combat discrimination against the elderly.[1]

Coping Skill 2: Maintaining Dignity and Pride ▲
· ·

[1] The Gray Panthers, 3635 Chestnut Street., Philadelphia, PA 19104. Write and ask about a chapter in your area.

Another stigma associated with old age is the use of aging as a metaphor for ill health and general decline (Newquist, 1985). When people take this kind of attitude toward aging, as noted above, they are vulnerable to a negative self-fulfilling prophecy. If we perceive our lives as going downhill as we get older, our belief may very well become a reality. We will probably become so preoccupied with our aches and pains that we will wake up every morning with stress and anxiety about the fact that our lives are no longer worthwhile. People around us will pick up the messages we are sending and will start treating us as if we have nothing more to offer.

Another problem is that elderly people are often reluctant to seek medical attention for legitimate ailments, fearing they won't be taken seriously. Family members and friends respond to complaining elderly people by urging them to take it easy and discouraging them from doing things for themselves. However, this is the time when it is most important for the elderly to use their assertiveness skills (see Chapter 8). It is true that we will all suffer various physical detriments as we get older. Some tips about how to master the physical challenges that come with aging are given later in this chapter. However, it is also true that taking a pessimistic view of aging is not in our best interest. Use the ideas in this chapter to develop coping skills so that aging will be a positive rather than negative self-fulfilling experience.

BEING FUTURE-ORIENTED

After years of using aging as a metaphor for decline, it shouldn't surprise you to learn that many elderly people find it difficult to be oriented toward the future. One research study found that a large proportion of elderly people were future-oriented to the extent that they looked forward to events related to their families (Reker & Wong, 1985). However, less than 10% of these people had any plans or expectations related to their own personal development. This is unfortunate. Old age is not a time to give up on ourselves. We must remain future-oriented. There are always skills to be learned and challenges to be mastered.

AGING AS A LIFE TASK

One way to remain future-oriented as we grow older is to view aging as a life task (Cantor, Norem, Niedenthal, Langston, & Brower, 1987). The value of this outlook is that it keeps us aware of goals to accomplish. Erik Erickson (1963) outlined stages of growth and development we go through during our lives. The stages relevant to this chapter on aging are those of middle age and later life:

> *Middle age:* The life task of middle age (ages 35 through 60) is *generativity versus stagnation.* Most people have accomplished the challenges of completing their educations, raising families, and settling on their careers. Our challenge during these years is to maintain a sense of usefulness and productivity. We need to involve ourselves in activities, hobbies, and personal relationships that offer a sense of satisfaction and accomplishment.
>
> *Later life:* The life task of later life (age 60 and older) is *integrity versus despair.* We want to look back on our lives and feel they were worthwhile. We must

now reconcile our satisfactions with our regrets and resolve the following issues (Peck, 1968): (1) We must realize that our worth does not depend on our job history or on how much money we made, but rather on our quality as a human being. (2) We must balance loss of physical strength and lowered resistance to illness against satisfying memories and meaningful interpersonal relationships. (3) We must come to terms with our mortality by caring for others.

As we can see, the best way to get through the stages of middle age and later life is to prepare for them ahead of time. We can begin by reviewing our lives now. Are you satisfied with what you are doing? If not, it is time to consider new directions.

Coping Skill 3: Being Future-Oriented ▲

A number of specific tasks that must be accomplished during later life are: (1) preparing a will, (2) making plans for our death and funeral, (3) completing "unfinished business" with people close to us, and (4) discussing with loved ones how we would like to be remembered. These are tasks we often avoid because they remind us of our mortality. However, facing and accomplishing them provides a sense of competence and self-efficacy.

Coping Skill 4: Completing Our Life Tasks ▲

The Importance of Continuity

It should be clear by now that old age is not the time for us to withdraw or to disengage ourselves from the lifestyle we have learned to prefer (Dreyer, 1989). We should maintain our times of activity, times of relaxation, and time spent alone at comfortable levels. Old age should not come as a shock where our whole sense of self is disrupted.

One common method for maintaining a feeling of continuity throughout life is the *life review* (Kamptner, 1989). We all have memories, and often photographs, diaries, and other mementos, to preserve the meaningfulness of our lives. It is important, especially in old age, to appreciate our identity as a person with values, attitudes, and experiences that have developed over the course of our life history (Erikson, J. M., Erikson, & Kivnick, 1986).

Coping Skill 5: Recognizing the Importance of Continuity ▲

FORGETFULNESS AS A BUM RAP

How do we explain why a young person forgets something very simple? We probably assume the person is preoccupied or, at worst, careless. But what if an elderly person makes the same mistake? We may very likely attribute it to senility. Elderly people get a bum rap because they are stigmatized for making many of the same errors we all make every day.

Research studies indicate that elderly people are sometimes slower on mental tasks but are able to compensate with thoughtfulness and experience (Cox, 1988, pp. 97–100; Meer, 1986). Many studies of memory and performance placed elderly people at a disadvantage by comparing them with college students who are in top form for performing mental tasks. Other studies unfairly compared elderly people with younger people who had the benefit of more education. But elderly people do very well on tasks requiring immediate memory and memory for things that happened in the past. They sometimes have difficulty remembering a list of things if something happens to distract them between the time they learn the list and are tested. However, even when they don't remember the list exactly, they can recall its meaning. For example, college students may do better than elderly people in reciting the exact words of a poem they have memorized. Elderly people, however, will do just as well in describing the poem's message. One fair conclusion from research on memory and problem solving is that young people do better than elderly people in cramming and coming up with quick responses. When elderly people are given the opportunity to take their time and use the knowledge they have gained throughout their lives, their performance shows little decline.

Coping Skill 6: Appreciating the Value of Thoughtfulness and Experience ▲
• •

Exercising Our Minds

Although the brain is not made of muscle that atrophies from disuse, we can suffer psychologically if we lose the opportunity to think creatively, solve problems, and experience the pleasure of being competent. This loss is not uncommon among the elderly and has been the focus of a research program undertaken by Ellen Langer (Langer, 1979, 1981). Langer worked with residents of nursing homes, who are in the peculiar position of being well cared for physically while often suffering mentally and psychologically. Residents in many nursing homes lead routine and regimented lives. All of their physical needs are met. They don't have to think about housekeeping and preparing meals. Unfortunately, many of them live in an environment with institutional furniture, uninspiring room decorations, and minimal stimulation. We are all aware of the value of providing young children with stimulating environments that offer the opportunity for mastering sounds and colors and learning how to put things together. Why does our society give up on elderly people and force them into a routine existence? Where is the "joy in being a cause" in most nursing home environments?

Langer and her associates (Langer, Rodin, Beck, Weinmen, & Spitzer, 1979) conducted an illuminating series of studies. They gave nursing home residents an opportunity to exercise their minds. Elderly people in one study had four visits by a young person who engaged them in personal conversations. The elderly residents were encouraged by their visitors to think of new ideas and to remember things from one visit to the next. This experience had a remarkable effect. Four stimulating conversations were enough to make these elderly people happier and more alert, sociable, and active. The four stimulating conversations also resulted in significant improvements on tests of memory.

In a second study, elderly people were provided with the opportunity to work on some challenging puzzles (Avorn & Langer, 1982). The elderly residents in one group were offered a lot of help with the puzzles. Those in a second group were encouraged but left to solve the puzzles on their own. It shouldn't be a surprise that participants in the second group did better. In addition to solving the puzzles more accurately, they experienced a significant increase in self-confidence. If we think about it, we can also understand why the performance of the elderly people in the first group actually got worse. Isn't it more fun to figure things out yourself?

A third study demonstrated the technique of attending to daily choices and decisions (Perlmuter & Langer, 1983). This might not sound very exciting to people with challenging and demanding lives. However, it can serve a good purpose for those who are restricted to routine lives. Even restricted people can recognize their ability to choose what they will wear, what they will eat or drink, and what they will read or watch on TV. By attending to daily choices, elderly people can reaffirm their ability to exercise control over their lives.

Coping Skill 7: Exercising Our Minds ▲
••

The Value of Competence

Let's return to the point about how elderly people are deprived of self-efficacy when their lives become routine and they no longer have challenges to master. Ellen Langer and Judith Rodin demonstrated how this false sense of incompetence can be overcome (Langer & Rodin, 1976; Rodin & Langer, 1977). They provided nursing home residents with an opportunity to experience competence. The residents were encouraged to exercise control by voicing their ideas for changes in the nursing home, deciding on their room decorations, and planning their free-time activities. The residents were also given a personal house plant to care for.

These opportunities for exercising competence might not seem very great. However, compared with the institutionalized life the residents had been living, they made a big difference. Compared with nursing home residents of equal age and health, residents who exercised this small amount of competence felt significantly more control over their lives. They were happier, more alert, and more sociable. Not only did the opportunity to exercise competence help these elderly people psychologically, it also helped them physically. Nursing home residents who exercised competence lived longer. The fact that having some control over their lives helped these people live longer is remarkable. However, it is not surprising when we consider the studies on helplessness described in Chapter 15 (see also Shupe, 1985).

The message from this research is loud and clear. Human beings thrive when they exercise competence and deteriorate when their opportunities for experiencing self-efficacy are lost. It is important for us to always have activities in our lives that we can control.

Coping Skill 8: Finding Opportunities for Experiencing Competence ▲
••

ADJUSTING TO OLD AGE

The remainder of this chapter will focus on suggestions about how to adjust to old age. The following factors have been correlated with successful adjustment to aging (Cox, 1988, p. 109; Clark, M., & Anderson, 1967):

1. A feeling of self-sufficiency and autonomy
2. A good social support system
3. A reasonable amount of physical comfort
4. A sufficiently stimulating lifestyle
5. Sufficient mobility to engage in satisfying activities
6. A sense of meaning and purpose in life

Some Useful Goals and Activities

An interview study with elderly people identified the following factors associated with successful aging: entertainment and diversions, socializing, and productive activities (Clark, M., & Anderson, 1967). Elderly people with low morale complained of feeling dependent, lonely, and bored. The skill of developing support systems and good interpersonal relationships is discussed later in this chapter. Here are some other skills that can make aging a good experience (Reker, 1985):

Stress control: We need to practice the self-relaxation skills described in Chapter 3. It is important to always take time to find inner peace and tranquility.

Self-responsibility: We should take as much responsibility for our own needs as possible. But we also need to remember that it is OK to ask for help when we need it. We are still in control of our lives when we take the initiative to ask for things we need (Zevon, Karuza, & Brickman, 1982).

Nutrition: We must make an effort to plan a diet that is both healthy and enjoyable.

Physical fitness: We need to consult a physician about how to maintain physical fitness.

Enjoying the process as well as the product: Our culture is product-oriented. People are valued for their speed in producing things. We are often so preoccupied with the outcome of work that we forget to take pleasure in the creative process. As we get older, we may not be able to work as quickly, or even as accurately, as we once did. However, we can still experience the pleasure in doing things (Langer et al., 1988; Piper & Langer, 1987).

Appreciating our life experiences: Many researchers have pointed out the value of taking time to review one's life experiences. This does not imply living in the past and neglecting our orientation toward the future. The point of this exercise is to appreciate the lessons we have learned and the things we have accomplished. A good way to put our lives into perspective is by sharing our autobiography. We can write it, narrate it on tape, or discuss it with others. An important reason for reviewing our life experiences is to remind ourselves that we have many dimensions. We want to avoid getting trapped in the role of an old person who has nothing to offer.

THE VALUE OF INDIVIDUALITY

Research has demonstrated quite clearly how people lose their individuality when they are lumped into groups and categories (Hamilton, 1979; Hamilton & Rose, 1980). We stereotype people who are different from us according to race, religion, nationality, and any other characteristic we can think of. Even though we know that *we* are individuals, we tend to see people from other groups as identical. This stereotyping also occurs with the elderly. Instead of looking at senior citizens as individuals, we often think of them as having similar characteristics. The challenge for elderly people, then, is to assert their individuality. But this is not easy because our society also resists nonconformists. Just look at the struggles experienced by people from racial and religious minorities who have attempted to maintain their identity over the course of history. Women have also faced resistance in gaining their rights and overcoming the negative stereotypes they suffer in U.S. society. Our society sees the model elderly person as docile, nondemanding, and invisible.

It is ironic that one method for asserting individuality in old age is to think unconventional thoughts. Unfortunately, while unconventional thinking is useful for making life interesting and exercising the mind, it can also be viewed as abnormal and a sign of senility. Langer and her colleagues make a convincing argument that one way to fight the boredom of old age is to think creatively and invent new ideas (Langer, Beck, Janoff-Bulman, & Timko, 1984). They found that elderly people who were labeled as "senile" (but who were actually in good health) were more creative problem solvers than elderly people of comparable age and health who were not labeled as senile. On top of this, the "senile" people who exercised their minds with creative and unusual ideas lived longer. Psychologists can appreciate the use of unconventional thinking for exercising individuality by relating it to the "crazy" behavior of patients with whom they work in clinical practice. Research indicates that crazy behavior is sometimes used to assert control over an otherwise intolerable or unmanageable life (Braginsky, Braginsky, & Ring, 1969; Fontana, Klein, Lewis, & Levine, 1968). Have you ever felt like acting out as a way of expressing yourself? As members of an outgroup in our society, elderly people must make the choice between conforming and losing their individuality or asserting themselves and facing some inevitable disapproval.

Coping Skill 9: Asserting Our Individuality ▲
. . . .

SOME USEFUL SUGGESTIONS ABOUT AGING

A good way to conclude this chapter is by considering some suggestions about aging provided by B. F. Skinner and Margaret Vaughan in their book *Enjoy Old Age* (Skinner & Vaughan, 1983). These suggestions can be divided into two sections. The first group of suggestions focuses on ways to master the physical detriments that occur as we grow older. The second group concerns methods for maximizing our relationships with other people.

Mastering Our Physical Limitations

It is hard to think of any way to view the physical detriments accompanying old age in a positive light. Unfortunately, our primary appraisal of physical decline tells us that it is inevitable. We therefore have to face physical limitations with a secondary appraisal that offers some good avenues for coping. Skinner and Vaughan give a list of practical suggestions. For example, when our vision gets weaker, we have to compensate by making sure we have good eyeglasses and comfortable lighting. A magnifying glass can help with small print, and a small flashlight is useful in restaurants and other places with low lighting. Libraries have books with large print, and many books and magazines are available on recordings. Many helpful devices are available for enhancing hearing.

Changes can also be made to make the home environment more comfortable (Simon, 1987). It is worthwhile to find household utensils and kitchen items that are manageable. Look for clocks that are not difficult to read and telephones that are easy to dial. Make sure stairs and doorway thresholds are well marked and lighted. Good shoes and a walking stick will help us get around with greater ease, and a comfortable chair can be a real pleasure.

The point of these suggestions is to get across the concept of mastery and competence. Elderly people are often embarrassed to wear hearing aids or to be seen using a cane. Instead, they sit at home and suffer. Successful coping results from facing physical detriments with a problem- solving attitude. We need to think about tools we can use and changes we can make in our environments to master our physical limitations.

Coping Skill 10: Mastering Physical Limitations ▲
• •

Maximizing Personal Relationships

Most communities have groups and activities that provide opportunities for elderly people to develop personal relationships with one another. When it comes to maximizing personal realtionships with those who are younger, the elderly face a challenge because people of different ages don't always have things in common. You are probably very aware of the generation gap between teenagers and parents. There is also a generation gap separating elderly people from those who are younger. How can this gap be overcome? One way for elderly people to approach this challenge is by considering what they want from their relations with younger people. Two needs that many elderly people share are to exercise control and to communicate affection.

When it comes to exercising control in personal relationships, elderly people are often at a disadvantage. Most young people want to be independent, and they can be impatient and nonreceptive to an older person's suggestions and advice. Probably the worst way for elderly people to exercise control in their relationships with younger people is by nagging and becoming a "backseat driver." It is more fruitful to take a problem-solving approach. A better way to relate with a younger person is by recognizing that person's need for independence and exercising self-control over our urge to give advice. Our challenge is to communicate our knowledge and experience in a manner that the young person can accept. This is not always easy, but it will certainly keep us thinking and exercising our mind. Real mastery comes not from nagging and fussing but from allowing young people a sense of independence. If we present ourselves as people with knowledge and experience, younger people will seek our advice when they are ready.

Two suggestions can be given for bridging generation gaps when communicat-ing affection. First, it is useful to learn about the interests of people who are important to us. Skinner and Vaughan recommend Jonathan Swift's resolution not to bore younger people by telling the same stories over and over. Elderly people must realize that although their roots and growth experiences are in the past, younger people are primarily oriented toward the future. When relating with younger people it is often necessary to tune in to their perspective.

A second suggestion for communicating affection with younger people is to help them understand us better. Young people don't know what it is like to be an elderly person. If, for example, we have trouble with our eyesight or hearing, it is helpful to let others know how to communicate with us. It is usually best to let our needs be known. If we try to hide the fact that we have trouble following conversations or being mobile, we will suffer in the long run. This doesn't mean that we should complain about every ache and pain. The challenge for us will be to exert competence and teach others the things they need to know so our interactions can be mutually gratifying.

Coping Skill 11: Maximizing Personal Relationships ▲

A CONCLUDING THOUGHT

By employing good coping skills we can face the challenge of aging with humor, dignity, tranquillity, and satisfaction. Rather than looking at old age with an attitude of helplessness, we want to maintain a life philosophy of being a coper (see Chapter 15). In this spirit, Dylan Thomas exhorts:

> Do not go gentle into that good night,
> Old age should burn and rave at close of day;
> Rage, rage against the dying of the light.[2]

▲ LIST OF SKILLS FOR COPING WITH AGING

Coping Skill 1: Making Aging a Positive Self-Fulfilling Experience

Coping Skill 2: Maintaining Dignity and Pride

Coping Skill 3: Being Future-Oriented

Coping Skill 4: Completing Life Tasks

Coping Skill 5: Recognizing the Importance of Continuity

Coping Skill 6: Appreciating the Value of Thoughtfulness and Experience

Coping Skill 7: Exercising Our Minds

Coping Skill 8: Finding Opportunities for Experiencing Competence

Coping Skill 9: Asserting Our Individuality

Coping Skill 10: Mastering Physical Limitations

Coping Skill 11: Maximizing Personal Relationships

---

[2] Dylan Thomas: *Poems of Dylan Thomas.* Copyright 1952 by Dylan Thomas. Reprinted by permission of New Directions Publishing Corporation.

SUGGESTIONS FOR FURTHER READING

BLAU, Z. (1973). *Old age in a changing society.* New York: New Viewpoints.

BUTLER, R. N. (1975). *Why survive? Being old in America.* New York: Harper & Row.

ERIKSON, J. M., ERICKSON, E. H., & KIVNICK, H. (1986). *Vital involvement in old age.* New York: Norton.

FRIES, J. F., & CRAPO, L. M. (1981). *Vitality and aging.* New York: W. H. Freeman.

KIMMEL, D. C. (1974). *Adulthood and aging.* New York: Wiley.

RUSSELL, C. H. (1989). *Good news about aging.* New York: Wiley.

SKINNER, B. F., & VAUGHAN, M. E. (1983). *Enjoy old age.* New York: Norton.

WARD, R. A. (1984). *The aging experience.* New York: Harper & Row.

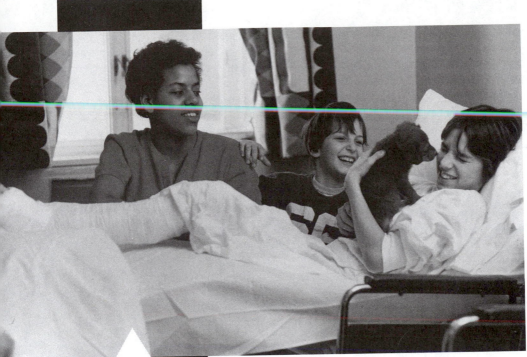

12

Coping with Pain

Pain is a private experience. We can't sense other people's pain, and there is no way to communicate to others exactly how our pain feels to us. This is what makes pain such a fascinating topic. Although everyone feels pain, each of us reacts in our own individual manner.

This chapter discusses two kinds of pain: acute and chronic. *Acute pain* is pain of relatively short duration. When we hit our head, cut ourself, or suffer some other kind of injury, we experience pain that we know will eventually go away. The same is true for dental work, surgery, and childbirth. Although the pain from these experiences can be severe, it has a limited duration. Coping with acute pain involves finding ways to bear up and "hang in there" until it is over. *Chronic pain,* on the other hand, is pain with which people have to live. Back problems, arthritis, and certain injuries and illnesses result in pain that is either almost always present or that can flare up at any moment. Coping with chronic pain requires learning how to live a meaningful and satisfying life that can outweigh and override the constant burden of pain.

INFLUENCES ON PAIN

Cultural Influences

The subjectivity of pain is apparent in studies of people's reactions to pain in various cultures (Zborowski, 1969). Some cultures are very open to expressions of pain and see nothing wrong with grimacing and moaning when experiencing pain. An example of this attitude is found in the following statement: "Sometimes it hurts so bad that you just have to yell and scream, or moan, or let it out in some way. It's a release. It makes you feel better." Other cultures are more stoic and encourage people to keep their pain to themselves. An example of this attitude is: "I don't yell or scream or fuss about it. That won't help. I just keep it to myself and live with it. Sometimes you just have to be tough and not act like a baby."

Motivational Influences

The subjectivity of pain is also demonstrated in studies of people's motivations for tolerating pain. Volunteers in one research study were exposed to pain from a pressure cuff placed around the upper arm (Lambert, Libman, & Posner, 1960). The cuff was designed with hard rubber projections that could be pressed into the arm with increasing force until the volunteers asked for the pain to be terminated. These volunteers were willing to tolerate more pain when they were motivated to make a good showing for the sake of the particular religious group with which they were affiliated. Participants in another study were exposed to electric shocks under one of two different conditions (Zimbardo, Cohen, Weisenberg, Dworkin, & Firestone, 1969). Participants in one group felt they were taking the shocks out of free choice. Participants in a second group felt pressured by the researchers to take the shocks. Which people were willing to tolerate the greatest shocks? You probably supposed that the participants who felt they were taking the shocks out of free choice demonstrated less pain than the participants who felt pressured to take the shocks. That is, when we are forced to put up with pain, we often have no qualms about complaining. When we feel we have in some way chosen to accept pain, we have some incentive to increase our tolerance before complaining.

MEASURING PAIN

The subjectivity of pain is further underscored by the fact that the only way to measure pain is by recording what people say or by observing how they act. There is no instrument for obtaining a purely objective and standard measure of pain. Pain is usually measured with one or more of the following three methods: rating scales, pain behaviors, and daily activity. An understanding of these methods will help us better appreciate how pain is experienced.

Pain Rating Scales

The most simple way to measure pain is to have people rate their pain on a scale of 0 to 10 or 1 to 100. The higher the rating, the greater the pain. However, if different researchers use different scales, it would be difficult to compare their results. For this reason, researchers and therapists have developed standardized pain rating scales. One of the most commonly used pain rating scales is the McGill Pain Questionnaire, developed by Ronald Melzack (1975). The McGill Pain Questionnaire has people rate their pain on two kinds of scales. The first scale is called Present Pain Intensity. For example, people rate the degree of pain they are presently experiencing on a scale of 0 to 5: no pain is 0, mild pain is 1, discomforting pain is 2, distressing pain is 3, horrible pain is 4, and excruciating pain is 5. The second scale of the McGill Pain Questionnaire is the Pain Rating Index. This scale measures the following three dimensions of pain: sensory aspects, affective aspects, and evaluative aspects. A shortened version of the Pain Rating Index is shown below:

Sensory Aspects of Pain

Throbbing _____	Jumping _____
Pounding _____	Flashing _____
Pinching _____	Shooting _____
Gnawing _____	Tugging _____
Crushing _____	Wrenching _____
Dull _____	Tender _____
Aching _____	Splitting _____
Radiating _____	Numb _____
Penetrating _____	Tearing _____
Squeezing _____	Hot _____
Cold _____	Burning _____
Pricking _____	Stabbing _____

Affective Aspects of Pain

Fearful _____	Punishing _____
Frightful _____	Grueling _____
Terrifying _____	Cruel _____

Vicious _____   Killing _____
Sickening _____   Exhausting _____

Evaluative Aspects of Pain

Annoying _____   Dreadful _____
Miserable _____   Unbearable _____

People are given a list of words and check the ones that describe their pain. Their score is determined by the number of words checked. Since the three Pain Rating Index scales overlap to some degree, it is possible to combine them into a total score representing the total number of words checked on all three scales (Turk, Rudy, & Salovey, 1985).

Pain Behaviors

Pain behaviors are behaviors that let us know that someone is in pain. We can see pain in people's facial expressions, in their body language, and in their vocal expressions. Pain behaviors have been measured in a systematic way by making videotapes of people as they go through various exercises, such as walking, picking up an object on the floor, side bends, toe touching, sit-ups, and leg raises. The videotapes are then scored on pain behaviors such as the following:

Guarded movement: Slow, cautious movement or jerky movement
Bracing: Bracing oneself on the floor, walls, or furniture or leaning on objects to move around
Position shifts: Wiggling or moving body to find "comfortable spot"
Partial movement: Limited range of motion or not making a complete movement
Grimacing: Grimacing facial expression or biting lip, gritting teeth
Limitation statements: Statements related to doubts about ability to complete exercise; or about pain, fatigue, stiffness, numbness; or about hesitation, fear, or unwillingness to attempt exercise
Sounds: Grunts, moans, or other pain-related sounds

Pain behaviors are scored on how often they occur in a specific time, and a total pain behavior score is derived by adding up a person's total on each of the pain behaviors (Follick, Ahern, & Aberger, 1985; Keefe & Block, 1982; Kleinke & Spangler, 1988b).

Daily Activity

Measures of daily activity are particularly relevant for people who suffer from chronic pain that interferes with their life functioning. The theory behind measures of daily activity is that although people may *feel* pain they still need to keep busy and get on with their lives. Daily activity is measured by having people keep a log of what they are doing during each hour of the day. Are they lying down, sitting, standing, or engaging in some kind of movement? The distinction is often made between "up-time," when the person is engaging in some kind of activity, and "down-time," when the person is lying down or in bed (Follick, Ahern, & Laser-Wolston, 1984; Fordyce, Lanske, Calsyn, Shelton, Stolov, & Rock, 1984).

COPING WITH ACUTE PAIN

When people are suffering from acute pain, they want to find strategies for holding their own and bearing up until the worst of it is over. Researchers have discovered a number of useful skills for coping with acute pain. Most research studies on coping with pain actually put volunteers through a painful experience. In some studies, volunteers were taught to use various coping skills, and the researchers determined which worked best. In other studies, volunteers were asked to employ their own methods for coping with the pain, and the researchers identified the kinds of people who were most successful. Several techniques were used to induce pain. One method was the pressure cuff described earlier. Electric shock and a heavy weight on the finger have also been used as pain stimuli. The most common method of manipulating pain was to have the volunteers put a hand in ice water and keep it there for as long as they could. Pain tolerance was measured by the number of minutes the volunteers could keep the hand in the cold water. In some studies the volunteers also rated the degree of their pain on a pain rating scale.

The researchers discovered eight useful skills for coping with pain: taking a coping attitude, self-relaxation, distraction, creative imagery, using ice, talking oneself through the pain, maintaining a sense of humor, and keeping realistic expectations. Let's learn how each of these coping skills works (Turk, Meichenbaum, & Genest, 1983).

Taking a Coping Attitude

What is the difference between people who are good and not so good at coping with pain? We have already seen how people's willingness to tolerate pain is affected by their motivation and culture. It is sometimes amazing what people can do when they *want* to. This is what a coping attitude is all about. It is an attitude of wanting to take control of our lives, to bolster our feelings of self-efficacy, and to follow a problem-solving orientation when faced with challenges such as pain (Bandura, O'Leary, Taylor, Gauthier, & Gossard, 1987; Litt, 1988).

People who are good at tolerating pain are referred to by researchers as *copers*. These people find ways to distract themselves from the painful feelings. Copers take the following kind of attitude when undergoing pain: "This really hurts. Let's see, what can I do to bear up to this pain? I have to distract myself . . . to think about other things. Relax. Think about something pleasant. Don't focus on the pain. Put my mind someplace else. I'll be able to tolerate the pain better this way."

People who are not good at tolerating pain are called *catastrophizers*. They lose control to the painful feelings. They focus on how much it hurts and convince themselves that they can't stand it and that there is nothing they can do to increase their tolerance. Catastrophizers take the following kind of attitude when undergoing pain: "This really hurts! I can't stand it! I can just feel the pain throbbing and getting worse. This is terrible! The pain keeps aching, and I can't escape it. There is no relief. It's more than I can bear."

There is no easy way to know why some people grow up to be copers while others grow up to be catastrophizers. However, understanding the difference between coping and catastrophizing can help all of us learn how to take a coping attitude (Spanos, Brown, Jones, & Horner, 1981; Spanos, Radtke-Bodorik, Ferguson, & Jones, 1979; Spanos, Stam, & Brazil, 1981; Stam & Spanos, 1980).

Coping Skill 1: Taking a Coping Attitude   ▲
••

Self-Relaxation

In a study comparing the effectiveness of several pain coping skills, self-relaxation was found to be most helpful for most people (Hackett & Horan, 1980). Self-relaxation is also one of the most preferred treatment modalities for people with chronic pain (Kleinke, 1987). This is because self-relaxation is relatively easy to learn and its benefits are felt soon after it is put to use. When we are in pain, it is a simple matter to remind ourselves to take a deep breath and begin using our relaxation skills. The more we practice the self-relaxation procedure outlined in Chapter 3, the better we will do. Of course, self-relaxation does not necessarily make the pain disappear. However, it can help us bear up and tolerate it better.

Coping Skill 2: Using Self-Relaxation   ▲
••

Distraction

In addition to calming us down, self-relaxation increases our coping capacity by taking our attention away from the pain, anxiety, anger, or whatever is bothering us. And we can gain even more control over our attention by learning how to use techniques of distraction. That is, we can take our attention away from the pain by focusing our mind on other things. What we think about is not as important as forcing ourselves to ignore the painful sensations. Researchers have tested the effects of distraction by exposing research participants to pain while they engaged in various activities such as solving problems, counting backward, looking at slides, listening to music, and thinking pleasant thoughts. Results of these studies showed that distraction generally helped people tolerate greater amounts of pain (McCaul & Malott, 1984).

Distractions that require a lot of involvement are usually better than minimal distractions because the former are more likely to keep our attention off the pain. Distractions that involve pleasant thoughts, such as thinking fond memories or making exciting plans, have the benefit of putting us in a positive mood. Distractions seem to work best for pain that is moderate, but not too severe. When pain sensations are very strong, it is hard to find distractions that will outweigh the pain. When the pain is too strong to ignore, we need to continue self-relaxation and use some of the techniques of creative imagery that are described in the following section (McCaul & Malott, 1984).

Distraction is a skill that requires practice. First of all, we have to ignore the painful sensations. Second, we must think of ways to keep our mind focused on other things. Some people find it easiest to distract themselves by having someone else keep them occupied or by attending to things that are going on around them. Others seek distraction by occupying their minds with thoughts and images. One way to keep your mind occupied is to engage in repetitive acts such as counting or repeating words and phrases. Another strategy is to let your thoughts wander to whatever images, memories, and fantasies come to mind. The point is that we need to actively work at and practice distraction as a coping skill (Farthing, Venturino, & Brown, 1984).

Coping Skill 3: Using Distraction   ▲

Creative Imagery

Techniques of creative imagery were devised by psychologists to help people use their mental power to greater advantage. As suggested earlier, creative imagery can be of value when we are coping with pain that is too severe to ignore with distraction. The idea behind creative imagery is to "flow with the pain." We can't fight it and we can't get rid of it. So, for as long as it lasts, we have to find a way to incorporate it into our lives. How can we ou do this? Here are some techniques that have been found effective in experimental research (Barber, Spanos, & Chaves, 1974; Chaves & Barber, 1974; Hackett & Horan, 1980; Singer, 1974; Spanos, Horton, & Chaves, 1975; Worthington & Shumate, 1981).

Disassociation
Imagine that the place that hurts is no longer a part of your body. If the pain is in your arm, visualize your arm as separate from the rest of your body. Your arm is detached and floating through the sky. If the pain is in your head, imagine working the pain out of your head, through your arms, and out the tips of your fingers. Or imagine undergoing surgery where the "infected" pain-ridden part of your brain is removed. When we use disassociation, the pain still exists, but it becomes a smaller factor in our overall being.

Fantasy
We can change the meaning of pain by fantasizing that we are suffering for a good cause. Imagine that you are a soldier, athlete, or other kind of hero. Your pain is a small price to pay for a major effort you have accomplished. You can also picture yourself as a superhuman being who has a very high tolerance for pain.

Imagining Numbness
Imagine that the part of your body that hurts is slowly becoming numb. You can feel the sensation of numbness starting in your extremities and slowly spreading to the place where you are feeling pain. As the feelings of numbness build, concentrate on them more and more. Eventually it will be difficult to distinguish between what is pain and what is numbness. You can enhance the feelings of numbness by imagining that Novocain has been injected into the painful area and that its effects are slowly spreading.

Focusing on Sensations

Since we can't escape the sensations of pain, we can focus on them and study what they are about. If you are having dental work, consider the pain as an indication that the dentist is repairing and removing the damaged, "rotten" parts of your teeth. The pain is a sign that good work is being done. If you have a headache, imagine the pain as caused by bands of steel around your head that you can slowly loosen as you relax. Focus on the pain as a message that your body is functioning properly. A good healthy body should feel pain under appropriate circumstances. An unhealthy, "dead" body does not feel pain. Pay attention to the pain as an interesting and unique sensation. Is it steady or intermittent? Is it throbbing or pulsating? Does it feel hot or cold? How could you describe the pain to others? How many different words can you think of that indicate exactly how it feels?

People differ widely in how much they use imagery in their lives. Some people will find that the above techniques for using creative imagery make perfect sense. To others the same techniques might seem strange and perhaps even bizarre.

There are two important points to be made about such differences between people. First, each of us has to devise a strategy for coping with pain that works best for us. Coping with pain is an individual matter that is based on one's particular personality, preferences, and strengths. A second point to consider is that new skills and ways of looking at the world can be learned. We want to adapt pain coping skills to fit our personality, but we can also benefit by remaining flexible and investing the time and effort to practice and master new techniques.

Coping Skill 4: Using Creative Imagery   ▲
• •

Using Ice

One effective method for taking the edge off many pains is to apply ice. Using an ice pack or even rubbing the painful area with an ice cube can provide a pleasant numbing sensation. The advantage of ice is that it helps to relieve pain without the harmful side effects of medication (Melzack, Jeans, Stratford, & Monks, 1980).

Coping Skill 5: Using Ice   ▲
• •

Talking Ourselves through the Pain

All three phases of talking ourselves through challenges that were outlined in Chapter 3 are useful for coping with pain. Coach yourself as you prepare for pain, confront pain, and reflect back on your performance. Learn how to make the following kinds of statements to yourself:

> "This is painful, but I can use my coping skills to handle it."
> "It hurts, but I know I will survive."
> "One step at a time. I won't let the pain get the best of me."
> "Relax. Think about how to cope with this pain."
> "Let me run through my list of coping skills and find the best ones for this situation."

"My coping skills might not get rid of the pain, but they will make it more tolerable."

Talking ourselves through pain can serve as a useful distraction, can bolster our feelings of self-efficacy, and can keep us on track as we pull together our resources to live through the painful experience.

Coping Skill 6: Talking Ourselves through the Pain ▲
• •

Maintaining a Sense of Humor

I recently underwent a painful medical procedure and was struck by the fact that the doctor kidded and joked with me as he pricked and probed. Apparently my doctor was aware of a recent research study that found that people were willing to tolerate greater pain if their sense of humor was enlivened with humorous tapes of comedians such as Lily Tomlin and Bill Cosby (Cogan, Cogan, Waltz, & McCue, 1987). Laughter helps increase our tolerance for pain in two ways. First, laughter is a good distraction. Second, laughter puts us in a positive frame of mind where the impact of the pain is not so great.

Coping Skill 7: Maintaining a Sense of Humor ▲
• •

Keeping Realistic Expectations

A final skill for coping with acute pain is to keep realistic expectations. Pain is a signal that our bodies are functioning properly and are warning us that they are hurt. Pain is unpleasant, but it is not an awful, terrible sensation that we can't bear. An interesting finding has come out of the pain research studies that is important for us to remember. Research participants often learn to use pain coping skills to increase their ability to bear up to and tolerate pain. However, these same people usually report that the pain still hurts. Coping skills do not make pain magically disappear. The coping skills described here are meant to bolster feelings of self-efficacy and internal control and to help us become copers. They should help us tolerate pain more effectively, and with some luck, they will make the pain less distressing (Hackett & Horan, 1980; Scott & Barber, 1977).

Coping Skill 8: Keeping Realistic Expectations ▲
• •

CHRONIC PAIN

Because chronic pain is likely to stay with a person for most of his or her life, it requires skills for coping with pain as well as skills for coping with life disruption. When it comes to coping with pain, all of the skills described above for coping with acute pain are useful. People with chronic pain will find it helpful to learn and practice these skills every day. Coping with life disruption requires an understanding of chronic pain and the psychological effects it has on people who are destined to spend much of their lives in pain.

The Prevalence of Chronic Pain

To get an idea of the prevalence of chronic pain, we can look at a community survey that was conducted in Canada in 1984 (Crook, Rideout, & Browne, 1984). This survey found that 15% of female and 12% of male adults were suffering from a chronic pain problem. The most common pain complaints were back problems and headaches. People with chronic pain spent an average of 12 days in the hospital per year, and they reported that pain interfered with their work and with their general health. People suffering from chronic pain had cut down on their daily activities, and they saw few options beside medication for pain relief.

The annual cost of chronic pain in the United States has been estimated at over $100 billion. This figure includes $45 billion for the costs of health care and $55 billion in employment losses. There are 40 million Americans with chronic headaches, 18 million Americans with chronic back pain, and almost 100 million more Americans with a variety of other chronic pain disorders. One out of three Americans sffers from some kind of chronic pain. People with chronic pain may have hundreds of hospital visits a year, numerous surgical procedures, and health care bills of up to $100,000 a year (Bonica & Black, 1974; *U.S. News and World Report,* 1987).

The Experience of Chronic Pain

People suffering from chronic pain must learn to cope not only with the daily experience of pain but also with the life disruption caused by their chronic pain problem. Chronic pain challenges people to come to terms with the fact that they must learn to live with their pain and pull themselves out of feelings of sadness and depression. Chronic pain also impinges on interpersonal relationships and requires special adjustments for pain sufferers and the people close to them.

Coming to terms with chronic pain   One of the most difficult challenges for people with chronic pain is to accept the fact that they must learn to live a satisfying and productive life in spite of their pain. It is tempting to get caught up in the hope of finding a magic cure or a miracle drug that will alleviate one's pain forever. Although the ability to fantasize and daydream can be healthy, people with chronic pain face the danger of putting their life on hold while they wait for a cure.

Coping Skill 9: Coming to Terms with Chronic Pain   ▲
• •

Dealing with sadness, depression, and anger   Being faced with chronic pain is a good reason for feeling depressed. Chronic pain inevitably requires one to give up activities that have been rewarding and meaningful. People with chronic pain must work through the grieving process described in Chapter 10. Chronic pain sufferers can make the mistake of closing themselves off emotionally, denying feelings of sadness, depression, and anger that are normal reactions to a major life disruption. But we can't learn to live with these feelings until we accept them as real (Blumer & Heilbronn, 1982; Hendler, 1984; Kleinke, 1988a).

Coping Skill 10: Dealing with Sadness, Depression, and Anger   ▲
• •

Adjustments in interpersonal relationships Chronic pain inevitably impinges on interpersonal relationships. Some chronic pain sufferers want to be tough and not ask for help and understanding from others. By keeping their suffering to themselves they avoid the discomfort that comes from asking favors. However, this kind of reaction also causes them to feel isolated and misunderstood. Other chronic pain sufferers get caught up in the role of being a "patient." They receive sympathy and attention but face the danger of taking on an attitude of helplessness and becoming a burden on others. People with chronic pain must learn to communicate that although they desire care and nurturance, they are also willing to hold up their end of a relationship to the best of their ability.

Coping Skill 11: Making Adjustments in Interpersonal Relationships ▲
• •

Coping Strategies Used by Chronic Pain Patients

A survey was taken of coping strategies used by people with chronic pain before they began a treatment program in a multidiscipline pain clinic (Kleinke, 1989). The coping strategies could be grouped into four categories: self-management, helplessness, medical remedies, and social support:

> *Self-management:* Think about other things, do something I enjoy (hobbies, etc.), try consciously to relax, increase my concentration on work or household activities, and/or go for a walk.
>
> *Helplessness:* Think about how awful it is, feel bad because I have to suffer, focus on how much it really hurts, feel I can't stand it any longer, and/or do nothing, since nothing really helps.
>
> *Medical remedies:* Use a heating pad or ice, elevate the painful area or use a pillow for support, lie down or go to bed, apply pain-reducing ointment, and/or take a shower or bath.
>
> *Social support:* Talk to friends, family, spouse; ask for help and support from others; try to be around other people; and/or let others know I am in pain.

At the time of admission to the pain clinic, the most effective pain-coping strategies were self-management and social support. The least effective strategies were helplessness and medical remedies. It seems clear that chronic-pain patients adjust most successfully when they take an active rather than passive approach toward their pain problem (Brown, K. G., & Nicassio, 1987; Brown, K. G., Nicassio, & Wallston, 1989).

While working in the pain treatment program, participants learned how to use the pain-coping strategies described in this chapter. By the time they completed the pain program, their pain ratings and pain behaviors had significantly decreased (Kleinke & Spangler, 1988a, 1988b).

THE PROMISE OF PAIN TREATMENT CLINICS

In recognition of the debilitating effects of chronic pain, more than 1000 pain treatment clinics have been set up throughout the United States. Many of these clinics are affiliated with hospitals and universities and incorporate teaching and research into their programs. Other clinics are operated by well-intentioned but less qualified therapists who are responding to an ever increasing market for treatment of chronic pain. People intending to seek the services of pain treatment clinics are advised to choose clinics that have been nationally certified (Block, 1982; Follick, Ahern, Attanasio, & Riley, 1985; Fordyce, 1976; Kerns, Turk, & Holzman, 1983; Roy, 1984, Turk, Holzman, & Kerns, 1986).

Goals of Pain Treatment Clinics

A pain treatment clinic is designed to help people who have chronic pain for which there is no medical cure. The clinics are geared toward teaching people skills they can use to live meaningful and satisfying lives that will outweigh their experience of chronic pain. That is, the participants in pain clinics are taught pain coping skills that will help them live more effectively with their pain but that in most cases will not make their pain disappear. The goal of pain treatment clinics is not to cure chronic pain (which is unfortunately not possible) but rather to help people suffering from chronic pain make a clear commitment to get on with their lives (Fordyce, 1988). The clinics have programs designed to help chronic pain sufferers accomplish the challenges described earlier: coming to terms with chronic pain; dealing with sadness, depression, and anger; and making adjustments in interpersonal relationships.

An Overview of the Pain Treatment Clinic

Pain treatment clinics offer both inpatient and outpatient programs. People participating in inpatient programs come to live in the pain clinic, which is usually a separate unit of a hospital. The pain treatment program lasts from 3 to 4 weeks. Participants live in a "community" where they are responsible for taking care of their rooms, making their beds, and doing various chores. They are more like students than patients because they are not in the program to be "treated" or "cured" but rather to learn useful coping skills. Participants in the outpatient programs attend classes several times a week and are taught skills that they practice daily at home.

The Pain Treatment Program

The pain treatment clinic is based on the concept of *multidisciplinary treatment* by professionals ranging from medical doctors, nurses, physical therapists, social workers, and clinical psychologists. Medical doctors make sure that all possible avenues of medical diagnosis have been covered, and they attend to any medical needs participants may have while they are in the program. Nurses work individually with the participants on all phases of their treatment program. Physical therapists teach the participants to understand their physical strengths and limitations. They provide an individualized treatment plan outlining exercises that the participants agree to practice every day. Social workers meet with the participants and their families to work out a plan that will help them live harmoniously in spite of the chronic pain problem. Clinical psychologists provide classes to teach the skills for coping with pain described earlier in this chapter. They also conduct group meetings where the participants can share their experiences and gain insight into effective ways for finding life satisfaction. Participants in pain treatment clinics also benefit from each other. They find a good source of support in their community living arrangement and often arrange to keep in touch after the pain treatment program is completed. Evaluation studies have shown that multidisciplinary pain clinics based on the above model are successful in helping the majority of chronic pain patients lead more productive lives (Fordyce, Brockway, Bergman, & Spengler, 1986; Kleinke & Spangler, 1988a; McArthur, Cohen, Gottlieb, Naliboff, & Schandler, 1987a, 1987b).

PRIMARY AND SECONDARY APPRAISAL OF PAIN

A good way to conclude this chapter is by relating our discussion of pain and pain coping skills to the processes of primary and secondary appraisal.

Primary Appraisal of Pain

It stands to reason that our primary appraisal of pain will usually be negative. It is not very often that people enjoy the experience of pain. However, when we make a primary appraisal of pain, we have to ask ourselves whether it is in our best interest to view the pain as horrible, unbearable, and catastrophic or rather as unpleasant, inconvenient, undesirable, but one of life's many challenges with which we can live. We don't want to deny our feelings of anger, fear, and depression since they are normal reactions to pain. But when we recognize these feelings, it will be useful to follow the suggestions for rational thinking in Chapter 2.

Secondary Appraisal of Pain

In this chapter we learned a number of coping skills to apply when making a secondary appraisal of pain and considering what we can do about it. When confronted with pain, we need to go through our list of coping skills and find the ones that will be most useful. We should use the kind of problem-solving approach described in Chapter 3. By mastering our pain coping skills, we will strengthen our feelings of self-efficacy and be better prepared to live with our next pain experience.

▲ LIST OF SKILLS FOR COPING WITH PAIN

Coping Skill 1: Taking a Coping Attitude

Coping Skill 2: Using Self-Relaxation

Coping Skill 3: Using Distraction

Coping Skill 4: Using Creative Imagery

Coping Skill 5: Using Ice

Coping Skill 6: Talking Ourselves Through the Pain

Coping Skill 7: Maintaining a Sense of Humor

Coping Skill 8: Keeping Realistic Expectations

Coping Skill 9: Coming to Terms with Chronic Pain

Coping Skill 10: Dealing with Sadness, Depression, and Anger

Coping Skill 11: Making Adjustments in Interpersonal Relationships

SUGGESTIONS FOR FURTHER READING

HENDLER, N., & FENTON, J. A.(1986). *How to cope with chronic pain.* Cockeysville, Md.: Liberty.

MELZACK, R., & WALL, P. D. (1982). *The challenge of pain.* New York: Basic Books.

SMOLLER, B., & SCHULMAN, B. (1982). *Pain control: The Bethesda Program.* Garden City, N.Y.: Doubleday.

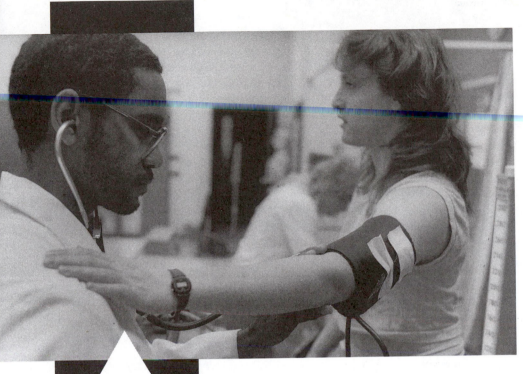

Coping with Illness and Maintaining Health

The remaining chapters of this book are different from Chapters 4 through 12 because they don't contain specific lists of coping skills. These chapters take a more personal approach by looking at particular experiences of people who have been confronted with difficult life experiences. In addition to reading about the personal experiences of copers, we will gain knowledge about conclusions reached from research on a number of important topics.

The focus of this chapter is on illness and maintaining health. The three major health issues discussed are headaches, cancer, and AIDS. Although these illnesses differ widely in their threats to life, they are in the consciousness and within the experience of many people. This chapter also teaches some principles of primary prevention and offers some useful suggestions about developing a hardy, low-stress personality. Chapter 14 is devoted to people's experiences with traumatic events. Chapter 15 summarizes the theme of this book by discussing coping as a lifestyle.

MAINTAINING HEALTH

In recent years there has been a growing attempt by health professionals to teach people how to decrease their risk of illness. Engaging in health-maintaining behaviors is called *primary prevention* (Caplan, 1964). Primary prevention makes good sense because it is obviously to our advantage to avoid illness and to maintain health by taking care of ourselves.

Although very few people disagree with the concept of primary prevention, consider the following negative health practices: cigarette smoking, alcohol and drug abuse, poor diet, failure to wear seat belts. This list only touches the surface of ways in which people place themselves in jeopardy. Recognition of the value of teaching good health practices has resulted in the development of the fields of behavioral medicine and health psychology (Krantz, Grunberg, & Baum, 1985; Pomerleau & Rodin, 1986; Taylor, 1986). *Behavioral medicine* is defined as "the broad interdisciplinary field of scientific investigation, education, and practice which concerns itself with health, illness, and related physiological dysfunctions" (Gatchel & Baum, 1983, p. 10). *Health psychology* refers to the particular contributions to behavioral medicine made by psychologists. A major goal of psychologists is to promote preventive health practices by emphasizing: "individual responsibility in the application of behavioral and biomedical science knowledge and techniques for the maintenance of health and the prevention of illness and dysfunction by a variety of self-initiated individual or shared activities" (Matarazzo, 1980, p. 813). This definition suggests that we are each responsible for taking care of our health by using coping skills that have been found effective by scientific research. These skills will be discussed in the following sections of this chapter.

Taking Control

Check whether you agree or disagree with the following statements:

	Strongly agree	Agree	Disagree	Strongly disagree
1. If I take care of myself, I can avoid illness.	____	____	____	____

	Strongly agree	Agree	Disagree	Strongly disagree
2. Good health is largely a matter of good fortune.	____	____	____	____
3. Whenever I get sick it is because of something I've done or not done.	____	____	____	____
4. No matter what I do, if I am going to get sick I will get sick.	____	____	____	____
5. People's ill health results from their own carelessness.	____	____	____	____
6. Most people do not realize the extent to which their illnesses are controlled by accidental happenings.	____	____	____	____
7. I am directly responsible for my health.	____	____	____	____
8. People who never get sick are just plain lucky.	____	____	____	____

These statements come from the Health Locus of Control Scale (Wallston, Wallston, Kaplan, & Maides, 1976). People who agree with statements 1, 3, 5, and 7 tend to have an internal locus of control regarding their health. They take responsibility for their health by seeking information about and engaging in good health practices. People who agree with statements 2, 4, 6, and 8 tend to have an external locus of control regarding their health. They don't recognize the value of preventive health, and they underestimate their responsibility for maintaining good health. Hopefully, this chapter will reinforce your feelings of internal control over your health.

Controlling Health

What percentage of people do you think would agree with this statement: I want to take better care of my health? Almost everybody. OK. Here are 12 things each of us can do right now to control our health (Matarazzo, 1984):

1. Get 7 to 8 hours of daily sleep.
2. Eat breakfast every day.
3. Get your weight to a normal level.
4. Don't smoke.
5. Use alcohol moderately or not at all.
6. Get regular physical activity.
7. Wear seat belts.
8. Don't drive at excessive speeds.
9. Learn good diets and follow them.
10. If you are a woman, learn how to do regular breast exams.
11. If you are a man, learn how to do regular prostate exams.
12. Find a physician with whom you can communicate.

Following the above recommendations will increase life expectancy. Yet, how many people who read this book will change their lifestyles? Very few. This shows how challenging the fields of behavioral medicine and health psychology can be. It is easy to agree that we should take control over our health. But how do we get ourselves to do it?

STRESS

Much has been written about how life stress can negatively affect physical and emotional health. Hundreds of research studies have been conducted to learn how people adapt when they are faced with stressful life events such as those below (Holmes & Rahe, 1967; Maddi, Bartone, & Puccetti, 1987):

Death of a loved one	Change in financial status
Divorce	Personal injury or illness
Marital separation	Injury or illness in family
Marriage	Starting school
Loss of job	Marriage of son or daughter
Pregnancy	Abortion
Gain of a new family member	Marital infidelity
Sexual difficulties	Assaulted or robbed
Change of job	Involved in accident
Change of residence	Involved in lawsuit
Loss of significant friendship	Violation of law

You can test your current life stress by checking off which life events are currently happening to you. The major conclusion of these research studies is that stressful events can be detrimental. People who are experiencing a number of stressful life events at one time are at particularly high risk. However, the negative effects of life changes depend on the person who is experiencing them and on her or his primary and secondary appraisals and coping skills. An awareness of stressful life events can help place difficult times in our life into perspective. We are not doomed to suffer ill effects from stressful events if we master the coping skills discussed in this book.

If we are undergoing stressful events, we need to give ourselves a break and not expect everything we do to be perfect. Our first coping skill during stressful life events is just to "hang in there." After we have a chance to appraise the situation, we can decide which coping skills are most appropriate (Holmes & Masuda, 1974; Kessler, Price, & Wortman, 1985; Krantz, Grunberg, & Baum, 1985; Maddi, Bartone, & Puccetti, 1987).

Developing a Low-Stress Personality

It was suggested in Chapter 3 that if human beings inhabit the earth long enough, they may develop a natural relaxation response instead of the fight-or-flight response that seems to characterize our reaction to challenges at the present time. Given the competitive nature of our present world, along with its noise, traffic jams, and pollution, a fight-or-flight response is not particularly adaptive. Many people, how-ever, utilize this style of coping without thinking much about it. And although they often get what they want in the short run, they pay an emotional and physical price in the long run. The kind of fight or flight response I have been talking about is referred to by psychologists as a *Type A* behavior pattern. For example, how closely do the following questions describe your lifestyle?

1. Does your job carry a heavy responsibility?
2. Do you drive yourself harder to accomplish things than most others?
3. Do you play games to win?
4. Does it make you restless to watch someone else taking too long with a job?
5. Do you eat rapidly?
6. Do you get frustrated and angry when waiting in lines?
7. Are you under a lot more pressure than most people?

These statements are adapted from an interview used to assess people who fit the Type A pattern (Rosenman, 1978). Type A people generally agree with these statements. Type As are characterized by the following traits:

Time urgency: Type A people are in a hurry. They feel like they never have enough time to accomplish everything being demanded from them.

Competitiveness: Type A people are habitually competitive. They don't know how to relax and have fun.

Hostility: Type A people's sense of time urgency causes them to feel angry when they are delayed or when others get in their way. Their competitiveness prevents close personal relationships because they are on guard against anyone who might try to get ahead of them.

The emotional and physical price paid by Type A people is high. They are less likely to have satisfactory personal relationships. They are also more susceptible to heart disease, and they have a higher risk of death (Gatchel & Baum, 1983; Matarazzo, 1984). One reason Type A people suffer so much from life stress is that they have difficulty accepting what they can and cannot control (Glass, D. C., 1976). We have been advised throughout this book that some life events are best "controlled" by our willingness to let them take their course. Type A people burn themselves out because their primary appraisals tell them that virtually *everything* is threatening, and their secondary appraisals don't accurately discriminate between life events they can and cannot change. It is a useful coping skill to practice the following kinds of responses (Gatchel & Baum, 1983, p. 212):

1. Be calm and attentive when relating to others.
2. Speak slowly in a low, mellow tone.
3. Don't interrupt when others are talking.
4. Don't get angry when someone disagrees with you.
5. Keep your body relaxed.
6. Breathe slowly.
7. Smile.

Developing an Attitude of Hardiness

Suzanne Kobasa and her colleagues discovered that people who adapt best to stressful life events are those who have developed an attitude of *hardiness* (Kobasa,

1979; Kobasa, Maddi, & Kahn, 1982; Kobasa, Maddi, Puccetti, & Zola, 1985). Developing a hardy attitude involves building a sense of commitment, control, and challenge.

Commitment: Commitment means taking an active role in our lives. When we are committed, our lives have a purpose. We are not passive bystanders. We assume responsibility for making our lives meaningful.

Control: Control refers to an internal locus of control on the Health Locus of Control Scale described above. Control is achieved by developing our internal control (Chapter 3) and self-efficacy (Chapter 2). Control is the opposite of helplessness (see Chapter 15). Control occurs when we take charge, make adaptive primary and secondary appraisals, and implement good coping skills.

Challenge: Challenge is realized by appreciating the benefits of growth and change. This requires us to be flexible. New experiences are often stressful, and it is tempting to seek stability to maintain our sense of security. Being open to change can be difficult at first, but it will make us stronger in the long run.

Using Support Systems

The skills for building a support system that were described in Chapter 3 can be beneficial to our physical and emotional well-being. A good support system can help moderate the effects of stressful life events. Support from others can also provide encouragement during rehabilitation and adaptation to illness and injury. Of course, the use of support systems is an individual matter. Some people are very open about sharing their stresses, and they derive benefit from a broad support system. Others prefer to keep their troubles to themselves and rely on a very small support system. However, it is important to recognize that it is not healthy to isolate ourselves during times of stress. It is in our best interest to build the kind of support system that works best for us (Cohen, S., & Syme, 1984; Kessler, Price, & Wortman, 1985; Pomerleau & Rodin, 1986; Reis, Wheeler, Nezlek, Kernis, & Spiegel, 1985; Wallston, Alagna, DeVellis, & DeVellis, 1983).

COPING WITH HOSPITALIZATION

Being hospitalized is stressful for most people. Hospitals instill a fear of the unknown, a loss of control over our lives, and a genuine concern about our well-being. It is difficult to cope because even though we want to maintain a sense of self-efficacy, we are often in a situation that makes us feel helpless. Shelly Taylor (1979) has described three coping styles commonly used by hospital patients, all of which have disadvantages:

Depersonalization: These patients cope by "tuning out" and turning off their emotions. Because of this, they are often treated as nonpersons and end up feeling anxious and confused.

Helplessness: These patients cope by being passive and compliant. They wait for the hospital staff to tell them what to do. They don't complain and don't ask questions. However, they are often neglected and end up feeling helpless and depressed.

Reactance: These patients cope by aggressively standing up for themselves. They ask questions, demand attention, and complain when their needs are not satisfied. Patients who respond with reactance often end up alienating the hospital staff, who then treat them in a condescending manner. As a result, the patients suffer frustration and anger.

The challenge when being confined in a hospital is finding the proper balance between being assertive, getting proper treatment, and maintaining good relations with the hospital staff, who are typically busy, tired, and feeling overworked. This is no small task, considering that our social supports are often not with us and that we are suffering a good deal of stress and worry ourselves. However, we can help ourselves with rational thinking, self-relaxation, humor, assertiveness, and talking ourselves through the challenge (see Chapter 3).

PREPARING FOR SURGERY

It is becoming more common for people to go through some kind of training or preparation before they have surgery. Many physicians have videotapes and pamphlets describing surgical procedures. Patients are often encouraged to visit the hospital before the surgery, so it won't seem like such a strange and scary place. There is a large body of research showing that it is beneficial for people to be prepared for surgery by gaining information about what will be done to them and what sensations, discomforts, and inconveniences they will experience (Anderson, K. O., & Masur, 1983; Taylor & Clark, 1986).

We can also prepare for surgery by using the coping skills outlined in Chapter 3. Self-relaxation, humor, and social support systems can be very beneficial. We also want to maintain a sense of internal control by talking ourselves through the challenge. A moderate amount of anxiety before surgery is OK. If we completely denied our concerns, we might not take the time to inform and prepare ourselves properly. But by practicing good coping skills we can tone down the really high levels of fear that are detrimental (Janis, 1958). Talking with others who have successfully coped with similar surgical procedures can also be helpful. Children (and presumably adults) benefit greatly when they have the opportunity to watch a film showing someone like them modeling good coping skills through all stages of the surgery experience (Melamed, 1984).

A good example of using coping skills to get through surgery can be found in a study of hospital patients who were about to undergo surgery (Langer, Janis, & Wolfer, 1975). The patients were trained to cope with their impending surgery by making adaptive primary and secondary appraisals. Although the surgery was inconvenient, they knew it would be beneficial in the long run. They were taught how they could maintain a feeling of control over their hospitalization by enjoying the attention they would receive from hospital staff and visitors and using the time to take stock of their lives and enjoy a vacation from outside pressures. The patients also practiced using the pain control strategies outlined in Chapter 12. As a result of their training in the use of coping skills, these patients recovered from their surgery more quickly than other patients undergoing the same surgical procedures. They were less anxious, more relaxed, and felt less need for pain-relieving medication.

Another example of the principles of coping with surgery is seen in childbirth. Although there are various approaches toward preparing women for childbirth, they all address the following goals:

1. Reducing anxiety by providing accurate expectations
2. Enhancing feelings of self-efficacy by teaching self-management skills
3. Teaching self-relaxation
4. Teaching women and their partners to use distraction
5. Encouraging social support before, during, and after birth

Use of coping skills such as those above has been shown to help women control their anxiety and pain and go through childbirth with a more positive experience (Leventhal, Leventhal, Shacham, & Easterling, 1989).

COPING WITH HEADACHES

Surveys have indicated that 15% of men and 25% of women experience regular debilitating headaches (Holroyd, 1986). Headaches are responsible for millions of dollars of lost work and for a sizable proportion of visits to doctors' offices. A large industry is supported by the market for headache remedies. The two most common types of headaches are *migraine headaches* and *tension headaches.*

Migraine Headaches

Migraine headaches are characterized by an intense throbbing and pounding pain that is felt in the forehead or temple, or around the ears or eyes. Migraines usually start on one side of the head and are often associated with nausea. Often there are visual disturbances, such as flashing lights and blurred sight. A migraine attack typically lasts from 1 to 2 days. Migraine headaches are thought to result from an irregular flow of blood in the brain, often preceded by a constriction of arteries and a reduced blood supply, followed by dilation of arteries with inflammation, swelling, and pain.

Tension Headaches

Tension headaches are characterized by a sensation of tightness, pressure, or constriction. They feel as if a vise or band of steel has been tightened around the head. Tension headaches can last for days, weeks, and even months. They are generally thought to result from muscle tension, although some researchers believe that changes in blood flow are also responsible.

Treating Headaches

People with severe and recurrent headaches are advised to take the following steps in seeking treatment:

1. Consult with a physician to rule out neurological complications and temporomandibular joint dysfunction, which is related to improper functioning of the jawbone.

2. Assess one's diet, particularly in the case of migraine headaches. Caffeine and alcohol can be especially problematical.

3. Assess current life stressors that may be precipitating the headaches.

4. Assess moods of anger and depression, which may both precipitate and result from headache suffering.

5. Become educated about headaches to instill a sense of self-efficacy and internal control.

6. Avoid misuse of medication.

7. Master self-relaxation.

Research studies have indicated that self-relaxation can be beneficial for both migraine and tension headaches. Biofeedback training is useful in some cases because it helps headache sufferers focus on the most crucial areas of their bodies (Adams, Feuerstein, & Fowler, 1980; Andrasik, Blanchard, Neff, & Rodichok, 1984; Blanchard, Andrasik, Ahles, et al., 1980; Blanchard, Andrasik, Neff, et al., 1982, 1983). It is also therapeutic for headache sufferers to look at their lifestyles. How do they handle interpersonal conflict? Are their appraisals of life challenges reasonable? Have they fallen into the Type A behavior pattern discussed earlier? Although it is not always possible to expect a complete cure, the steps outlined here have provided relief for many headache sufferers.

COPING WITH CANCER

Cancer is a stressful life event that affects one out of three individuals and nearly three out of four families in the United States (American Cancer Society, 1985). Due to its pervasiveness and the uncertainty of its causes and prognosis, cancer is one of the most serious and long-lasting stresses facing many people.

We can learn a good deal about coping by recognizing the resiliency and willpower of those who have been forced to cope with cancer. To this end, Shelley Taylor and her colleagues conducted extensive interviews to learn how people cope with cancer and to identify effective styles of coping (Taylor, 1983; Taylor, Lichtman, & Wood, 1984; Wood, Taylor, & Lichtman, 1985). Participants in one series of studies were women with breast cancer and their family members. The women ranged in age from 29 years to 78 years. Almost all of them had undergone surgery, and the prognosis of their illness ranged from very good to poor. The coping skills employed by these women to adjust to their experience of having cancer fell into three major categories: searching for meaning, maintaining self-efficacy, and building self-esteem.

Searching for Meaning

Human beings have a need to find meaning in their lives and to feel they have some understanding about why things are the way they are. Finding meaning in our lives is a coping skill because it helps us understand why we exist. A sense of life meaning provides a reason for enjoying good times and tolerating bad ones. The women with cancer did two things to reaffirm their sense of meaning. First, they searched for an explanation of why their cancer occurred. Some women felt their cancer was due to stress. Others believed it was caused by diet or carcinogens. Another group of women attributed their cancer to heredity. Although the causes of cancer are not completely understood by medical science, these women had the need to find a reason for their cancer. The particular kind of explanation adopted did not seem to make a great difference. What was important was finding an explanation that gave personal meaning to the cancer experience.

A second approach the women took to search for meaning was to reevaluate their lives and recognize what they had learned from their illness. For example, one woman said: "The ability to understand myself more fully is one of the greatest changes I have experienced. I have faced what I went through. It's a bit like holding a mirror up to one's face when one can't turn around" (Taylor, 1983, p. 1163). Another woman explained her search for meaning in this way: "You take a long look at your life and realize that many things that you thought were important before are totally insignificant. What you do is put things into perspective. You find out that things like relationships are really the most important things you have—the people you know and your family—everything else is just way down the line. It's very strange that it takes something so serious to make you realize that" (Taylor, 1983, p. 1163).

We can see from these responses that the ability to search out a meaningful life experience in the face of a devastating illness is a beneficial coping skill.

Maintaining Self-Efficacy

Many of the women coped with their cancer by maintaining their feelings of self-efficacy. Two-thirds of the cancer victims believed they had at least some control over their cancer. This is interesting because, in strict medical terms, the women's chances of affecting the outcome or recurrence of their cancer was very limited. However, believing they continued to have power to take charge of their lives, both physically and psychologically, was a valuable coping skill. The cancer victims maintained their self-efficacy in a number of ways. Many of them resolved to live with a positive attitude, and they refused to take on an identity of helplessness and passivity. They also exercised their self-efficacy by keeping busy. They practiced self-relaxation, they involved themselves in exercise programs, and they added more healthy foods to their diet. Another activity that helped the women maintain a sense of control over their lives was seeking information and knowledge about cancer. They acquired books and pamphlets and attended groups with the goal of actively confronting the major life event of cancer that was threatening them.

Information seeking is a useful skill for coping with chronic illness because it reinforces the feeling that we are taking control over our lives and doing something instead of passively waiting for things to get better (Felton & Revenson, 1984).

Building Self-Esteem

The women attempted to fight against feelings of depression and despair by engaging in thoughts and activities that would bolster their self-esteem. One strategy used by many women was to compare themselves with those who were less fortunate. For example, An older woman compared herself with women who were younger. "The people I really feel sorry for are these young gals. To lose a breast when you're so young must be awful. I'm 73; what do I need a breast for?" (Taylor, 1983, p. 1166). A young married woman compared herself with women who were single. "If I hadn't been married, I think this thing would have really gotten to me. I can't imagine dating or whatever knowing you have this thing and not knowing how to tell the man about it" (Taylor, 1983, p. 1166).

The ability to boost one's self-esteem and life appreciation by recognizing those who are less fortunate is a universal coping skill (Perloff, 1987; Wood et al., 1985).

The women also bolstered their self-esteem by recognizing their bout with cancer as a valuable life experience. Many of the women gained the impetus to make the changes in their jobs, living situations, and personal relationships they had been putting off. Other women took the opportunity to travel, to read new books, and to treat themselves to enjoyable activities. These women who attempted to build their self-esteem in the face of their serious illness said to themselves, in one way or another, "Life has presented me with a difficult challenge. What can I do to make the most of it?"

Using Support Systems

Another coping skill employed by people with chronic illness is use of support systems (see Chapter 3). Cancer patients reach out for support from the medical profession, from their friends and families, and from organized support groups. Interviews with cancer patients indicate that using support systems as a coping skill is an individual manner (Taylor, Falke, Shoptaw, & Lichtman, 1986). Some patients benefit from having many support people. Others limit their support people to just a few. Some patients prefer individual support people. Others prefer groups. It does not appear that everyone suffering a severe illness should necessarily join a support group. However, the ability to seek support according to one's individual preferences and needs is a useful coping skill.

Another way to understand the value of support people is by understanding how people can help. Dakof and S. E. Taylor (1990) asked men and women cancer patients what kinds of actions were helpful and unhelpful from the following people: spouse and family, friends, physicians, and nurses (see Table 13.1). It is interesting to see that the most helpful actions from loved ones included expressing concern, empathy, and affection and accepting the patient's cancer. Good care and useful information and advice were valued from physicians and nurses. Also instructive is the fact that people's attempts to minimize the patients' illness were viewed as unhelpful. As we learned in Chapter 10, it is rather thankless when others trivialize your distress (Lazarus, 1984).

Balancing Self-Efficacy and Acceptance

A good way to sum up our discussion of skills for coping with chronic illness is by appreciating the need to balance the benefits of self-efficacy against the reality of accepting things you can't control. On the one hand, we don't want to blame

TABLE 13.1   Helpful and unhelpful actions reported by cancer patients

Support people	Helpful actions	Unhelpful actions
Spouse	Physical presence (just being there)	Critical of patient's response to cancer
	Expressing concern, empathy, and affection	Minimizing impact of cancer on patient
	Calmly accepting patient's cancer	Expressing too much worry and pessimism
Family	Expressing concern, empathy, and affection	Minimizing impact of cancer on patient
	Physical presence (just being there)	Critical of patient's response to cancer
	Providing practical assistance	Expressing little concern, empathy, and affection
Friends	Expressing concern, empathy, and affection	Avoiding social contact with patient
	Providing practical assistance	Expressing too much worry and pessimism
	Calmly accepting patient's cancer	Minimizing impact of cancer on patient
Nurses	Expressing concern, empathy, and affection	Providing technically incompetent medical care
	Providing practical assistance	Minimizing impact of cancer on patient
	Being pleasant and kind	Expressing little concern, empathy, and affection
Physicians	Providing useful information or advice	Providing insufficient information
	Expressing optimism about prognosis and patient's ability to cope	Expressing little concern, empathy, and affection
	Providing technically competent medical care	Providing technically incompetent medical care

From "Victim's Perceptions of Social Support: What Is Helpful from Whom?" by G. A. Dakof and S. E. Taylor, 1990, *Journal of Personality and Social Psychology, 58,* 80–89. Copyright 1990 by the American Psychological Association.

ourselves for our illness and avoid responsibility by passively wishing that things would get better. On the other hand, we must be realistic about what we can and cannot change. We want to devote our energy to activities that will give meaning to our lives and help us feel good about ourselves. We also want to avoid beating our head against the wall and focusing only on symptoms of chronic illness that are part of life and out of our control (Folkman, 1984; Folkman, Lazarus, Gruen, & DeLongis, 1986; Manne & Sandler, 1984).

COPING WITH AIDS

AIDS is one of the world's major health problems. In early 1989 there were more than 75,000 people afflicted with AIDS in the United States (Batchelor, 1988). It has been estimated that if AIDS cases continue to grow at their present rate, there will be 450,000 Americans suffering from this disease by 1993 (Matarazzo, Bailey, Kraut, & Jones, 1988).

Two factors make AIDS particularly devastating and challenging. First, because there is presently no cure, its victims face certain death. Second, AIDS is a communicable disease that could be confined if people practiced preventive behaviors. In the United States, the majority of AIDS victims are homosexual and bisexual people and intravenous drug users. However, AIDS also afflicts heterosexuals, and the number of AIDS cases contracted through heterosexual sex is likely to grow (Batchelor, 1988; Herek & Glunt, 1988). Everyone is vulnerable to this disease, and it is important that we all work together to reduce its impact.

The Importance of Prevention

Because AIDS is a communicable disease, it can be confined with primary prevention. But, how can people be convinced to practice protected sex and (if addicted to drugs) to use sterilized needles? Education is the first step. A number of school districts have developed AIDS education programs for adolescents with good success (Brooks-Gunn, Boyer, & Hein, 1988; Flora & Thoresen, 1988). It is also important to get at factors controlling people's behaviors, such as group norms and personal responsibility (Des Jarlais & Friedman, 1988; Fisher, 1988; Morin, 1988). Health care programs promoting education, group support, and personal efficacy have successfully influenced people to engage in AIDS prevention behavior (Stall, Coates, & Hoff, 1988).

The Burdens of AIDS Victims

AIDS victims bear a terrible burden. As well as facing death, they suffer stigma and blame. They are given less respect than people suffering from other serious illnesses (Herek & Glunt, 1988; Weiner, Perry, & Magnusson, 1988). Why is this so? For one reason, because AIDS is a communicable disease, it is easier to blame AIDS victims for being irresponsible. Second, AIDS is often associated with stigmatized people in our society. Another reason for blaming AIDS victims is to rationalize our own fears. By "blaming the victim" we can externalize this devastating disease and pretend it can't happen to us (Kleinke, 1986, chap. 4; Ryan, 1971; Walster, 1966).

In addition to stigma, AIDS forces catastrophic changes in a person's life. AIDS victims frequently lose their jobs and face eviction. They are often denied police and health care services, and they suffer prejudice from insurance companies. They may experience impairment in their thinking and motor coordination. It is no wonder that AIDS victims feel like "walking time bombs existing in limbo" (Tross & Hirsch, 1988).

Some Useful Coping Strategies

The coping strategies discussed earlier in this chapter for people with cancer are useful for AIDS victims. AIDS victims can also benefit from the skills for coping with loss outlined in Chapter 10. They must maintain their self-esteem and avoid self-blame. Support groups and psychotherapy are often helpful in achieving these goals (McKusick, 1988).

A CONCLUDING THOUGHT

A major theme of this chapter is that there are many life events affecting our health and well-being. Some of these we can control and others we can't control. Life events beyond our control require development of good coping skills for maintaining our feelings of competence, hope, and self-efficacy. Health care practices that we can freely choose for extending our lives pose a special challenge. We need to learn how to encourage people not to place their health and safety in jeopardy. And we need to learn to become more reliable in taking care of ourselves and those we love.

SUGGESTIONS FOR FURTHER READING

DELOACH, C., & GREER, B. G. (1981). *Adjustment to severe physical disability: A metamorphosis.* New York: McGraw-Hill.

FRIEDMAN, M., & ROSENMAN, R. H. (1974). *Type A behavior and your heart.* New York: Knopf.

GATCHEL, R. J., & BAUM, A. (1983). *An introduction to health psychology.* New York: Random House.

HOLROYD, K. A., & CREER, T. L. (Eds.). (1986). *Self-management of chronic disease.* New York: Academic Press.

LEVITT, P. M., & GURALNICK, E. S. (1985). *You can make it back: Coping with serious illness.* New York: Facts on File Publications.

TAYLOR, S. E. (1986). *Health psychology.* New York: Random House.

U.S. Public Health Service. (1979). *Healthy people: The Surgeon General's report on health promotion and disease prevention* (Stock Number 017-001-00416-2). Washington, D.C.: U.S. Government Printing Office.

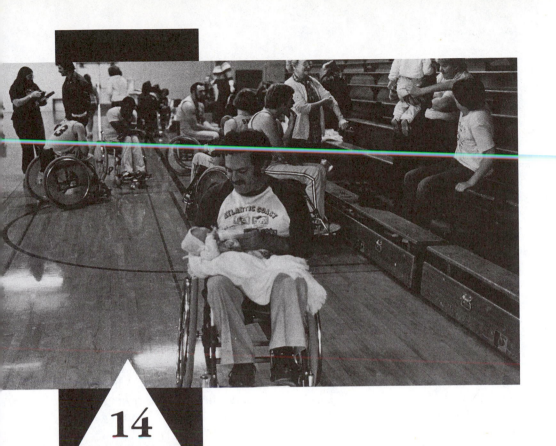

Coping with Injury and Trauma

There are many examples in life where people have borne up to traumas, tragedies, accidents, and disasters. Stories about individuals who maintained their will to survive such difficult challenges are an inspiration to all of us. The purpose of this book is to teach coping skills derived from research on large groups of people, and I therefore have not recounted personal anecdotes about human fortitude and heroism. However, since much can be learned from people who have gone through traumatic events, some examples of such coping experiences are explored in this chapter. The challenges of injury and trauma are good topics for discussion because they are commonly experienced and people's coping responses to these life events have been studied in scientific research.

We will begin with an overview of research on people's experiences coping with serious injury. We will then look at studies of traumatic events that range from noise, crowding, and pollution to human-caused disasters, rape, and the horror of concentration camps. The chapter will conclude with a discussion of post traumatic stress disorder and a summary of experiences common to people who have suffered from injury and trauma.

COPING WITH INJURY

The fortitude shown by people who have been disabled in accidents is inspiring. When we see disabled people exercising their willpower to make their lives meaningful and productive, we often wonder, "Where do they find the strength?" Let's begin by looking at some of the difficulties and challenges faced by victims of serious injury.

Suffering a severe injury is a devastating experience. In many cases, the individual loses the ability to lead a normal life. This loss requires the person to go through the stages of grief work described in Chapter 10. Injury victims are vulnerable to hopelessness and depression (see Chapter 5). They often suffer stigma because others are uncomfortable with their disability. They are at high risk for drug abuse because they are often given addictive pain-relieving medication. Coping with all of this is a tremendous challenge.

Two major needs of injury victims are social support and an opportunity for building self-esteem. Successful adjustment requires virtually all of the coping skills outlined in Chapter 3.

Researchers have attempted to understand how injury victims cope by interviewing victims of serious accidents who were destined to spend the rest of their lives with major disabilities (Bulman & Wortman, 1977; Frank et al., 1987; Schulz & Decker, 1985).

The first challenge for the accident victims was to find a meaningful answer to the question "Why me?" Some victims found the answer in God's will. Others felt their injury was a calculated risk for engaging in a dangerous but pleasurable activity. Victims also understood their injury as a natural risk of living in a dangerous and unpredictable world. It didn't matter so much what kind of answer was found to the "why me" question as long as the answer was meaningful and satisfying. Victims who suffered most were those who could not find a meaningful reason for their accident.

A second challenge for the accident victims was to maintain a sense of self-efficacy and control over their lives. This is difficult because it requires the ability to find a balance between what is and what is not controllable in one's life. It is not adaptive to fault others, and it is important not to feel helpless and sink into depression. These accident victims were able to adapt by acknowledging their choice of engaging in the behavior that resulted in the accident. They also worked hard to maintain control over their lives by involving themselves in rehabilitation and meaningful activities once the reality of their disability was accepted.

A third challenge for accident victims was to find a good support system. Having a good support system was one of the most useful coping skills for providing victims with a positive sense of well-being.

COPING WITH NOISE, CROWDING, AND POLLUTION

Noise, crowding, and pollution are not usually thought of as disasters, but they do represent stressors caused by human technological development. Are these stressors detrimental to our health? The best way to answer this question is to look at each of them separately.

Noise

One of the most comprehensive studies of the effects of noise on health and psychological functioning is the Los Angeles Noise Project (Cohen, S., Evans, Stokols, & Krantz, 1986). The purpose of this study was to learn how the noise from Los Angeles International Airport affected children who attended schools in the direct vicinity of the airport. These children, who were exposed to high levels of aircraft noise approximately every 2.5 minutes, were compared with children of comparable ages and backgrounds who attended schools in other areas of the city. On the average, the children exposed to the high levels of noise had higher blood pressures and poorer performance on learning tasks requiring attention and memory. This research and other studies cited by its authors leave little doubt that constant exposure to noise can be detrimental. One of the most disturbing things about noise pollution is that it is usually unpredictable and beyond our control. We are distressed not only from the distraction caused by the noise, but also by the frustration of not being able to stop it.

Crowding

Crowding disturbs us most when it interferes with what we are trying to do. Most of us have been in situations, such as parties and social gatherings, where being crowded was not a problem. On the other hand, when close proximity with others hampers our daily activities, crowding can be disturbing. In psychiatric hospitals and prisons, where close proximity intensifies other maladaptive behaviors, crowding has been implicated with higher than average rates of illness, emotional problems, suicide, and death (Cox, V. C., Paulus, & McCain, 1984; Paulus, McCain, & Cox, 1978).

Andrew Baum and his colleagues examined the reactions of college students who found themselves living in crowded dormitories (Baum, Aiello, & Calesnick, 1978; Baum, Fisher, & Solomon, 1981; Baum & Gatchel, 1981; Rodin & Baum, 1978).

One of the most disturbing experiences for students living in crowded environments was their reduced feeling of personal control. Students who were living in crowded rooms found it troublesome to have such limited privacy. Those in dormitories with long corridors had little choice over their social contacts and were not able to develop a sense of community. As a result of the loss of personal control resulting from their crowded living conditions, the students tended to become withdrawn. They were dissatisfied with their living situation and they had difficulties cooperating and being friendly with others. To assist students living in dormitories with long corridors, Baum and G. Davis (1980) persuaded the university to remodel the space into two suites of rooms separated by a lounge. This change in living space had a very positive effect on the morale and social interactions of the students.

Although the students suffering from crowding in the above study were assisted by the researchers, there are many occasions where we can cope with crowding by helping ourselves. Here are some suggestions (Kleinke, 1986, chap. 6):

1. *Set priorities:* If being in a crowded situation interferes with our concentration, it is useful to focus on specific goals. By setting priorities we can protect ourselves from feeling overwhelmed.

2. *Think adaptively.* It helps to talk ourselves through stressful situations (see Chapter 3), and crowding can sometimes be stressful.

3. *Take action.* We want to do something to enhance our sense of control over an uncomfortable situation. Sometimes we can modify the physical setting. If this is not possible, we want to maintain a sense of competence by maintaining our composure and engaging others in a polite and assertive manner.

Pollution

The first thing that must be acknowledged about pollution is its direct threat to our physical health:

> The health effects of air pollution include respiratory infection, irritation, and disease. Photochemical oxidants (smog) produce irritation and respiratory discomfort at ambient levels. Some upper respiratory impairment has also been noted. . . . Ambient ranges of sulfur dioxide irritate upper respiratory passages, reduce mucosal clearance activity, and reduce pulmonary function. Sulfur dioxide has also been associated with upper respiratory infections, bronchitis, and asthma. Oxides of nitrogen reduce pulmonary function and resistance to some diseases, inflame bronchial passages, and interfere with hemoglobin peroxidation. Some respiratory illnesses may be associated with nitrogen oxides as well. Carbon monoxide has been associated with cardiovascular disease, reduced birth weights, and in cases of acute exposure, with headaches, dizziness, and nausea. Research on various particulates including toxic metals like lead and mercury have revealed various human impacts including pulmonary lesions, carcinoma, mesothelial tissue damage, and pulmonary cancer for mercury; gastrointestinal disturbances, anemia, retardation, and impaired neural functioning for lead; thyroid disturbances, and cancer for asbestos (Cohen, S., et al., 1986, pp. 129–130).

This is bad enough. When we add to these health risks the stress resulting from the knowledge that we are being poisoned and that there is little we are doing about it, we can begin to appreciate the devastating impact of human-caused pollution.

Some Conclusions

One problem that noise, crowding, and pollution have in common is the threat they pose to our sense of personal control. When our ability to control our lives becomes too limited, we suffer from the kinds of helplessness discussed in Chapter 15. What can we do to cope? When it is possible to alter the conditions causing noise, crowding, and pollution, we, of course, would like to do so. However, while we want to be effective and constructive in working toward environmental reform, we don't want to exacerbate our stress with unrealistic expectations and unfocused anger. It is also important to remember that even though the world is often difficult to change, we can always manage our own reactions. The following coping skills described in Chapter 3 should help us cope successfully with environmental stressors:

> Support systems can encourage us to improve our environment.
> Problem solving can help us identify viable ways to improve our environment and strategies for making this happen.
> Self-relaxation is good for controlling our bodily arousal when faced with environmental stress.
> Internal control can help us prevent feelings of helplessness.
> We can maintain our composure when faced with environmental stress by talking ourselves through the challenge.

COPING WITH DISASTERS

The development of health psychology and behavioral medicine has stimulated a growing interest in how people cope with disasters. We will look at the outcome of research on two disasters that occurred in the United States: Buffalo Creek and Three Mile Island. These disasters were particularly detrimental because they were caused by humans and were therefore potentially avoidable.

Buffalo Creek

The Buffalo Creek disaster occurred in 1972 as a result of corporate negligence. For some time, a mining company had dumped coal waste into a mountain stream in West Virginia, causing an artificial dam that was incapable of holding back the mass of water building up behind it. After several days of rain the dam gave way, causing a devastating flood that wiped out entire communities as it roared down the valley. The Buffalo Creek disaster had a traumatic impact on survivors that they will carry with them for the rest of their lives. Interviews with survivors indicated they were suffering from the following psychological and emotional problems (Lifton & Olson, 1976).

> *Death imprint and death anxiety:* Two years after the disaster, survivors were still vividly reliving the devastating experience of destruction and death. For some, it was as if the flood had just happened yesterday. Many survivors reported having anxiety attacks whenever it rained. Terrifying dreams were also common. Psychiatric symptoms of depression, obsessive fear, and changes in character and lifestyle were common (Titchener & Kapp, 1976).

Death guilt: Survivors had a need to ask themselves why they survived while others died. They also ruminated about their inability to save their loved ones. They had trouble accepting the fact that they were helpless bystanders to human-caused death and destruction.

Psychic numbing: One common defensive reaction to disasters is psychic numbing. The trauma is so painful that the anxiety, sadness, guilt, and anger are denied. This is a useful coping response in the short run because it offers immediate respite (it's like going into shock). However, remaining numb and emotionally withdrawn causes problems in the long run by preventing people from living full and meaningful lives.

Unfocused rage: Because the disaster was caused by human negligence, it is understandable that the victims would feel rage. Unfortunately, it was difficult to get satisfaction and obtain justice. Those who died could not be returned, and the people responsible were anonymous members of a powerful corporation.

Difficulty in finding a meaning: As we will see in the discussion of the Three Mile Island disaster, human-caused disasters are particularly difficult to accept because they have no meaning. Natural disasters can be accepted as an uncontrollable act of nature. Human-caused disasters, in contrast, remind us of our vulnerability to uncontrolled technology. The Buffalo Creek victims were also in the discomforting position of being dependent on a mining company for their employment—for their food and housing. Yet, this mining company had betrayed them.

Five Sources of Trauma

Five factors related to the Buffalo Creek disaster made it particularly difficult for its victims to cope in a successful manner (Lifton & Olson, 1976). It will be useful to outline these factors as a way of understanding the human reaction to traumas.

1. The disaster was sudden. There was no idea that it could happen. It caused complete terror.

2. The disaster was caused by irresponsibility and lack of consideration by fellow human beings.

3. It was difficult for the survivors to put the disaster behind them. The same coal company responsible for the disaster was still in business, and the destruction caused by the flood would be visible for years to come.

4. The victims lived in an isolated community, and they had little political power. They saw no opportunity to reform the powerful coal company that controlled their lives, and they did not have the resources to move away.

5. The destruction was total. Small hamlets were completely destroyed. Those who died were known to everyone. There was a feeling of total loss and breakdown of the community structure. Since everyone was a victim, it was difficult to find social support.

Later in this chapter we will see why the Buffalo Creek survivors were vulnerable to post traumatic stress disorder. It is a tragedy that these people were trapped in such a difficult situation. Hopefully, we can learn from their experience.

Three Mile Island

In 1979 there was an accident at the Three Mile Island nuclear plant in Pennsylvania, exposing people living nearby to dangerous levels of radiation. A series of studies conducted after this accident focused on three interesting and important questions.

How Did the Victims Suffer?

The psychological effects of the accident were studied by comparing people living within 5 miles of the damaged nuclear plant with comparable groups of people living either within 5 miles of an undamaged nuclear plant or a coal-fired power station. The reason for choosing these comparison groups was to control for whatever stress may naturally result from living near a power plant. Although victims of the Three Mile Island disaster were similar in age, education, and income to the other groups, they suffered significantly more physical and psychological stress. Several years after the nuclear accident, victims of the Three Mile Island disaster were still more depressed and psychologically disturbed than comparable people living near undamaged power plants. The Three Mile Island victims also continued to suffer higher levels of physiological stress (Baum, Gatchel, & Schaeffer, 1983; Collins, Baum, & Singer, 1983; Davidson & Baum, 1986).

How Did the Victims Cope?

Although the stress suffered by the victims of the Three Mile Island disaster was severe, some victims coped more successfully than others. People who stood up best to the disaster employed the following coping skills (Baum, 1988; Baum, Fleming, & Singer, 1983):

1. They engaged in emotion-focused coping (see Chapter 1). They dealt with their emotions by talking themselves through the disaster (see Chapter 3) and appraising it in a way that protected them from feeling overwhelmed.

2. They focused their energies on things they could change, such as their feelings of personal responsibility about taking care of themselves and planning their future.

3. They did not insist on changing things beyond their control, and they did not waste much energy blaming others.

4. They used social support systems (see Chapter 3).

What Did We Learn?

One important conclusion coming out of the Three Mile Island studies is that disasters caused by human error often result in more long-lasting stress than disasters caused by nature. Why is this so? We know that natural disasters are beyond our control. When a natural disaster strikes, there is nobody to blame. Technological disasters are more stressful because they remind us of our fallibilities. The technologies we create to fulfill the needs of our society can backfire and cause hardship and suffering. Human-caused disasters remind us of our precarious control over our own creations. Technological disasters also tend to result in longer-lasting stress because they often don't have a clear beginning or end. Most natural disasters strike swiftly and then are over. In contrast, our technology poses a constant, nagging threat.

We live under the shadows of nuclear plants, toxic waste dumps, and hazardous industries that may wreak havoc at any time (Baum, 1988).

COPING WITH RAPE

Being raped is a traumatic experience that often has long-lasting negative consequences. Rape victims commonly suffer from anxiety, sexual dissatisfaction, depression, and family problems (Atkeson, Calhoun, Resick, & Ellis, 1982; Ellis, E. M., Atkeson, & Calhoun, 1981; Feldman-Summers, Gordon, & Meagher, 1979; Kilpatrick, Resick, & Veronen, 1981). Because rape is a serious crime in the United States, it is important for everyone to participate in programs designed to reduce the incidence of rape. It is also useful to understand how victims manage to cope when they have been raped.

Some Facts about Rape

Rape is defined as:

> a sexual invasion of the body by force, an incursion into the private, personal inner space without consent—in short an internal assault from one of several avenues and by one of several methods that constitutes a deliberate violation of emotional, physical, and rational integrity and is a hostile, degrading act of violence (Brownmiller, 1975, p. 376).

Rape must be understood in light of the following facts (Gilliland & James, 1988):

1. *Rape is not sex:* Rape is power, dominance, and violence.
2. *Rape is an uninvited act:* Rape victims are violated against their will.
3. *Rape may happen to anyone:* Although we may stigmatize rape victims, the fact is that we are all vulnerable.
4. *Rapists come from every segment of society:* We might like to believe that rapists come from the lower strata of society. However, the truth is that anyone is capable of committing rape.
5. *Many sexual assaults go unreported:* Rape is a far greater problem than realized because many sexual assaults are never reported.
6. *Most perpetrators of sexual assault are men:* Men between the ages of 18 and 35 inflict 99% of the sexual assaults in the United States.

A final important fact about rape is that victims can be assisted in their recovery with good coping skills and strong support systems.

How Women Cope with Rape

Researchers have studied skills for coping with rape by interviewing women rape victims about their experiences and their attempts to adjust and get on with their lives. Women rape victims report that they cope by using the following methods (Burgess & Holmstrom, 1979):

> Seeking reasons for why the rape occurred
> Minimizing the impact of the rape by telling themselves that it was not really so terrifying
> Suppressing their reactions to the rape by refusing to think about it

Keeping busy and engaging in activities
Using self-relaxation and meditation to reduce stress
Withdrawing from other people
Using drugs and alcohol

It is apparent that some of these methods of coping with rape are more adaptive than others. To learn more about the effectiveness of various coping skills, another group of researchers interviewed women rape victims and correlated their choice of coping styles with the following three measures of personal adjustment (Meyer & Taylor, 1986): depression, anxiety, sexual dissatisfaction. Among the least effective coping responses were withdrawing from others and staying isolated. Suppressing one's feelings and minimizing the impact of the rape didn't seem to hurt, but it also did not help. Use of drugs and alcohol was not measured in this study, but it is likely that this is not an effective coping strategy—especially in the long run.

Among the most effective coping responses were techniques that involved some form of stress reduction, such as self-relaxation, physical activity, and rational thinking. Using support systems is also likely to be an effective coping strategy.

The researchers were particularly interested in learning how the rape victims explained their traumatic experience to themselves. How is it possible to give meaning to a crime such as this? The most reasonable explanation for crimes such as rape appears to be that we live in an imperfect world. Accepting the fact that the world is sometimes a bad place doesn't necessarily make us feel better, but it keeps us from falling into depression and putting ourselves down. But we need to remember that because we accept the world as imperfect doesn't mean that we might not want to take an active role in making it better.

Explanations for rape that were not adaptive were those related to self-blame. Women who suffered most from depression, anxiety, and sexual dissatisfaction were those who said the following kinds of things to themselves: "I should have been more cautious." "I am too trusting." "I was raped because I made some kind of mistake." "I can't take care of myself." "Maybe I deserved it." "It was my fault." These kinds of self-downing statements are similar to those described in Chapter 5 for people who are depressed. They are also similar to statements made by people who are poor at coping with failure (see Chapter 4). It is clearly not adaptive to find meaning in the experience of being a crime victim by blaming oneself. Given this fact, it might surprise you to learn that at least half of women rape victims do just that. They take personal responsibility for the fact that someone raped them. Why is this so? Much of this self-blame results from the fact that people like to believe that they live in a fair and just world. In order to believe in this kind of world, it is necessary to convince oneself that victims must somehow deserve their plight. Women rape victims also blame themselves because our society has a history of sexism that excuses men for sexual misconduct and encourages women to accept their misfortunes.

The Attitudes Toward Rape Victims Scale

Check how much you agree or disagree with the following items from the Attitudes Toward Rape Victims Scale (Ward, 1988).

	Strongly agree	Agree	Disagree	Strongly disagree
1. A raped woman is a less desirable woman.	____	____	____	____
2. Most women secretly desire to be raped.	____	____	____	____
3. A healthy woman can successfully resist a rape if she really tries.	____	____	____	____
4. Sexually experienced women are not really damaged by rape.	____	____	____	____
5. A woman should blame herself for rape.	____	____	____	____
6. In most cases when a woman was raped, she deserved it.	____	____	____	____
7. Accusations of rape by bar girls, dance hostesses, and prostitutes should be viewed with suspicion.	____	____	____	____
8. Women provoke rape by their appearance and behavior.	____	____	____	____

A survey of the Attitudes Toward Rape Victims Scale found that neither men nor women agreed with the above statements (Ward, 1988). However, men were not offended by these statements nearly as much as were women.

Raising Our Consciousness
Research on rape is valuable because it raises our consciousness about rape victims. We can appreciate the importance of helping rape victims maintain their sense of worthiness and self-esteem after suffering a traumatic crime.

COPING IN THE CONCENTRATION CAMPS

It is almost impossible to conceive of coping with the horrors imposed on human beings in the Nazi concentration camps. Yet, prisoners in these camps did cope, and some lived to tell about it. In this section we will learn about the strategies used by concentration camp prisoners to maintain their self-esteem and will to live. Attention is also paid to the psychological and emotional strains suffered by concentration camp survivors and the ways they are coping with them. This section is followed by one on post traumatic stress disorder, which is relevant to all of the traumas discussed in this chapter.

Seven major coping skills were used by prisoners during their internment in Nazi concentration camps: differential focus on the good, survival for some purpose, psychological distancing, mastery, will to live, hope, and social support (Dimsdale, 1974).

Differential focus on the good: In spite of the horrible events occurring, some prisoners attempted to focus their attention on whatever good they could find, such as finding a small carrot in the field or seeing a sunset.

Survival for some purpose: The will to survive is a strong source of motivation. It was a remarkable strength shown by prisoners who were determined to live, if for no other reason than to bear witness to the world about what happened.

Psychological distancing: There were a number of ways prisoners distanced themselves from the experiences suffered in the camps:

1. *Intellectualizing:* Bruno Bettelheim (1943) described how he coped with being interned in a Nazi prison by taking the role of an observer who would study this situation and write about it.
2. *Religious conviction:* Religious convictions were a source of strength because they made the suffering less personal and in some cases provided hope of some kind of existence after death.
3. *Time focus:* It was possible to distance oneself from the magnitude of the horror by living 1 day, 1 hour, or even 1 minute at a time.
4. *Humor:* In the hardest of times, prisoners still maintained their capacity to salve their pain with humor.

Mastery: The theme of mastery and self-efficacy has appeared throughout this book. It is important to always find something we can do to demonstrate our competence. Although the lives of prisoners were extremely limited, there were still opportunities to use one's mind and to devote one's energies toward helping others and maintaining a sense of worthiness and self-esteem.

Will to live: You will understand this concept more fully after reading the examples of helplessness in Chapter 15. Human beings have a powerful source of strength when they refuse to give up and are determined to survive.

Hope: In Chapter 15 you will also learn about the power of hope: "Where there is life there is hope." It often doesn't matter how realistic the hope is so long as it is held and nurtured.

Social support: Social support was a major source of strength for prisoners, whether it came from groups or individual friendships.

Due to the extreme harshness, horror, and cruelty suffered by prisoners, it is not surprising that many became totally overwhelmed and gave up. A poignant example of helplessness exhibited by these victims is described in Chapter 15. Also not surprising is that those who were lucky enough to survive are still carrying scars of this terrible experience. Researchers have identified a number of stresses suffered by Nazi concentration camp survivors (Ehrlich, 1988; Marmar & Horowitz, 1988). For example: difficulty concentrating, nervousness and irritability, sleep disturbances and nightmares, feelings of helplessness and depression, intrusive memories and flashbacks, survivor guilt, feelings of isolation, and/or loss of identity.

Researchers have also identified coping skills used by the survivors who have been most successful in adjusting to their concentration camp experience (Ehrlich, 1988; Kahana, Harel, & Kahana, 1988). These adaptive coping skills include the following:

Seeking support people with whom they can share the Holocaust experiences
(having a spouse who was also a concentration camp survivor was particu-
larly helpful)
Devoting physical and emotional energy to care for other people
Use of problem-focused coping (see Chapter 1) as a way of taking active steps
to maintain one's self-esteem and sense of competence and efficacy
Having meaningful employment or other gratifying life activities
Being future-oriented

Useful therapy for Holocaust survivors includes social support, family counseling, and grief work (Ehrlich, 1988).

COPING WITH POST TRAUMATIC STRESS DISORDER (PTSD)

Post traumatic stress disorder (PTSD) has become familiar to many people since the
Vietnam War. Individuals who suffer PTSD were exposed to a traumatic event that
continues to interfere with their lives. They usually experience the following symptoms (Gilliland & James, 1988):

1. Reexperiencing the trauma through flashbacks, recurrent intrusive thoughts
or dreams, or the sudden notion that the traumatic event is happening right now
2. Withdrawal, numbing of feelings, detachment from others
3. Strong desire for love and support conflicting with outbursts of anger
4. Hyperalertness, problems sleeping, guilt, memory impairment, trouble concentrating, avoidance of activities that arouse recollection of the traumatic event

Studies of World War II veterans found that soldiers who were exposed to heavy
combat still feel this experience helped them to value their lives and to learn how
to cope with adversity. However, these same veterans suffered many long-lasting
emotional and psychological problems, including nightmares, flashbacks, anxiety,
bad memories, depression, and guilt (Elder & Clipp, 1988, 1989). The Vietnam War
was even more debilitating. It has been estimated that 33% to 60% of Vietnam combat
veterans suffer from PTSD (Brende & Parson, 1985, p. 1). This is not surprising when
one considers the following kinds of trauma to which Vietnam veterans were
exposed (Gilliland & James, 1988):

Hypervigilance: Soldiers had long tours of duty where they were in constant
danger. They never knew from one moment to the next when they might
be attacked, injured, or killed.
Lack of goals: Because the war dragged on there was rarely a feeling of accomplishment. No territory was ever "won." The only measure of victory was a
"body count" (MacPherson, 1984).
Victim/victimizer role: This was a guerrilla war where civilians were friends as
well as enemies. Soldiers were thrown into the role of being both victims
and victimizers.
Lack of debriefing: A soldier could be sweating for his life in the jungle one day
and a couple of days later be sitting on his porch at home (MacPherson,
1984). This was a war in which soldiers were motivated to survive their tour
of duty and get home alive. For this reason, survivors often felt guilty about

those who died or were injured. They were happy to go home but felt bad about leaving their comrades behind.

Antiwar sentiment: The impact of antiwar sentiment on returning veterans was devastating. These men had suffered and risked their lives, many returning with disabling injuries. However, they were not regarded as heroes and were often treated with disdain. Many soldiers had extreme difficulty starting a new life after returning from the war.

Although PTSD has received greater recognition since the Vietnam War, it is not new. The fact that people can suffer long-lasting psychological disturbance after trauma has been known for hundreds of years (Trimble, 1985). All of the traumas discussed in this chapter can be severe enough to result in PTSD. The following ten factors influence the onset and course of PTSD (Wilson, J. P., Smith, & Johnson, 1985):

1. *Degree of life-threat:* Traumatic events threatening one's life are likely to be most debilitating and to invoke the kind of death imprint described in the discussion of the Buffalo Creek disaster.

2. *Loss of significant others:* Bereavement is associated with prolonged stress responses. The death of significant others is a source of grief, guilt, rage, and depression.

3. *Suddenness of onset:* Traumas that occur without warning are particularly likely to instill a feeling of helplessness and loss of external control.

4. *Duration of trauma:* It is most difficult to adjust to traumas that are prolonged and that continue for a long time.

5. *Displacement from one's community:* It is particularly detrimental to be exposed to traumatic events that occur away from one's community or that result in community disintegration. Traumatic events are times when we desperately need the love and belongingness that come from our support systems.

6. *Potential for recurrence:* Traumatic events that are unpredictable, that might recur, and that cause distrust and hypervigilance are particularly disturbing.

7. *Exposure to death, dying, and destruction:* Exposure to death, dying, and destruction exacerbates intrusive imagery, psychic numbing, isolation, and guilt.

8. *Degree of moral conflict:* It is bad enough to experience traumatic events that have some reason or justification. It is even more difficult to adjust to traumatic events that threaten one's personal values and instill moral conflict.

9. *Personal role:* In some situations, people are placed in a role where they must react and cope with destruction. This is difficult. In other situations, people are obliged not only to react, but also to perpetrate destruction. This is even more difficult.

10. *Natural versus human trauma:* It is usually easier to accept and cope with natural disasters than disasters caused by one's fellow human beings.

What kinds of therapy are helpful for people suffering with PTSD? The following five factors appear to help people cope more effectively (Scurfield, 1985):

1. *A trusting relationship with a therapist or support group:* PTSD victims suffer from emotions ranging from shame, guilt, and depression to anger and rage. They need to feel safe before these feelings can be recognized, accepted, and explored.

2. *Education about the stress recovery process:* It is reassuring to understand the reasons for our suffering and to realize that it is a human condition and not a sign of personal weakness.

3. *Learning and practicing stress management techniques:* Coping skills such as those discussed in Chapter 3 are useful for stress management, as are the skills of rational thinking and self-efficacy outlined in Chapter 2.

4. *Reexperiencing and desensitizing oneself from trauma:* This is a powerful but often effective process involving the methods of desensitization, flooding, and thought-stopping described in Chapter 7 (Cooper & Clum, 1989; Keane, Fairbank, Caddell, & Zimmering, 1989; Keane, Fairbank, Caddell, Zimmering, & Bender, 1985). With the support of trained professionals, people suffering from PTSD vividly relive the traumatic experience until they are in control of the experience rather than suffering by having experience control them.

5. *Reconciling oneself to the traumatic experience:* As we will learn in the next section, we all have the need to find meaning in life and to believe in ourselves as worthwhile people. With professional guidance, victims can find a way to integrate the trauma they suffered into their total life experience.

SOME COMMON EXPERIENCES

Although the illnesses and injuries described in this chapter are very different, people coping with them share several common experiences. When we are confronted with a traumatic experience or injury, our feelings about the "goodness of life" are threatened. We are forced to reconcile our suffering with our desire to maintain the following beliefs (Janoff-Bulman & Thomas, 1988): "The world is basically a good place. Life is meaningful. I am a worthwhile person." Much of this chapter is about how people who have suffered injury and trauma go about doing this. Three things people commonly experience when trying to regain their faith in the above beliefs are searching for meaning, recurrent thoughts, and self-blame (Janoff-Bulman & Thomas, 1988; Tait & Silver, 1989).

Searching for Meaning
Check whether you agree or disagree with the following statements:

	Agree	Disagree
1. Basically, the world is a just place.	_____	_____
2. It is a common experience for a guilty person to get off free in U.S. courts.	_____	_____
3. The political candidate who sticks up for personal principles rarely gets elected.	_____	_____
4. It is rare for an innocent person to be sent to jail.	_____	_____
5. By and large, people get what they deserve.	_____	_____
6. Good deeds often go unnoticed and unrewarded.	_____	_____

	Agree	Disagree
7. In almost any business or profession, people who do their job will rise to the top.	___	___
8. Many people suffer through absolutely no fault of their own.	___	___

These statments come from the Just World Scale (Rubin & Peplau, 1975). People who believe in a just world agree with statements 1, 4, 5, and 7 and disagree with statements 2, 3, 6, and 8. People with a high belief in a just world view the world as a just place where people are rewarded for good deeds and punished for bad deeds (Lerner, 1980). Of course, all would like to live in a just world where everything is fair. Unfortunately, this is not the case. Tragedies and traumas can happen to anyone. It is important to find a satisfactory answer for these negative events. We must reconcile our desire to live in a just world with life's unfairness. This is not always easy to do, but it is a necessary first step to getting on with our lives. Part of the solution is to develop the kind of coping attitude toward life discussed in Chapter 15.

Recurrent Thoughts

It is common for people who have suffered major tragedies and even minor setbacks to keep thinking about them (Tait & Silver, 1989). These ruminations sometimes continue to occur for years and even for a lifetime. It is hard to get the negative experience out of mind. We think about it over and over and relive the negative emotions hundreds and even thousands of times.

There are three things to bear in mind regarding ruminations about negative events. First, recurrent thoughts are experienced by almost everyone. Recurrent thoughts serve a useful purpose because we need time to put things into perspective. We can't ignore a setback, injury, or trauma and pretend that it didn't happen. We must accept its reality and find a way to assimilate it into our lives. Second, it is helpful to discuss our thoughts and feelings with a support person. If our feelings are complex and will require some time to sort out, we may benefit from working with a professional therapist. Third, we can prevent recurrent thoughts from getting the best of us by keeping busy and focused on meaningful activities.

Self-Blame

There are a number of things to understand before we blame ourselves for an illness or injury. Self-blame is a common human experience. So, if we blame ourselves, we are no different from most other people. Self-blame can even serve a useful purpose if it motivates us to take responsibility for our actions. Self-responsibility will reinforce our feelings of being a competent and worthwhile person. However, self-blame can be destructive if we use it to undermine our character. It is important to recognize the distinction between accepting a mistake in our behavior and doubting our value as a person (Kiecolt-Glaser & Williams, 1987; Nielson & MacDonald, 1988).

WHAT WE CAN LEARN FROM COPERS

The previous chapters of this book focused on coping skills researchers have found to be effective for different kinds of challenging life events. This chapter took a more personal approach by looking at the experiences of those who have lived through life crises. People who are good copers have learned how to use effective coping skills. They have also developed a self-identity as survivors. This theme will be continued in Chapter 15 as you learn about the life philosophy of being a coper. When you are through reading this book, you should have a good understanding about how to combine these aspects of being a good coper in a way that best matches your personal style.

SUGGESTIONS FOR FURTHER READING

BENEDICT, H. (1985). *Recovery: How to survive sexual assault— For women, men, teenagers, their friends and families.* Garden City, N.Y.: Doubleday.

FIGLEY, C. R. (Ed.). (1985). *Trauma and its wake: The study and treatment of post-traumatic stress disorder.* New York: Brunner/Mazel.

GIL, E. (1984). *Outgrowing the pain.* Palo Alto, Calif.: Consulting Psychologists Press.

GROSSMAN, R., & SUTHERLAND, J. (1983). *Surviving sexual assault.* New York: Congdon & Weed.

LERNER, M. J. (1980). *The belief in a just world: A fundamental delusion.* New York: Plenum.

MEDEA, A., & THOMPSON, K. (1974). *Against rape. A survival manual for women: How to avoid entrapment and how to cope with rape physically and emotionally.* New York: Farrar, Straus, & Giroux.

VIORST, J. (1986). *Necessary losses.* New York: Simon & Schuser.

WILSON, J. P., HAREL, Z., & KAHANA, B. (Eds.) (1988). *Human adaptation to extreme stress: From the Holocaust to Vietnam.* New York: Plenum.

15

Coping as a
Life Philosophy

While reading this book you have become familiar with terms such as self-efficacy, competence, and mastery. All of these concern coping because they suggest a life philosophy of believing in oneself as a coper. When faced with a life challenge, copers take the attitude that although the experience might not be pleasant, they can use their problem solving skills to seek the best possible outcome. Copers refuse to be passive and helpless. They look for ways to take active control over their lives.

This chapter focuses on coping as a life philosophy. We will begin by looking at the opposite extreme of coping—helplessness. Helplessness occurs when people give up and allow external circumstances to take over their lives. An insight into the phenomenon of helplessness will give us a different perspective on self-efficacy, competence, and mastery and a deeper appreciation of what it means to be a coper.

HELPLESSNESS

Helplessness is a term that can be used to describe conditions where we cannot control certain events in our lives. Students would be helpless if their grades were determined randomly and had nothing to do with their performance. Infants would be helpless if their cries for nurturance were always ignored. Sick and elderly people are helpless when they are given no opportunity to do things for themselves. After reading this book it should be clear to you that these kinds of helplessness often result in passivity and depression.

There is also another kind of helplessness—*learned helplessness.* Learned help-lessness is a term used by Martin Seligman (1975) to describe conditions where we believe we are helpless or have learned to feel helpless when we really are not. Women in U.S. society have traditionally been taught to feel helpless about their mechanical and physical skills. Men have traditionally been taught to feel helpless about homemaking and nurturing young children. There are even more severe examples of helplessness where people give up complete control over their lives and die. It is important to emphasize that these cases of helplessness are *learned.* They result from complete acceptance of a belief that we are doomed and there is nothing we can do about it. Consider the following cases of helplessness described by anthropologists who studied people who believed they were destined by certain life events to death:

> A Brazilian Indian condemned and sentenced by a so-called medicine man is helpless against his own emotional response to this pronouncement—and dies within hours. In Africa a young Negro unknowingly eats the inviolably banned wild hen. On discovery of his "crime," he trembles, is overcome by fear, and dies within 24 hours.
>
> In New Zealand a Maori woman eats fruit that she only later learns has come from a tabooed place. Her chief has been profaned. By noon of the next day she is dead.
>
> In Australia a witch doctor points a bone at a man. Believing that nothing can save him, the man rapidly sinks in spirits and prepares to die. He is saved only at the last moment when the witch doctor is forced to remove the curse.
>
> The man who discovers that he is being boned by an enemy is, indeed, a pitiable sight. He stands aghast with his eyes staring at the treacherous pointer, and with his hands lifted to ward off the lethal medium, which he imagines is pouring into his

body. His cheeks blanch, and his eyes become glassy, and the expression of his face becomes horribly distorted. He attempts to shriek but usually the sound chokes in his throat, and all that one might see is froth at his mouth. His body begins to tremble and his muscles twitch involuntarily. He sways backward and falls to the ground, and after a short time appears to be in a swoon. He finally composes himself, goes to his hut and there frets to death. (Basedow, 1925; Cannon, 1957, p. 184; Richter, 1957, p. 191)

Bruno Bettelheim (1960) has described how he coped with being a prisoner in a Nazi concentration camp by telling himself that he was a scientist who was going to study this terrible event. By looking at his experience in this way, Bettelheim was able to maintain a sense of self-efficacy. Many other prisoners felt completely helpless and gave up control over their lives:

Prisoners who came to believe the repeated statements of the guards—that there was no hope for them, that they would never leave the camp except as a corpse—who came to feel that their environment was one over which they could exercise no influence whatsoever, these prisoners were in a literal sense, walking corpses. In the camps they were called "moslems" (*Muselmänner*) because of what was erroneously viewed as a fatalistic surrender to the environment, as Mohammedans are supposed to blandly accept their fate. But these people had not, like real Mohammedans, made an act of decision and submitted to fate out of free will. On the contrary, they were people that were so deprived of affect, self-esteem, and every form of stimulation, so totally exhausted, both physically and emotionally, that they had given the environment total power over them. (Bettelheim, 1960, pp. 151–152)

Seligman (1975) recounts a story told to him about a tough marine corporal who was a prisoner in a North Vietnamese POW camp. The North Vietnamese had a practice of releasing Americans from their POW camps from time to time if they had proven themselves as "model prisoners." This marine survived the brutal conditions of the POW camp by holding on to the hope that if he worked hard and cooperated he would win such a release. He submitted to forced labor and carried loads of rocks on his back barefoot without complaining. He gratefully ate his daily ration of vermin-infested rice and dutifully followed his captors' orders. His faith that hard work and stoicism would result in freedom kept him alive. After several years in the POW camp this marine faced the harsh truth that the North Vietnamese had no intention of letting him go. His attempt to gain freedom by being a model prisoner was wasted. He became depressed, stopped eating, and refused to get out of bed. His fellow prisoners tried to help by giving him care and nurturance. When that didn't work, they attempted to pull him out of his depression by using physical force. It became clear that he had lost all sense of control over his life and within a few weeks he was dead.

The above examples of helplessness are extreme, but they relate to the theme of this book because they demonstrate the importance of finding ways of maintaining a sense of mastery and self-efficacy in our lives. It is true that people who are prisoners or who are afflicted with a terminal illness have little power over matters of life and death. However, as copers these people seek other ways to exercise self-efficacy by using their minds, thoughts, dreams, and hopes. The purpose of learning the coping skills described in this book is to develop tools to fall back on when things get tough. When faced with difficult life challenges we can use our problem-solving skills to sort out our goals and decide which coping skills will help us to hold our own and make the best out of this experience.

SELF-PRESERVATION

Human beings have a remarkable capacity for adapting to difficult situations. We saw many examples in Chapters 13 and 14 of how people survived tragedies, disasters, and threats to their health. They did this by finding ways to overcome feelings of helplessness. People who are survivors have learned how to use coping skills such as those described in this book. They have also developed a life philosophy oriented toward self-preservation. Self-preservation is the opposite of helplessness. It involves approaching life in ways that bolster feelings of self-efficacy, mastery, and control. It will be useful to look at the research on self-preservation and learn how it can be employed as a coping skill.

Coping with Victimization

Shelley Taylor and her colleagues studied responses of people who were victims of negative life events and arrived at a number of conclusions that have important implications for self-preservation as a coping strategy (Taylor & Brown, 1988; Taylor, Wood, & Lichtman, 1983). People for the most part don't want to feel like victims. Taking on the role of a victim means focusing on suffering and reminding ourselves of our inability to prevent the cause of our victimization. Seeing oneself as a victim lowers self-esteem because victims are often stigmatized as people who can't care for themselves.

Because seeing oneself as a victim often has negative implications, people who have suffered harm are inclined to protect themselves by interpreting their victimization in a manner that will protect their self-esteem. This is done in the following ways:

Comparing oneself with less fortunate others: Like the cancer patients who were described in Chapter 13, some victims maintain their identity as effective people by comparing themselves with others who are less fortunate. No matter how bad the situation, there is always someone who is worse off. It is tempting to view our suffering as unique and more terrible than anybody else's. However, this kind of thinking is likely to make us feel like a victim who is passive and depressed. Recognizing that there are people who are less fortunate gives us a more positive attitude toward our lives.

Seeing the positive side: Victims often overcome helplessness by feeling thankful that things are not worse. It is ironic to think of a victim as being thankful. Yet, seeing the positive side that our suffering is not as bad as it could have been helps us maintain our optimism and hope.

Using victimization as a learning experience: Another way some victims overcome helplessness is by appreciating what they learned as a result of their negative experience. Traumatic events give us an opportunity to discover new sides of ourselves, to reevaluate our life priorities, and to interact with others in a mutually supportive manner. It is unfortunate that it sometimes takes a catastrophic event to force people to take an honest look at themselves. On the other hand, it is a tribute to the human capacity for self-preservation that people are able to gain new meanings even from terrible experiences.

Finding strength in being a survivor: It is easier to cope with being a victim when we find strength in being a survivor. It boosts our self-esteem to recognize that we are handling the situation better than others.

Self-Preservation as a Way of Looking at Life

People who are copers have learned how to look at life in ways that enhance their feelings of self-preservation. Looking at life as a coper means finding the right balance between realism and optimism in how we view ourselves, our control over our environment, and our future (Taylor & Brown, 1988):

Viewing ourselves: You have learned from reading this book that being a good coper means not being too hard on yourself. When there is a choice between focusing on our faults or appreciating our virtues, it is usually more adaptive to appreciate our virtues. Appreciating our virtues doesn't mean that we should be grandiose and blind to our shortcomings. It means taking a balanced view of our strengths and weaknesses, but not bringing ourselves down by focusing on our imperfections.

Viewing our control over the environment: There are some events in our lives that we realistically cannot control and it would be foolish to believe otherwise. However, even when faced with uncontrollable events, there is always some way of exercising mastery. Although we may not be able to change the life event, we can always control how we think and how we react. Copers overcome helplessness by not insisting on controlling things they can't. When faced with difficult challenges they use their problem-solving skills to identify some piece or aspect of this life event where they can take charge and feel competent.

Viewing our future: Copers are future-oriented. Negative experiences in the past cannot be undone, but there is always hope for better times in the future. The future provides an opportunity for using our learning experiences and coping skills to improve in relation to past mistakes and to experience satisfaction. Looking forward to the future inspires hope and optimism about new opportunities for exercising mastery and competence.

COPING AS A SELF-FULFILLING PROPHECY

Viewing ourselves as copers is a self-fulfilling prophecy. When we expect ourselves to use good coping skills, we are more likely to do so. Check whether you agree or disagree with the following statements.

	Strongly agree	Agree	Disagree	Strongly disagree
1. In uncertain times, I usually expect the best.	____	____	____	____

	Strongly agree	Agree	Disagree	Strongly disagree
2. I always look on the bright side of things.	____	____	____	____
3. I'm always optimistic about the future.	____	____	____	____
4. I'm a believer in the idea that "every cloud has a silver lining."	____	____	____	____
5. If something can go wrong for me, it will.	____	____	____	____
6. I hardly ever expect things to go my way.	____	____	____	____
7. Things never work out the way I want them to.	____	____	____	____
8. I rarely count on good things happening to me.	____	____	____	____

These statements come from the Life Orientation Test, which measures people's positive expectancies and general feelings of optimism (Scheier & Carver, 1985). Optimists agree with statements 1 through 4 and disagree with statements 5 through 8. Research indicates that optimists make use of adaptive coping skills, such as problem solving and building support systems (see Chapter 3). Optimists also focus on achieving their goals in the face of hindrances and distractions. Because their energies are devoted to developing self-efficacy, optimists have positive expectations about the future. As a result of their more effective coping skills, they suffer less from life stresses and have fewer physical and psychological complaints than pessimists (Reker & Wong, 1985; Scheier & Carver, 1985; Scheier, Weintraub, & Carver, 1986).

In contrast to optimists, pessimists cope less adaptively by focusing on negative feelings, withdrawing, and avoiding. The kinds of negative thinking engaged in by pessimists causes a number of potential problems (Goodhart, 1985). For example:

Negative thinking interferes with selection of effective coping strategies.
Negative thinking lowers self-esteem.
Negative thinking reinforces feelings of vulnerability.
Negative thinking causes increased stress.

Another way to understand the difference between optimists and pessimists is by looking at how they view their lives in terms of three dimensions that were discussed in Chapter 5: stability, globality, and internality.

Stability versus instability: An attitude of stability means that we think that things in our lives are predetermined and that there is not much we can do about them. An attitude of instability means that we believe events in our lives can change. Things won't always be the way they are now.

Globality versus specificity: Globality describes the attitude that a single experience can affect our entire life. Specificity means putting things into perspective. When we believe in specificity we realize we will have good and bad experiences throughout our lives and that we don't have to be overwhelmed by any of them.

Internality versus externality: This lifestyle was explained in Chapter 3. An attitude of internality encourages us to take responsibility for getting what we need out of life. An attitude of externality places us in a more passive role because we give the world more control over our destiny.

Researchers have found that people who view the world with a generally pessimistic outlook are characterized by attitudes of stability, globality, and externality and often have poorer health than those who are more optimistic with attitudes of instability, specificity, and internality (Peterson, 1988; Peterson & Seligman, 1987). It has also been found that men who expressed attitudes of stability, globality, and externality in college had poorer physical health 20 to 40 years later than did men whose attitudes in college were oriented toward instability, specificity, and internality (Peterson, Seligman, & Vaillant, 1988). This finding is important because it suggests that attitudes of pessimism and optimism can have a direct influence on physical health.

Viewing ourselves as copers provides a boost to our self-esteem. Self-esteem is a durable source of strength because we carry it around with us. We can use our feelings of self-worth and competence to cope with life challenges even when other avenues of support are not available (Hobfoll & Leiberman, 1987).

THE IMPORTANCE OF HOPE

Most of us are reminded about the harsh realities of life on a daily basis. We need to maintain a sense of reality to cope with the hassles that confront us. However, it also helps to nurture an attitude of hope—a belief that somehow we can make things turn out OK. Check how much you agree or disagree with the following statements:

	Strongly agree	Agree	Disagree	Strongly disagree
1. I can think of many ways to get out of a jam.	____	____	____	____
2. Even when others get discouraged, I know I can find a way to solve the problem.	____	____	____	____
3. There are lots of ways around any problem.	____	____	____	____
4. I can think of many ways to get things in life that are important to me.	____	____	____	____
5. I've been pretty successful in my life.	____	____	____	____
6. My past experiences have prepared me well for the future.	____	____	____	____

	Strongly agree	Agree	Disagree	Strongly disagree
7. I meet the goals I set for myself.	_____	_____	_____	_____
8. I energetically pursue my goals.	_____	_____	_____	_____

These statements come from the Hope Scale (Snyder, 1989). The Hope Scale is a good predictor of physical and mental health because it assesses two qualities that are essential for getting needs met. Statements 1 through 4 measure our flexibility in finding *pathways* for getting what we want. Statements 5 through 8 measure how positive we are about our ability to *attain* our goals. Good copers take responsibility to pursue their goals actively, and they are open to finding the best coping strategies.

TAKING APPROPRIATE RESPONSIBILITY

Taking appropriate responsibility means taking charge of things we can control in our lives without suffering needless stress and self-blame for life events beyond our control. Table 15.1 outlines four models applying to life events where we are either responsible or not responsible for: (1) the cause of the problem and (2) the solution for the problem (Brickman et al., 1982).

Moral Model

In the moral model, we are responsible for a problem's cause and solution. Some examples of problems fitting the moral model are:

Doing poorly on a test because we didn't study hard enough
Someone's being angry because we behaved badly
Failing to engage in good health practices
Failing to make constructive plans for our future

In the moral model it is up to us to assert ourselves and make an active effort to do what is in our best interest. We follow the moral model when it is appropriate for us to take care of ourselves.

Enlightenment Model

The enlightenment model holds us responsible for a problem's cause but not for its solution. Some examples of the enlightenment model are:

Using our support system
Finding support in organized religion
Participating in individual or group therapy

The enlightenment model applies to problems we might have caused but that are best solved with the help of others. Some examples of these problems include alcohol and drug abuse and eating disorders. We follow the enlightenment model when we realize it is not in our best interest to isolate ourselves and that we can benefit by using help from others.

TABLE 15.1   Four Models of Responsibility

Responsibility for problem	Responsibility for solution	
	High	Low
High	Moral model	Enlightment model
Low	Compensatory model	Medical model

From "Models of Helping and Coping" by P. Brickman, V. C. Rabinowitz, J. Karuza, D. Coates, E. Cohen, and L. Kidder, 1982, *American Psychologist, 37,* 368–384. Copyright 1982 by the American Psychological Association. Adapted with permission.

Compensatory Model

The compensatory model applies to problems that we didn't cause but that we must solve. Some examples of the compensatory model are:

Rehabilitating ourselves after an injury or illness
Pursuing an education
Bargaining, negotiating, and being assertive
Coping with catastrophes and disasters
Learning new skills

The compensatory model encourages us to take an active role in solving problems without blaming ourselves for their cause.

Medical Model

The medical model is relevant for problems we didn't cause and that we can't solve. This model is called the medical model because it applies primarily to illnesses and injuries where we must depend on trained professionals for assistance. We also follow the medical model when we pay an expert for a consultation or to provide services we can't do ourselves. The medical model encourages us to rely on others for assistance without feeling weak or guilty because we can't solve the problem on our own.

These four models of responsibility are valuable because they can help us sort out the best strategies for dealing with problems in our lives. We can see how rigidly following only one or two of these models can result in needless guilt and self-blame (for example, by leaning inappropriately on others) or loneliness and alienation (for example, by trying to solve everything for ourselves).

BEING A WELL-ROUNDED PERSON

It is easier to be a good coper when we are well rounded. Being a well-rounded person means having a multidimensional identity, being flexible, and taking an interest in others.

Having a Multidimensional Identity

Having a multidimensional identity is a valuable coping skill (Linville, 1987). People who have a one-dimensional view of themselves are very limited. They don't have a broad foundation of personal resources to fall back on when facing difficult challenges. For example, an athlete who bases his full identity on being a jock will find it difficult to maintain a sense of personal effectiveness when his athletic career is over. A businessperson who puts her entire life into her position will feel at a loss when she reaches the top and has no more competitive challenges. People who put the bulk of their self-value in raising children lose their sense of purpose when their children grow up and leave home to pursue their own lives. And lovers who derive all of their self-esteem from a single person feel empty and worthless when the love relationship ends.

Good copers have a life philosophy of developing their personal identity along many dimensions. It is important to learn how to gain a sense of self-fulfillment in more than one area of life. We need to pursue life activities that will give us many interests. That way, if one part of our life is challenged we will have other dimensions of self-identity to rely on for feelings of self-esteem, mastery, and competence.

Being Flexible

Good copers have learned how to be flexible in their thinking and in their actions.

Thinking Flexibly

We were urged in Chapter 11 to be flexible in our perceptions about what it means to grow old and to avoid the self-fulfilling prophecy that aging means going downhill. This advice about thinking flexibly applies not only to aging. When we find ourselves in a situation that is not in our best interest, it doesn't have to be that way. Of course, refusing to accept roles that are expected of us and getting out of harmful relationships requires pain and effort. We must sometimes decide whether it is worth suffering in the short run for the sake of being satisfied with ourselves in the long run. Being a flexible thinker means we are at least willing to consider this choice. To live our lives with a sense of competence and self-esteem is often difficult, but it is a *possibility*.

Acting Flexibly

To be flexible in our actions, we must have a large arsenal of coping skills and know how to use them appropriately in challenging situations (Paulhus & Martin, 1988). For example, when faced with a challenge, we will have a variety of responses at our disposal. Think about the ways you have already mastered in relating to people: being assertive, nurturant, or sympathetic; being a leader; being a follower; being a talker; being a listener; expressing anger; expressing consideration; bargaining; and compromising. You also know how to use coping skills such as those discussed in this book. Being competent in all of these ways of facing challenges and relating to people provides a feeling of self-confidence. It is reassuring to have more than one option when confronted with a problem to solve.

We know we can skillfully match the coping strategies and interpersonal skills we have mastered to the situation—and we are not afraid to use them. We are not restricted by responding to all challenges in the same manner.

Taking an Interest in Others

We become severely limited when we spend a lot of time thinking and worrying about ourselves. Too much self focus causes us to avoid valuable experiences because we are preoccupied with guarding our self-esteem. When, on the other hand, we devote time and energy to others, we are less apt to ruminate about our own problems. We find ourselves taking a more active role in life, and as a result, we become healthier and happier people (Crandall, 1980, 1984; Crandall & Putman, 1980).

Choosing Healthy Friendships

Everyone is familiar with the admonition that people are judged by their choice of friends. However, we often overlook the benefits we gain by associating with good role models. It is much more uplifting when we are in jeopardy to have friends who are examples of adaptive rather than maladaptive coping. Being a well-rounded person means taking control over our lives by associating with people whose lifestyles have a positive impact (Taylor & Lobel, 1989).

RAISING CHILDREN TO BE COPERS

One of the best ways to master new ideas, concepts, and skills is to teach them to someone else. You might find it useful to put together what you have learned in this book by considering what it takes to grow up as a person who knows how to cope with life challenges. A good place to start is by looking at coping from its opposite extreme. How could you raise a child to be incompetent and helpless? One way is by raising a child in a world where he or she has little or no opportunity to experience success. Although, hopefully, you would not want to do this, it is clear that many children grow up just this way. Children who are not prepared with the fundamentals they need for school fall behind and come to see themselves as "slow," "dumb," or "learning disabled." Children who grow up in poverty have little opportunity for experiencing mastery and competence, unless it is by engaging in activities that are antisocial or illegal. Kenneth Clark (1964) provides the following description of helplessness in the poverty of Harlem:

> In short, the Harlem ghetto is the institutionalization of powerlessness. Harlem is made up of the socially engendered ferment, resentment, stagnation, and potentially explosive reactions to powerlessness and continued abuses. The powerless individual and community reflect this fact by increasing dependency and by difficulty in mobilizing even the latent power to counter the most flagrant abuses. Immobility, stagnation, apathy, indifference, and defeatism are among the more obvious consequences of personal and community impotence. Random hostility, aggression, self-hatred, suspiciousness, seething turmoil, and chronic personal and social tensions also reflect self-destructive and non-adaptive reactions to a pervasive sense and fact of powerlessness. (Clark, in Seligman, 1975, pp. 160–161)

After considering the above description and the lessons you have learned in this book, it should be easy to appreciate the value of providing children with opportunities for experiencing self-efficacy, competence, and mastery. Children need to explore, to try things out, and to learn that they can have an effect on their social and physical environment.

Another way to teach children to be helpless is by making things too easy for them. Human beings need challenges to master and obstacles to overcome. It is through this process that they learn how to set meaningful goals and develop an ability to tolerate failure. Our fast-food–quick-fix society encourages helplessness by making life simple, shallow, and easy (Skinner, 1986). If we want entertainment we flip on the TV or read magazines that don't require much thought or concentration. If we are hungry we indulge in frozen dinners. It takes a concerted effort to maintain a sense of self-efficacy and competence by pursuing hobbies, interests, and activities that require self-discipline and practice. Being a competent person in our society means spending the time to develop our own sense of self-sufficiency and individuality. Children need good role models to teach them how to grow into well-rounded adults.

Children become copers by learning how to use coping skills such as those described in this book. When faced with life challenges, children can be taught to take responsibility for finding the best solution. A problem-solving orientation toward problems is a healthy substitute for throwing tantrums or giving up.

THE BENEFITS OF BEING A COPER

Being a coper means making the effort to learn and practice coping skills such as those taught in this book. Copers face challenges with perseverance. When they can't control difficult situations, they work on their own strategies, thinking styles, and emotional reactions. A coping attitude toward life provides copers with a heightened sense of competence and self-efficacy. But it requires personal energy. Is it worth the effort?

We can reach the following conclusions about the benefits of being a coper from a research review completed by Albert Bandura (1989):

1. Copers set high goals because they know how to use problem-solving skills when things get tough.
2. Because copers have learned how to put self-doubts into perspective, they are able to stay focused on the challenges before them.
3. Copers find strength in visualizing their possibilities for success.
4. The skills mastered by copers give them confidence to persevere and not to settle for mediocre outcomes.
5. Copers are future-oriented. They know how to make long-term plans by delaying immediate gratifications.
6. Copers know how to reward themselves for success.
7. Because of their problem-solving attitude, copers are less troubled by physical and emotional stress.

A coping attitude is a philosophy that says life will not always be the way we want it to be, but our coping skills can help us make the best of it.

SUGGESTIONS FOR FURTHER READING

ELLIS, A. (1971). *Growth through reason*. North Hollywood, Calif.: Wilshire Books.

ELLIS, A., & BECKER, I. (1982). *A guide to personal happiness*. North Hollywood, Calif.: Wilshire Books.

KLEINKE, C. L. (1978). *Self-perception: The psychology of personal awareness*. New York: W. H. Freeman.

KLINGER, E. (1975). *Meaning and void: Inner experience and the incentives in people's lives*. Minneapolis: University of Minnesota Press.

LAZARUS, A. A., & FAY, A. (1975). *I can if I want to*. New York: Morrow.

SELIGMAN, M. E. P. (1975). *Helplessness: On depression, development, and death*. New York: W. H. Freeman.

TAYLOR, S. E. (1989). *Positive illusions: Creative self-deception and the healthy mind*. New York: Basic Books.

References

••

ABBEY, A. (1982). Sex differences in attributions for friendly behavior: Do males misperceive females' friendliness? *Journal of Personality and Social Psychology, 42,* 830–838.

ABBEY, A. (1987). Misperceptions of friendly behavior as sexual interest: A survey of naturally occurring incidents. *Psychology of Women Quarterly, 11,* 173–194.

ADAMS, H. E., FEUERSTEIN, M., & FOWLER, J. L. (1980). Migraine headache: Review of parameters, etiology, and intervention. *Psychological Bulletin, 87,* 217–237.

ALDEN, L., & CAPPE, R. (1986). Interpersonal process training for shy clients. In W. H. Jones, J. M. Cheek, & S. R. Briggs (Eds.), *Shyness: Perspectives on research and treatment* (pp. 343–355). New York: Plenum.

AMERICAN CANCER SOCIETY. (1985). *Cancer facts and figures 1985.* New York: American Cancer Society.

AMERICAN PSYCHIATRIC ASSOCIATION. (1986). *Diagnostic and statistical manual of mental disorders* (3rd ed.). Washington, D.C.: American Psychiatric Association.

ANDERSEN, S. M., & WILLIAMS, M. (1985). Cognitive/affective reaction in the improvement of self-esteem: When thoughts and feelings make a difference. *Journal of Personality and Social Psychology, 49,* 1086–1097.

ANDERSON, C. A. (1983). Motivational and performance deficits in interpersonal settings: The effect of attributional style. *Journal of Personality and Social Psychology, 45,* 1136–1147.

ANDERSON, C. A., & ARNOULT, L. H. (1985). Attributional style and everyday problems in living: Depression, loneliness, and shyness. *Social Cognition, 3,* 16–35.

ANDERSON, C. A., HOROWITZ, L. M., & FRENCH, R. DES. (1983). Attributional style of lonely and depressed people. *Journal of Personality and Social Psychology, 45,* 127–136.

ANDERSON, K. O., & MASUR, F. T. (1983). Psychological preparation for invasive medical and dental procedures. *Journal of Behavioral Medicine, 6,* 1–40.

ANDRASIK, F., BLANCHARD, E. B., NEFF, D. F., & RODICHOK, L. D. (1984). Biofeedback and relaxation training for chronic headache: A controlled comparison of booster treatments and regular contacts for long-term maintainence. *Journal of Consulting and Clinical Psychology, 52,* 609–615.

ARKIN, R. M., & BAUMGARDNER, A. H. (1985). Self-handicapping. In J. H. Harvey & G. Weary (Eds.), *Attribution: Basic issues and applications* (pp. 169–202). New York: Academic Press.

ARKIN, R. M., LAKE, E. A., & BAUMGARDNER, A. H. (1986). Shyness and self-presentation. In W. H. Jones, J. M. Cheek, & S. R. Briggs (Eds.), *Shyness: Perspectives on research and treatment* (pp. 189–203). New York: Plenum.

ATKESON, B., CALHOUN, K., RESICK, P., & ELLIS, B. (1982). Victims of rape: Repeated assessment of depressive symptoms. *Journal of Consulting and Clinical Psychology, 50,* 96–102.

ATKINSON, J. W. (1957). Motivational determinants of risk-taking behavior. *Psychological Review, 64,* 359–372.

ATKINSON, J. W. (1964). *An introduction to motivation.* New York: Van Nostrand.

ATONOVSKY, A. (1979). *Health, stress and coping.* San Francisco: Jossey-Bass.

AVERILL, J. R. (1979). Anger. In H. Howe & R. Dienstbier (Eds.), *Nebraska symposium on motivation* (Vol. 26, pp. 1–80). Lincoln: University of Nebraska Press.

AVERILL, J. R. (1983). Studies on anger and aggression: Implications for theories of emotion. *American Psychologist, 38,* 1145–1160.

AVORN, J., & LANGER, E. J. (1982). Induced disability in nursing home patients: A controlled trial. *Journal of the American Geriatrics Society, 30,* 397–400.

BANDURA, A. (1977). Self-efficacy: Toward a unifying theory of behavioral change. *Psychological Review, 84,* 191–215.

BANDURA, A. (1989). Human agency in social cognitive theory. *American Psychologist, 44,* 1175–1184.

BANDURA, A., ADAMS, N. E., & BEYER, J. (1977). Cognitive processes mediating behavioral change. *Journal of Personality and Social Psychology, 35,* 125–139.

BANDURA, A., & CERVONE, D. (1983). Self-evaluative and self-efficacy mechanisms governing the motivational effects of goal systems. *Journal of Personality and Social Psychology, 45,* 1017–1028.

BANDURA, A., O'LEARY, A. O., TAYLOR, C. B., GAUTHIER, J., & GOSSARD, D. (1987). Perceived self-efficacy and pain control: Opioid and nonopioid mechanisms. *Journal of Personality and Social Psychology, 53,* 563–571.

BANDURA, A., REESE, L., & ADAMS, N. E. (1982). Microanalysis of action and arousal as a function of differential levels of perceived self-efficacy. *Journal of Personality and Social Psychology, 43,* 5–21.

BANDURA, A., & SCHUNK, D. H. (1981). Cultivating competence, self-efficacy, and intrinsic interest through proximal self-motivation. *Journal of Personality and Social Psychology, 41,* 586–598.

BARBER, T. X., SPANOS, N. P., & CHAVES, J. F. (1974). *Hypnotism, imagination, and human potentialities.* New York: Pergamon Press.

BARNETT, P. A., & GOTLIB, I. H. (1988). Psychosocial functioning and depression: Distinguishing among antecedents, concomitants, and consequences. *Psychological Bulletin, 104,* 97–126.

BARON, R. A., & BYRNE, D. (1987). *Social psychology.* Boston: Allyn & Bacon.

BARTLETT, J. (1982). *Familiar quotations.* Boston: Little, Brown.

BATCHELOR, W. F. (1988). AIDS 1988: The science and the limits of science. *American Psychologist, 43,* 853–858.

BAUM, A. (1988, April). Disasters, natural & otherwise. *Psychology Today,* pp.56–60.

BAUM, A., AIELLO, J., & CALESNICK, L. (1978). Crowding and personal control: Social density and the development of learned helplessness. *Journal of Personality and Social Psychology, 36,* 1000–1011.

BAUM, A., & DAVIS, G. (1980). Reducing the stress of high-density living: An architectural intervention. *Journal of Personality and Social Psychology, 38,* 471–481.

BAUM, A., FISHER, J., & SOLOMON, S. (1981). Type of information, familiarity, and the reduction of crowding stress. *Journal of Personality and Social Psychology, 40,* 11–23.

BAUM, A., FLEMMING, R., & SINGER, J. E. (1983). Coping with victimization by technological disaster. *Journal of Social Issues, 39,* 119–140.

BAUM, A., & GATCHEL, R. J. (1981). Cognitive determinants of reaction to uncontrollable events: Development of reactance and learned helplessness. *Journal of Personality and Social Psychology, 40,* 1078–1089.

BAUM, A., GATCHEL, R. J., & SCHAEFFER, M. A. (1983). Emotional, behavioral, and physiological effects of chronic stress at Three Mile Island. *Journal of Consulting and Clinical Psychology, 51,* 565–572.

BAUM, A., & NESSELHOF, S. E. A. (1988). Psychological research and the prevention, etiology, and treatment of AIDS. *American Psychologist, 43,* 900–906.

BAUMEISTER, R. F., & SCHER, S. J. (1988). Self-defeating behavior patterns among normal individuals: Review and analysis of common self-destructive tendencies. *Psychological Bulletin, 104,* 3–22.

BAUMGARDNER, A. H., HEPPNER, P. P., & ARKIN, R. M. (1986). Role of causal attribution in personal problem solving. *Journal of Personality and Social Psychology, 50,* 636–643.

BAZERMAN, M. H. (1986, June). Why negotiations go wrong. *Psychology Today,* pp. 54–58.

BECK, A. T. (1979). *Cognitive therapy and the emotional disorders.* New York: International Universities Press.

BECK, A. T., & EMERY, G. (1985). *Anxiety disorders and phobias.* New York: Basic Books.

BECK, A. T., EPSTEIN, N., BROWN, G., & STEER, R. A. (1988). An inventory for measuring clinical anxiety: Psychometric properties. *Journal of Consulting and Clinical Psychology, 56,* 893–897.

BECK, A. T., RUSH, A. J., SHAW, B. F., & EMERY, G. (1979). *Cognitive therapy of depression.* New York: Guilford.

BECK, A.T., WEISSMAN, A., LESTER, D., & TREXLER, L. (1974). The measurement of pessimism: The hopelessness scale. *Journal of Consulting and Clinical Psychology, 42,* 861–865.

BECKER, E. (1973). *The denial of death.* New York: Free Press.

BENSON, H. (1976). *The relaxation response.* New York: Avon.

BERGLAS, S., & JONES, E. E. (1978). Drug choice as a self-handicapping strategy in response to noncontingent success. *Journal of Personality and Social Psychology, 36,* 405–407.

BERSCHEID, E., & FEI, J. (1986). Romantic love and sexual jealousy. In G. Clanton & L. G. Smith (Eds.), *Jealousy* (pp. 101–109). Lanham, Md.: University Press of America.

BETTELHEIM, B. (1943). Individual and mass behavior in extreme situations. *Journal of Abnormal and Social Psychology, 38,* 417–452.

BETTELHEIM, B. (1960). *The informed heart—Autonomy in a mass age.* Glencoe, Ill.: Free Press.

BILLINGS, A. G., & MOOS, R. H. (1981). The role of coping responses and social resources in attenuating the stress of life events. *Journal of Behavioral Medicine, 4,* 139–157.

BILLINGS, A. G., & MOOS, R. H. (1985). Life stressors and social resources affect posttreatment outcomes among depressed patients. *Journal of Abnormal Psychology, 94,* 140–153.

BLANCHARD, E. B., ANDRASIK, F., AHLES, T. A., TEDERS, S. J., & O'KEEFE, D. (1980). Migraine and tension headache: A meta-analytic review. *Behavior Therapy, 11,* 613–631.

BLANCHARD, E. B., ANDRASIK, F., NEFF, D. F., ARENA, J. G., AHLES, T. A., JURISH, S. E., PALLMEYER, T. P., SAUNDERS, N. L., TEDERS, S. J., BARRON, K. D., & RODICHOK, L. D. (1982). Biofeedback and relaxation training with three kinds of headache: Treatment effects and their prediction. *Journal of Consulting and Clinical Psychology, 50,* 562–575.

BLANCHARD, E. B., ANDRASIK, F., NEFF, D. F., SAUNDERS, N. L., ARENA, J. G. PALLMEYER, T. P., TEDERS, S. J., & JURISH, S. E., (1983). Four process studies in the behavioral treatment of chronic headache. *Behaviour Research and Therapy, 21,* 1–12.

BLANKSTEIN, K. R., TONER, B. B., & FLETT, G. L. (1989). Test anxiety and the contents of consciousness: Thought-listing and endorsement measures. *Journal of Research in Personality, 23,* 269–286.

BLATT, S. J., QUINLAN, D. M., CHEVRON, E. S., & MCDONALD, C. (1982). Dependency and self-criticism: Psychological dimensions of depression. *Journal of Consulting and Clinical Psychology, 50,* 113–124.

BLOCK, A. R. (1982). Multidisciplinary treatment of chronic low back pain: A review. *Rehabilitation Psychology, 27,* 51–63.

BLUMBERG, S. R., & HOKANSON, J. E. (1983). The effects of another person's response style on interpersonal behavior in depression. *Journal of Abnormal Psychology, 92,* 196–209.

BLUMER, D., & HEILBRONN, M. (1982). Chronic pain as a variant of depressive disease. *Journal of Nervous and Mental Disease, 170,* 381–406.

BONICA, J. J., & BLACK, R. G. (1974). The management of a pain clinic. In M. Swerdlow (Ed.), *Relief of intractable pain* (pp. 116–129). Amsterdam: Excerpta Medica.

BRADBURN, N. (1969). *The structure of well-being.* Chicago: Aldine.

BRADBURY, T. N., & FINCHAM, F. D. (1987). Affect and cognition in close relationships: Towards an integrative model. *Cognition and Emotion, 1,* 59–87.

BRADBURY, T. N., & FINCHAM, F. D. (1988). Individual difference variables in close relationships: A contextual model of marriage as an integrative framework. *Journal of Personality and Social Psychology, 54,* 713–721.

BRAGINSKY, B., & BRAGINSKY, D. (1967). Schizophrenic patients in the psychiatric interview: An experimental study of their effectiveness at manipulation. *Journal of Consulting Psychology, 31,* 546–551.

BRAGINSKY, B., BRAGINSKY, D., & RING, K. (1969). *Methods of madness: The mental hospital as a last resort.* New York: Holt, Rinehart & Winston.

BRAGINSKY, D., GROSSE, M., & RING, K. (1966). Controlling outcomes through impression management: An experimental study of the manipulative tactics of mental patients. *Journal of Consulting Psychology, 30,* 295–300.

BRANTLEY, P. J., DIETZ, L. S., MCKNIGHT, G. T., JONES, G. N., TULLEY, R. (1988). Convergence between the Daily Stress Inventory and endocrine measures of stress. *Journal of Consulting and Clinical Psychology, 56,* 549–551.

BRANTLEY, P. J., WAGGONER, C. D., JONES, G. N., & RAPPAPORT, N. B. (1987). A daily stress inventory: Development, reliability, and validity. *Journal of Behavioral Medicine, 10,* 61–74.

BREHM, S. S. (1987). Coping after a relationship ends. In C. R. Snyder & C. E. Ford (Eds.), *Coping with negative life events* (pp. 191–212). New York: Plenum.

BRENDE, J. O., & PARSON, E. R. (1985). *Vietnam veterans: The road to recovery.* New York: Plenum.

BRICKMAN, P., & HENDRICKS, M. (1975). Expectancy for gradual or sudden improvement and reactions to success and failure. *Journal of Personality and Social Psychology, 32,* 893–900.

BRICKMAN, P., RABINOWITZ, V. C., KARUZA, J., COATES, D., COHN, E., & KIDDER, L. (1982). Models of helping and coping. *American Psychologist, 37,* 368–384.

BROOKS-GUNN, J., BOYER, C. B., & HEIN, K. (1988). Preventing HIV infection and AIDS in children and adolescents: Behavioral research and intervention strategies. *American Psychologist, 43,* 958–964.

BROWN, J. D., & SIEGEL, J. M. (1988a). Attributions for negative life events and depression: The role of perceived control. *Journal of Personality and Social Psychology, 54,* 316–322.

BROWN, J. D., & SIEGEL, J. M. (1988b). Exercise as a buffer of life stress: A prospective study of adolescent health. *Health Psychology, 7,* 341–353.

BROWN, K. G., & NICASSIO, P. M. (1987). Development of a questionnaire for the assessment of active and passive coping strategies in chronic pain patients. *Pain, 31,* 53–64.

BROWN, K. G., NICASSIO, P. M., & WALLSTON, K. A. (1989). Pain coping strategies and depression in rheumatoid arthritis. *Journal of Consulting and Clinical Psychology, 57,* 652–657.

BROWN, R. A., & LEWINSOHN, P. M. (1984). A psychoeducational approach to the treatment of depression: Comparison of group, individual, and minimal contact procedures. *Journal of Consulting and Clinical Psychology, 52,* 774–783.

BROWNMILLER, S. (1975). *Against our will: Men, women, and rape.* New York: Simon & Schuster.

BRUHN, J. G., & PHILLIPS, B. U. (1984). Measuring social support: A synthesis of current approaches. *Journal of Behavioral Medicine, 7,* 151–169.

BULMAN, R. J., & WORTMAN, C. B. (1977). Attributions of blame and coping in the "real world": Severe accident victims react to their lot. *Journal of Personality and Social Psychology, 35,* 351–363.

BURGESS, A., & HOLMSTROM, L. (1979). *Rape crisis and recovery.* Bowie, Md.: Brady.

BURNS, D. D. (1980). *Feeling good: The new mood therapy.* New York: Signet/New American Library.

BUSS, D. M., GOMES, M., HIGGINS, D. S., & LAUTERBACH, K. (1987). Tactics of manipulation. *Journal of Personality and Social Psychology, 52,* 1219–1229.

CANNON, W. B. (1929). *Bodily changes in pain, hunger, fear, and rage.* New York: Appleton.

CANNON, W. B. (1942). "Voodoo" death. *American Anthropologist, 44,* 169–181.

CANNON, W. B. (1957). "Voodoo" death. *Psychosomatic Medicine, 19,* 182–190.

CANTOR, N., NOREM, J. K., NIEDENTHAL, P. M., LANGSTON, C. A., & BROWER, A. M. (1987). Life tasks, self-concept ideals, and cognitive strategies in a life transition. *Journal of Personality and Social Psychology, 53,* 1178–1191.

CAPLAN, G. (1964). *Principles of preventive psychiatry.* New York: Basic Books.

CARVER, C. S., & SCHEIER, M. F. (1986). Analyzing shyness: A specific application of broader self-regulatory principles. In W. H. Jones, J. M. Cheek, & S. R. Briggs (Eds.), *Shyness: Perspectives on research and treatment* (pp. 173–185). New York: Plenum.

CHAMBLESS, D. L., & GRACELY, E. J. (1989). Fear of fear and the anxiety disorders. *Cognitive Therapy and Research, 13,* 9–20.

CHAPIN, M., & DYCK, D. G. (1976). Persistence in children's reading behavior as a function of N length and attribution retraining. *Journal of Personality and Social Psychology, 35,* 511–515.

CHAVES, J. F., & BARBER, T. X. (1974). Cognitive strategies, experimenter modeling, and expectation in the attenuation of pain. *Journal of Abnormal Psyhology, 83,* 356–363.

CHEEK, J. M., MELCHIOR, L. A., & CARPENTIERI, A. M. (1986). Shyness and self-concept. In L. M. Hartman & K. R. Blankstein (Eds.), *Perception of self in emotional disorder and psychotherapy* (pp. 113–131). New York: Plenum.

CLARK, K. A. (1964). *Youth in the ghetto: A study of the consequences of powerlessness and a blueprint for change.* New York: Haryou.

CLARK, M., & ANDERSON, B. C. (1967). *Culture and aging.* Springfield, Ill.: Charles C Thomas.

COGAN, R., COGAN, D., WALTZ, W., & MCCUE, M. (1987). Effect of laughter and relaxation on discomfort thresholds. *Journal of Behavioral Medicine, 10,* 139–144.

COHEN, D. R., SHERROD, D. R., & CLARK, M. S. (1986). Social skills and the stress-protective role of social support. *Journal of Personality and Social Psychology, 50,* 963–973.

COHEN, S., EVANS, G. W., STOKOLS, D., & KRANTZ, D. S. (1986). *Behavior, health, and environmental stress.* New York: Plenum.

COHEN, S., & SYME, L. (Eds.). (1984). *Social support and health.* New York: Academic Press.

COHEN, S., & WILLS, T. A. (1985). Stress, social support, and the buffering hypothesis. *Psychological Bulletin, 98,* 310–357.

COLLINS, D. L., BAUM, A., & SINGER, J. E. (1983). Coping with chronic stress at Three Mile

Island: Psychological and biochemical evidence. *Health Psychology, 2,* 149–166.

COLLINS, K. W., DANSEREAU, D. F., GARLAND, J. C., HOLLEY, C. D., & MCDONALD, B. A. (1981). Control of concentration during academic tasks. *Journal of Educational Psychology, 73,* 122–128.

CONGER, J. C., & FARRELL, A. D. (1981). Behavioral components of heterosocial skills. *Behavior Therapy, 12,* 41–55.

CONN, M. K., & PETERSON, C. (1989). Social support: Seek and ye shall find. *Journal of Social and Personal Relationships, 6,* 345–358.

COOPER, N. A., & CLUM, G. A. (1989). Imaginal flooding as a supplementary treatment for PTSD in combat veterans: A controlled study. *Behavior Therapy, 20,* 381–391.

COX, H. G. (1988). *Later life: The realities of aging.* Englewood Cliffs, N.J.: Prentice-Hall.

COX, H. G., SEKHON, G., & NORMAN, C. (1978). Social characteristics of the elderly in Indiana. *Proceedings/Indiana Academy of the Social Sciences* (Vol. 13, pp. 186–197).

COX, V. C., PAULUS, P. B., & MCCAIN, G. (1984). Prison crowding research. *American Psychologist, 39,* 1148–1160.

COYNE, J. C., & GOTLIB, I. H. (1983). The role of cognition in depression: A critical appraisal. *Psychological Bulletin, 94,* 472–505.

COYNE, J. C., KESSLER, R. C., TAL, M., TURNBULL, J., WORTMAN, C. B., & GREDEN, J. F. (1987). Living with a depressed person. *Journal of Consulting and Clinical Psychology, 55,* 347–352.

CRANDALL, J. E. (1980). Adler's concept of social interest: Theory, measurement, and implications for adjustment. *Journal of Personality and Social Psychology, 39,* 481–495.

CRANDALL, J. E. (1984). Social interest as a moderator of life stress. *Journal of Personality and Social Psychology, 47,* 164–174.

CRANDALL, J. E., & PUTMAN, E. L. (1980). Social interest and psychological well-being. *Journal of Individual Psychology, 36,* 151–168.

CROOK, J., RIDEOUT, E., & BROWNE, G. (1984). The prevalence of pain complaints in a general population. *Pain, 18,* 299–314.

CUNNINGHAM, M. (1989). Reactions to heterosexual opening lines: Female selectivity and male responsiveness. *Personality and Social Psychology Bulletin, 15,* 27–41.

CUTRONA, C. E. (1986). Objective determinants of perceived social support. *Journal of Personality and Social Psychology, 59,* 349–355.

DAKOF, G. A., & TAYLOR, S. E. (1990). Victim's perceptions of social support: What is helpful from whom? *Journal of Personality and Social Psychology, 58,* 80–89.

DAVIDSON, L. M., & BAUM, A. (1986). Chronic stress and posttraumatic stress disorders. *Journal of Consulting and Clinical Psychology, 54,* 303–308.

DAVIS, D., & HOLTGRAVES, T. (1984). Perceptions of unresponsive others: Attributions, attraction, understandability, and memory of their utterances. *Journal of Experimental Social Psychology, 20,* 383–408.

DAVIS, D., & PERKOWITZ, W. T. (1979). Consequences of responsiveness in dyadic interaction: Effects of probability of response and proportion of content-related responses on interpersonal attraction. *Journal of Personality and Social Psychology, 37,* 534–550.

DAVIS, K. (1986). Jealousy and sexual property. In G. Clanton & L. G. Smith (Eds.), *Jealousy* (pp. 129–134). Lanham, Md.: University Press of America.

DAVIS, M. H., & OATHOUT, H. A. (1987). Maintenance of satisfaction in romantic relationships: Empathy and relational competence. *Journal of Personality and Social Psychology, 53,* 397–410.

DEFFENBACHER, J. L. (1980). Worry and emotionality in test anxiety. In I. G. Sarason (Ed.), *Test anxiety: Theory, research, and applications* (pp. 111–128). Hillsdale, N.J.: Erlbaum.

DEFFENBACHER, J. L., DEMM, P. M., & BRANDON, A. D. (1986). High general anger: Correlates and treatment. *Behavior Research and Therapy, 24,* 481–489.

DEFFENBACHER, J. L., & SUINN, R. M. (1985). Concepts and treatment of the generalized anxiety syndrome. In L. M. Ascher & L. Michelson (Eds.), *International handbook of assessment and treatment of anxiety disorders.* New York: Guilford.

DEGREE, C. E., & SNYDER, C. R. (1985). Adler's psychology (of use) today: Personal history of traumatic life events as a self-handicapping strategy. *Journal of Personality and Social Psychology, 48,* 1512–1519.

DELONGIS, A., COYNE, J. C., DAKOF, G., FOLKMAN, S., & LAZARUS, R. S. (1982). Relationship of daily hassles, uplifts, and major life events to health status. *Health Psychology, 1,* 119–136.

DELONGIS, A., FOLKMAN, S., & LAZARUS, R. S. (1988). The impact of daily stress on health and mood: Psychological and social resources as mediators. *Journal of Personality and Social Psychology, 54,* 486–495.

DES JARLAIS, D. C., & FRIEDMAN, S. R. (1988). The psychology of preventing AIDS among intravenous drug users: A social learning conceptualization. *American Psychologist, 43,* 865–870.

DIENER, C. I., & DWECK, C. S. (1978). An analysis of learned helplessness: Continuous changes in performance, strategy, and achievement cognitions following failure. *Journal of Personality and Social Psychology, 36,* 451–462.

DIMSDALE, J. E. (1974). The coping behavior of Nazi concentration camp survivors. *American Journal of Psychiatry, 131,* 792–797.

DOHRENWEND, B. S., & DOHRENWEND, B. P. (Eds.). (1974). *Stressful life events: Their nature and effects.* New York: Wiley.

DOKA, K. J. (Ed.). (1989). *Disenfranchised grief: Recognizing hidden sorrow.* Lexington, Mass.: Lexington Books.

DOYNE, E. J., CHAMBLESS, D. L., & BEUTLER, L. E. (1983). Aerobic exercise as a treatment for depression in women. *Behavior Therapy, 14,* 434–440.

DREYER, P. H. (1989). Postretirement life satisfaction. In S. Spacapon & S. Oskamp (Eds.), *The social psychology of aging* (pp. 109–133). Newbury Park, Calif.: Sage.

DWECK, C. S. (1975). The role of expectations and attributions in the alleviation of learned helplessness. *Journal of Personality and Social Psychology, 31,* 674–685.

DWECK, C. S., & BUSH, E. S. (1976). Sex differences in learned helplessness: I. Differential debilitation with peer and adult evaluators. *Developmental Psychology, 12,* 147–156.

DWECK, C. S., DAVIDSON, W., NELSON, S., & ENNA, B. (1978). Sex differences in learned helplessness: II. The contingencies of evaluative feedback in the classroom. III. An experimental analysis. *Developmental Psychology, 14,* 268–276.

DWECK, C. S., & GILLIARD, D. (1975). Expectancy statements as determinants of reactions to failure: Sex differences in persistence and expectancy change. *Journal of Personality and Social Psychology, 32,* 1077–1084.

DWECK, C. S., GOETZ, T. E., & STRAUSS, N. L. (1980). Sex differences in learned helplessness: IV. An experimental and naturalistic study of failure generalization and its mediators. *Journal of Personality and Social Psychology, 38,* 441–452.

DWECK, C. S., & LEGGETT, E. L. (1988). A social-cognitive approach to motivation and personality. *Psychological Review, 95,* 256–273.

DWECK, C. S., & REPPUCCI, N. D. (1973). Learned helplessness and reinforcement responsibility in children. *Journal of Personality and Social Psychology, 25,* 109–116.

DYCK, D. G., VALLENTYNE, S., & BREEN, L. J. (1979). Duration of failure, causal attributions for failure, and subsequent reactions. *Journal of Experimental Social Psychology, 15,* 122–132.

D'ZURILLA, T. J., & NEZU, A. (1982). Social problem solving in adults. In P. C. Kendall (Ed.), *Advances in cognitive-behavioral research and therapy* (Vol. 1, pp. 202–274). New York: Academic Press.

EAVES, G., & RUSH, A. J. (1984). Cognitive patterns in symptomatic and remitted unipolar major depression. *Journal of Abnormal Psychology, 93,* 31–40.

EDELSON, R. I., & SEIDMAN, E. (1975). Use of videotaped feedback in altering interpersonal perceptions of married couples: A therapy analogue. *Journal of Consulting and Clinical Psychology, 43,* 244–250.

EHRLICH, P. (1988). Treatment issues in the psychotherapy of Holocaust survivors. In J. P. Wilson, Z. Harel, & B. Kahana (Eds.), *Human adaptation to extreme stress: From the Holocaust to Vietnam* (pp. 285–303). New York: Plenum.

EIDELSON, R. J., & EPSTEIN, N. (1982). Cognition and relationship maladjustment: Development of a measure of dysfunctional relationship beliefs. *Journal of Consulting and Clinical Psychology, 50,* 715–720.

EISLER, R. M., & FREDERIKSEN, L. W. (1980). *Perfecting social skills: A guide to interpersonal behavior.* New York: Plenum.

ELDER, G. H., JR., & CLIPP, E. C. (1988). Combat experience, comradeship, and psychological health. In J. P. Wilson, Z. Harel, & B. Kahana, (Eds.), *Human adaptation to extreme stress: From the Holocaust to Vietnam* (pp. 131–156). New York: Plenum.

ELDER, G. H., JR., & CLIPP, E. C. (1989). Combat experience and emotional health: Impairment and resilience in later life. *Journal of Personality, 57,* 311–341.

ELLIOTT, E. S., & DWECK, C. S. (1988). Goals: An approach to motivation and achievement. *Journal of Personality and Social Psychology, 54,* 5–12.

ELLIS, A. (1962). *Reason and emotion in psychotherapy.* New York: Lyle Stuart.

ELLIS, A. (1987). The impossibility of achieving consistently good mental health. *American Psychologist, 42,* 364–375.

ELLIS, A., & HARPER, R. A. (1975). *A new guide to rational living.* Englewood Cliffs, N.J.: Prentice-Hall.

ELLIS, E. M., ATKESON, B. M., & CALHOUN, K. S. (1981). An assessment of long-term reaction to rape. *Journal of Abnormal Psychology, 90,* 263–266.

EPICTETUS. (1899). *The works of Epictetus.* Boston: Little, Brown.

EPSTEIN, N., PRETZER, J. L., & FLEMING, B. (1987). The role of cognitive appraisal in self-reports of marital communication. *Behavior Therapy, 18,* 51–69.

ERIKSON, E. H. (1963). *Childhood and society* (2nd ed.). New York: Norton.

ERIKSON, J. M., ERIKSON, E. H., & KIVNICK, H. (1986). *Vital involvement in old age.* New York: Norton.

EWART, C. K., TAYLOR, C. B., KRAEMER, H. C., & AGRAS, W. S. (1984). Reducing blood pressure reactivity during interpersonal conflict: Effects of marital communication training. *Behavior Therapy, 15,* 473–484.

FALBO, T. (1977). Multidimensional scaling of power strategies. *Journal of Personality and Social Psychology, 35,* 537–547.

FARTHING, G. W., VENTURINO, M., & BROWN, S. W. (1984). Suggestion and distraction in the control of pain: Test of two hypotheses. *Journal of Abnormal Psychology, 93,* 266–276.

FELDMAN-SUMMERS, S., GORDON, P. E., & MEAGHER, J. R. (1979). The impact of rape on sexual satisfaction. *Journal of Abnormal Psychology, 88,* 101–105.

FELTON, B. J., & REVENSON, T. A. (1984). Coping with chronic illness: A study of illness controllability and the influence of coping strategies on psychological adjustment. *Journal of Consulting and Clinical Psychology, 52,* 343–353.

FINCHAM, F. D. (1985). Attribution processes in distressed and nondistressed couples: 2. Responsibility for marital problems. *Journal of Abnormal Psychology, 94,* 183–190.

FINCHAM, F. D., BEACH, S. R., & BAUCOM, D. H. (1987). Attribution processes in distressed and nondistressed couples: 4. Self-partner attribution differences. *Journal of Personality and Social Psychology, 52,* 739–748.

FINCHAM, F. D., BEACH, S. R., & NELSON, G. (1987). Attribution processes in distressed and nondistressed couples: 3. Causal and responsibility attributions for spouse behavior.

Cognitive Therapy and Research, 11, 71–86.

FINCHAM, F. D., & BRADBURY, T. N. (1988). The impact of attributions in marriage: Empirical and conceptual foundations. *British Journal of Clinical Psychology, 27,* 77–90.

FINCHAM, F. D., & O'LEARY, K. D. (1983). Causal inferences for spouse behavior in maritally distressed and nondistressed couples. *Journal of Social and Clinical Psychology, 1,* 42–57.

FISHER, J. D. (1988). Possible effects of reference group-based social influence on AIDS-risk behavior and AIDS prevention. *American Psychologist, 43,* 914–920.

FLORA, J. A., & THORESEN, C. E. (1988). Reducing the risk of AIDS in adolescents. *American Psychologist, 43,* 965–970.

FOLKINS, C. H., & SIME, W. E. (1981). Physical fitness training and mental health. *American Psychologist, 36,* 373–389.

FOLKMAN, S. (1984). Personal control and stress and coping processes: A theoretical analysis. *Journal of Personality and Social Psychology, 46,* 839–852.

FOLKMAN, S., & LAZARUS, R. S. (1980). An analysis of coping in a middle-aged community sample. *Journal of Health and Social Behavior, 21,* 219–239.

FOLKMAN, S., & LAZARUS, R. S. (1988). Coping as a mediator of emotion. *Journal of Personality and Social Psychology, 54,* 466–475.

FOLKMAN, S., LAZARUS, R. S., DUNKEL-SCHETTER, C., DELONGIS, A., & GRUEN, R. J. (1986). Dynamics of a stressful encounter: Cognitive appraisal, coping, and encounter outcomes. *Journal of Personality and Social Psychology, 50,* 992–1003.

FOLKMAN, S., LSAZARUS, R. S., GRUEN, R. J., & DELONGIS, A. (1986). Appraisal, coping, health status, and psychological symptoms. *Journal of Personality and Social Psychology, 50,* 571–579.

FOLLICK, M. J., AHERN, D. K., & ABERGER, E. W. (1985). Development of an audiovisual taxonomy of pain behavior: Reliability and discriminant validity. *Health Psychology, 4,* 555–568.

FOLLICK, M. J., AHERN, D. K., ATTANASIO, V., & RILEY, J. F. (1985). Chronic pain programs: Current aims, strategies, and needs. *Annals of Behavioral Medicine, 7,* 17–20.

FOLLICK, M. J., AHERN, D. K., & LASER-WOLSTON, N. (1984). Evaluation of a daily activity diary for chronic pain patients. *Pain, 19,* 373–382.

FONTANA, A. F., KLEIN, E. B., LEWIS, E., & LEVINE, L. (1968). Presentation of self in mental illness. *Journal of Consulting and Clinical Psychology, 32,* 110–119.

FORDYCE, W. E. (1976). *Behavioral methods in chronic pain and illness.* St. Louis: C. V. Mosby.

FORDYCE, W. E. (1988). Pain and suffering: A reappraisal. *American Psychologist, 43,* 276–283.

FORDYCE, W. E., BROCKWAY, J., BERGMAN, J. A., & SPENGLER, D. (1986). Acute back pain: A control-group comparison of behavioral vs. traditional management methods. *Journal of Behavioral Medicine, 9,* 127–140.

FORDYCE, W. E., LANSKE, D., CALSYN, D. A., SHELTON, J. L., STOLOV, W. C., & ROCK, D. L. (1984). Pain measurement and pain behavior. *Pain, 18,* 53–69.

FRANK, J. D. (1973). *Persuasion and healing* (rev. ed.). Baltimore, Md.: John Hopkins University Press.

FRANK, R. G., UMLAUF, R. L., WONDERLICH, S. A., ASKANAZI, G. S., BUCKELEW, S. P., & ELLIOTT, T. R. (1987). Differences in coping styles among persons with spinal cord injury: A cluster-analytic approach. *Journal of Consulting and Clinical Psychology, 55,* 727–731.

FUCH, C. Z., & REHM, L. P. (1977). A self-control behavior therapy program for depression. *Journal of Consulting and Clinical Psychology, 45,* 206–215.

GAELICK, L., BODENHAUSEN, G. V., & WYER, R. S., JR. (1985). Emotional communication in close relationships. *Journal of Personality and Social Psychology, 49,* 1246–1265.

GATCHEL, R. J., & BAUM, A. (1983). *An introduction to health psychology.* New York: Random House.

GILLILAND, B. E., & JAMES, R. K. (1988). *Crisis intervention strategies.* Pacific Grove, Calif.:

Brooks/Cole.

GLASS, C. R., & SHEA, C. A. (1986). Cognitive therapy for shyness and social anxiety. In W. H. Jones, J. .M. Cheek, & S. R. Briggs (Eds.), *Shyness: Perspectives on research and treatment* (pp. 315–327). New York: Plenum.

GLASS, D. C. (1976). *Behavior patterns, stress and coronary disease.* Hillsdale, N.J.: Erlbaum.

GLOVER, B., & SHEPARD, J. (1978). *Runner's training diary.* New York: Penguin.

GOLD, J. A., RYCKMAN, R. M., & MOSLEY, N. R. (1984). Romantic mood induction and attraction to a dissimilar other: Is love blind? *Personality and Social Psychology Bulletin, 10,* 358–368.

GOLDFRIED, M. R. (1971). Systematic desensitization as training in self-control. *Journal of Consulting and Clinical Psychology, 37,* 228–234.

GOLDFRIED, M. R., & DAVISON, G. C. (1976). *Clinical behavior therapy.* New York: Holt, Rinehart & Winston.

GOLDFRIED, M. R., DECENTECEO, E., & WEINBERG, L. (1974). Systematic rational restructuring as a self-control technique. *Behavior Therapy, 5,* 247–254.

GOLDFRIED, M. R., PADAWER, W., & ROBINS, C. (1984). Social anxiety and the semantic structure of heterosocial interactions. *Journal of Abnormal Psychology, 93,* 87–97.

GOLEMAN, D. (1985, April 16). Marriage: Research reveals ingredients of happiness. *New York Times,* p. 19.

GOODHART, D. E. (1985). Some psychological effects associated with positive and negative thinking about stressful event outcomes: Was Pollyanna right? *Journal of Personality and Social Psychology, 48,* 216–232.

GORDON, W. A., FREIDENBERGS, I., DILLER, L., HIBBARD, M., WOLF, C., LEVINE, L., LIPKINS, R., EZRACHI, O., & LUCIDO, D. (1980). Efficacy of psychosocial intervention with cancer patients. *Journal of Consulting and Clinical Psychology, 48,* 743–759.

GOSWICK, R. A., & JONES, W. H. (1981). Loneliness, self-concept, and adjustment. *Journal of Psychology, 107,* 237–240.

GOTLIB, I. H., & ROBINSON, L. A. (1982). Responses to depressed individuals: Discrepancies between self-report and observer-rated behavior. *Journal of Abnormal Psychology, 91,* 231–240.

GOTTMAN, J. G. (1979). *Empirical investigation of marriage.* New York: Academic Press.

GOUGH, H. G., & THORNE, A. (1986). Positive, negative, and balanced shyness. In W. H. Jones, J. M. Cheek, & S. R. Briggs (Eds.), *Shyness: Perspectives on research and treatment* (pp. 205–225). New York: Plenum.

GREENWALD, D. P. (1977). The behavioral assessment of differences in social skill and social anxiety in female college students. *Behavior Therapy, 8,* 925–937.

GREIST, J. H., JEFFERSON, J. W., & MARKS, I. M. (1986). *Anxiety and its treatment.* New York: Warner Books.

HACKETT, G., & HORAN, J. J. (1980). Stress inoculation for pain: What's really going on? *Journal of Counseling Psychology, 27,* 107–116.

HAEMMERLIE, F. M., & MONTGOMERY, R. L. (1984). Purposefully biased interactions: Reducing heterosocial anxiety through self-perception theory. *Journal of Personality and Social Psychology, 47,* 900–908.

HAHLWEG, K., & MARKMAN, H. J. (1988). Effectiveness of behavioral marital therapy: Empirical status of behavioral techniques in preventing and alleviating marital distress. *Journal of Consulting and Clinical Psychology, 56,* 440–447.

HAMILTON, D. L. (1979). A cognitive-attributional analysis of stereotyping. In L. Berkowitz (Ed.), *Advances in experimental social psychology* (Vol. 12, pp. 53–84). New York: Academic Press.

HAMILTON, D. L., & ROSE, T. L. (1980). Illusory correlation and the maintenance of stereotypic beliefs. *Journal of Personality and Social Psychology, 39,* 832–845.

HAMMEN, C. L., & COCHRAN, S. D. (1981). Cognitive correlates of life stress and depression in college students. *Journal of Abnormal Psychology, 90,* 23–27.

HANSSON, R. O. (1989). Old age: Testing the parameters of social psychological assumptions. In S. Spacapan & S. Oskamp (Eds.), *The social psychology of aging* (pp. 25–51). Newbury Park, Calif.: Sage.

HANSSON, R. O., & JONES, W. H. (1981). Loneliness, cooperation, and conformity among American undergraduates. *Journal of Social Psychology, 115,* 103–108.

HARRIS, L., & ASSOCIATES. (1975). *The myth and reality of aging in America.* Washington, D.C.: National Council on the Aging.

HARRIS, R. N., & SNYDER, C. R. (1986). The role of uncertain self-esteem in self-handicapping. *Journal of Personality and Social Psychology, 51,* 451–458.

HARVEY, J. H., WELLS, G. L., & ALVAREZ, M. D. (1978). Attribution in the context of conflict and separation in close relationships. In J. H. Harvey, W. J. Ickes, & R. F. Kidd (Eds.), *New directions in attribution research* (Vol. 2, pp. 235–260). Hillsdale, N.J.: Erlbaum.

HAZALEUS, S. L., & DEFFENBACHER, J. L. (1986). Relaxation and cognitive treatments of anger. *Journal of Consulting and Clinical Psychology, 54,* 222–226.

HEIBY, E. M. (1983). Assessment of frequency of self-reinforcement. *Journal of Personality and Social Psychology, 44,* 1304–1307.

HEIMBERG, R. G., KELLER, K. E., & PECA-BAKER, T. (1986). Cognitive assessment of social-evaluative anxiety in the job interview: Job Interview Self-Statement Schedule. *Journal of Counseling Psychology, 33,* 190–195.

HENDLER, N. (1984). Depression caused by chronic pain. *Journal of Clinical Psychiatry, 45,* 30–36.

HENRY, L. C. (Ed.). (1959). *Best quotations for all occasions.* New York: Fawcett.

HEPPNER, P. P., & PETERSON, C. H. (1982). The development and implications of the Personal Problem-Solving Inventory. *Journal of Counseling Psychology, 29,* 66–75.

HEREK, G. M., & GLUNT, E. K. (1988). An epidemic of stigma: Public reactions to AIDS. *American Psychologist, 43,* 886–891.

HOBFOLL, S. E., & LEIBERMAN, J. R. (1987). Personality and social resources in immediate and continued stress resistance among women. *Journal of Personality and Social Psychology, 52,* 18–26.

HOFFMAN, M. A., & TEGLASI, H. (1982). The role of causal attributions in counseling shy subjects. *Journal of Counseling Psychology, 29,* 132–139.

HOLAHAN, C. J., & MOOS, R. H. (1987). Personal and contextual determinants of coping strategies. *Journal of Personality and Social Psychology, 52,* 946–955.

HOLLON, S. D., & KENDALL, P. C. (1980). Cognitive self-statements in depression: Development of an automatic thoughts questionnaire. *Cognitive Therapy and Research, 4,* 383–395.

HOLMES, T. H., & MASUDA, M. (1974). Life change and illness susceptibility. In B. S. Dohrenwend & D. P. Dohrenwend (Eds.), *Stressful life events: Their nature and effects* (pp. 45–72). New York: Wiley.

HOLMES, T. H., & RAHE, R. H. (1967). The Social Readjustment Rating Scale. *Journal of Psychosomatic Research, 11,* 213–218.

HOLROYD, K. A. (1986). Recurrent headache. In K. A. Holroyd & T. L. Creer (Eds.), *Self-management of chronic disease* (pp. 373–413). New York: Academic Press.

HOLTZWORTH-MUNROE, A., & JACOBSON, N. S. (1985). Causal attributions of married couples: When do they search for causes? What do they conclude when they do? *Journal of Personality and Social Psychology, 48,* 1398–1412.

HUFF, J. G., VAN TREUREN, R. R., & PROPSOM, P. M. (1988). Attributional style and the components of hardiness. *Personality and Social Psychology Bulletin, 14,* 505–513.

HUGHES, J. R., CASAL, D. C., & LEON, A. S. (1986). Psychological effects of exercise: A randomized cross-over trial. *Journal of Psychosomatic Research, 30,* 355–360.

HUNSLEY, J. (1987). Internal dialogue during academic examinations. *Cognitive Therapy and Research, 11,* 653–664.

INGRAM, R. E., & WISNICKI, K. S. (1988). Assessment of positive automatic thoughts. *Journal of Consulting and Clinical Psychology, 56,* 898–902.

JACOBSON, E. (1938). *Progressive relaxation.* Chicago: University of Chicago Press.

JACOBSON, N. S., FOLLETTE, W. C., & MCDONALD, D. W. (1982). Reactivity to positive and negative behavior in distressed and nondistressed married couples. *Journal of Consulting and Clinical Psychology, 50,* 706–714.

JACOBSON, N. S., MCDONALD, D. W., FOLLETTE, W. C., & BERLEY, R. A. (1985). Attributional processes in distressed and nondistressed couples. *Cognitive Therapy and Research, 9,* 35–50.

JANIS, I. L. (1958). *Psychological stress: Psychoanalytic and behavioral studies of surgical patients.* New York: Wiley.

JANOFF-BULMAN, R., & THOMAS, C. E. (1988). Towards an understanding of self-defeating responses following victimization. In R. C. Curtis (Ed.), *Self-defeating behaviors: Experimental research and practical implications.* New York: Plenum.

JASNOSKI, M. L., HOLMES, D. S., SOLOMON, S., & AGUIAR, C. (1981). Exercise, changes in aerobic capacity, and changes in self-perceptions: An experimental investigation. *Journal of Research in Personality, 15,* 460–466.

JONES, E. E., & RHODEWALT, F. (1982). *The Self-Handicapping Scale.* Princeton N.J.: Princeton University, Department of Psychology.

JONES, W. H. (1982). Loneliness and social behavior. In L. A. Peplau & D. Perlman (Eds.), *Loneliness: A sourcebook of current theory, research, and therapy* (pp. 238–252). New York: Wiley-Interscience.

JONES, W. H., CARPENTER, B. N., & QUINTANA, D. (1985). Personality and interpersonal predictors of loneliness in two cultures. *Journal of Personality and Social Psychology, 48,* 1503–1511.

JONES, W. H., HOBBS, S. A., & HOCKENBURY, D. (1982). Loneliness and social skill deficits. *Journal of Personality and Social Psychology, 42,* 682–689.

JONES, W. H., SANSONE, C., & HELM, B. (1983). Loneliness and interpersonal judgments. *Personality and Social Psychology Bulletin, 9,* 437–441.

KAHANA, B., HAREL, Z., & KAHANA, E. (1988). Predictors of psychological well-being among survivors of the Holocaust. In J. P. Wilson, Z. Harel, & B. Kahana (Eds.), *Human adaptation to severe stress: From the Holocaust to Vietnam* (pp. 171–192). New York: Plenum.

KAMPTNER, N. L. (1989). Personal possessions and their meanings in old age. In S. Spacapan & S. Oskamp (Eds.), *The social psychology of aging* (pp. 165–196). Newbury Park, Calif.: Sage.

KANFER, R., & ZEISS, A. M. (1983). Depression, interpersonal standard setting, and judgments of self-efficacy. *Journal of Abnormal Psychology, 92,* 319–329.

KANNER, A. D., COYNE, J. C., SCHAEFER, C., & LAZARUS, R. S. (1981). Comparison of two modes of stress measurement: Daily hassles and uplifts versus major life events. *Journal of Behavioral Medicine, 4,* 1–39.

KAPLAN, H. B. (1970). Self-derogation and adjustment to recent life experiences. *Archives of General Psychiatry, 22,* 324–331.

KAPLAN, H. B., JOHNSON, R. J., & BAILEY, C. A. (1986). Self-rejection and the explanation of deviance: Refinement and elaboration of a latent structure. *Social Psychology Quarterly, 49,* 110–128.

KAPLAN, H. B., MARTIN, S. S., & JOHNSON, R. J. (1986). Self-rejection and the explanation of deviance: Specification of the structure among latent constructs. *American Journal of Sociology, 92,* 384–411.

KAPLAN, H. B., & POKORNY, A. D. (1969). Self-derogation and psychosocial adjustment. *Journal of Nervous and Mental Disease, 149,* 421–434.

KAPLAN, H. B., & POKORNY, A. D. (1976a). Self-derogation and suicide—I: Self-derogation as an antecedent of suicidal responses. *Social Science and Medicine, 10,* 113–118.

KAPLAN, H. B., & POKORNY, A. D. (1976b). Self-derogation and suicide—II: Suicidal responses, self-derogation, and accidents. *Social Science and Medicine, 10,* 119–121.

KAVANAUGH, R. (1974). *Facing death.* Baltimore: Penguin.

KEANE, T. M., FAIRBANK, J. A., CADDELL, J. M., & ZIMERING, R. T. (1989). Implosive (flooding) therapy reduces symptoms of PTSD in Vietnam combat veterans. *Behavior Therapy, 20,* 245–260.

KEANE, T. M., FAIRBANK, J. A., CADDELL, J. M., ZIMERING, R. T., & BENDER, M. E. (1985). A behavioral approach to assessing and treating post-traumatic stress disorder in Vietnam veterans. In C. R. Figley (Ed.), *Trauma and its wake* (pp. 257–294). New York: Brunner/Mazel.

KEEFE, F. J., & BLOCK, A. R. (1982). Development of an observation method for assessing pain behavior. *Behavior Therapy, 13,* 363–375.

KELLER, S., & SERAGANIAN, P. (1984). Physical fitness level and autonomic reactivity to psychosocial stress. *Journal of Psychosomatic Research, 28,* 279–287.

KELLEY, K., BYRNE, D., PRZBYLA, D. P. J., EBERLY, C., EBERLY, B., GREENDLINGER, V., WAN, C. K., & GORSKY, J. (1985). Chronic self-destructiveness: Conceptualization, measurement, and initial validation of the construct. *Motivation and Emotion, 9,* 135–151.

KELLEY, K., CHEUNG, F. M., RODRIGUEZ-CARRILLO, P., SINGH, R., WAN, C. K., & BECKER, M. A. (1986). Chronic self-destructiveness and locus of control in cross-cultural populations. *Journal of Social Psychology, 126,* 573–577.

KERNS, R. D., TURK, D., & HOLZMAN, A. D. (1983). Psychological treatment for chronic pain: A selective review. *Clinical Psychology Review, 3,* 15–26.

KESSLER, R. C., PRICE, R. H., & WORTMAN, C. B. (1985). Social factors in psychopathology: Stress, social support, and coping processes. In M. R. Rosenzweig & L. W. Porter (Eds.), *Annual review of psychology* (Vol. 39, pp. 531–572). Palo Alto, Calif.: Annual Reviews.

KIECOLT-GLASER, J. K., & WILLIAMS, D. A. (1987). Self-blame, compliance, and distress among burn patients. *Journal of Personality and Social Psychology, 53,* 187–193.

KILPATRICK, D. G., RESICK, P. A., & VERONEN, L. J. (1981). Effects of a rape experience. *Journal of Social Issues, 37,* 105–122.

KING, A. C., TAYLOR, C. B., HASKELL, W. L., & DEBUSK, R. F. (1989). Influence of regular aerobic exercise on psychological health: A randomized, controlled trial of healthy middle-aged adults. *Health Psychology, 8,* 305–324.

KIRSCH, I. (1982). Efficacy expectations or response predictions: The meaning of efficacy ratings as a function of task characteristics. *Journal of Personality and Social Psychology, 42,* 132–136.

KLEIN, D. C., FENCIL-MORSE, E., & SELIGMAN, M. E. P. (1976). Learned helplessness, depression, and the attribution of failure. *Journal of Personality and Social Psychology, 33,* 508–510.

KLEIN, D. C., & SELIGMAN, M. E. P. (1976). Reversal of performance deficits and perceptual deficits in learned helplessness and depression. *Journal of Abnormal Psychology, 85,* 11–26.

KLEINKE, C. L. (1978). *Self-perception: The psychology of personal awareness.* New York: W. H. Freeman.

KLEINKE, C. L. (1984a). Comparing depression coping strategies of schizophrenic men and depressed and nondepressed college students. *Journal of Clinical Psychology, 40,* 420–426.

KLEINKE, C. L. (1984b). Two models for conceptualizing the attitude-behavior relationship. *Human Relations, 37,* 333–350.

KLEINKE, C. L. (1986). *Meeting and understanding people.* New York: W. H. Freeman.

KLEINKE, C. L. (1987). Patients' preference for pain treatment modalities in a multidisciplinary pain clinic. *Rehabilitation Psychology, 32,* 113–120.

KLEINKE, C. L. (1988a). How chronic pain patients cope with depression: Relation to treatment outcome in a multidisciplinary pain clinic. Poster presented at the Association for Advancement of Behavior Therapy, N.Y.

KLEINKE, C. L. (1988b). The depression coping questionnaire. *Journal of Clinical Psychology, 44,* 516–526.

KLEINKE, C. L. (1989). Coping strategies used by chronic pain patients. Poster presented at the Association for the Advancement of Behavior Therapy, Washington, D.C.

KLEINKE, C. L., & DEAN, G. O. (1990). Evaluation of men and women receiving positive and negative responses with various acquaintance strategies. *Journal of Social Behavior and Personality, 5,* 369–377.

KLEINKE, C. L., KAHN, M. L., & TULLY, T. B. (1979). First impressions of talking rates in opposite-sex and same-sex interactions. *Social Behavior and Personality, 7,* 81–91.

KLEINKE, C. L., MEEKER, F. B., & STANESKI, R. A. (1986). Preference for opening lines: Comparing ratings by men and women. *Sex Roles, 15,* 585–600.

KLEINKE, C. L., & SPANGLER, A. S., JR. (1988a). Predicting treatment outcome of chronic back pain patients in a multidisciplinary pain clinic: Methodological issues and treatment implications. *Pain, 33,* 41–48.

KLEINKE, C. L., & SPANGLER, A. S., Jr. (1988b). Psychometric analysis of the audiovisual taxonomy for assessing pain behavior in chronic back-pain patients. *Journal of Behavioral Medicine, 11,* 83–94.

KLEINKE, C. L., STANESKI, R. A., & MASON, J. K. (1982). Sex differences in coping with depression. *Sex Roles, 15,* 877–889.

KOBASA, S. C. (1979). Stressful life events, personality, and health: An inquiry into hardiness. *Journal of Personality and Social Psychology, 37,* 1–11.

KOBASA, S. C., MADDI, S. R., & KAHN, S. (1982). Hardiness and health: A prospective study. *Journal of Personality and Social Psychology, 42,* 168–177.

KOBASA, S. C., MADDI, S. R., PUCCETTI, M. C., & ZOLA, M. A. (1985). Effectiveness of hardiness, exercise and social support as resources against illness. *Journal of Psychosomatic Research, 29,* 525–533.

KOESTENBAUM, P. (1976). *Is there an answer to death?* Englewood Cliffs, N.J.: Prentice-Hall.

KONECNI, V. J. (1984). Methodological issues in human aggression research. In R. M. Kaplan, V. J. Konecni, & R. W. Novaco (Eds.), *Aggression in children and youth.* The Hague, Netherlands: Nijhoff.

KRANTZ, D. S., GRUMBERG, N. E., & BAUM, A. (1985). Health psychology. In M. R. Rosenzweig & L. W. Porter (Eds.), *Annual review of psychology* (Vol. 39, pp. 349–383). Palo Alto, Calif.: Annual Reviews.

KRESSEL, K. (1986). Patterns of coping in divorce. In R. H. Moos (Ed.), *Coping with life crises: An integrated approach* (pp. 145–153). New York: Plenum.

KÜBLER-ROSS, E. (1969). *On death and dying.* New York: Macmillan.

KUPKE, T. E., CALHOUN, K. S., & HOBBS, S. A. (1979). Selection of heterosocial skills. II. Experimental validity. *Behavior Therapy, 10,* 336–346.

KUPKE, T. E., & HOBBS, S. A. (1979). Selection of heterosocial skills. I. Criterion-related validity. *Behavior Therapy, 10,* 327–335.

KYLE, S. O., & FALBO, T. (1985). Relationships between marital stress and attributional preferences for own and spouse behavior. *Journal of Social and Clinical Psychology, 3,* 339–351.

L'ABATE, L., & MILAN, M. A. (Eds.). (1985). *Handbook of social skills training and research.* New York: Wiley.

LAMBERT, W. E., LIBMAN, E., & POSNER, E. G. (1960). The effect of increased salience of a membership group on pain tolerance. *Journal of Personality, 28,* 350–357.

LANGE, A. J., & JAKUBOWSKI, P. (1976). *Responsible assertive behavior*. Champaign, Ill.: Research Press.

LANGER, E. J. (1979). The illusion of incompetence. In L. C. Perlmuter & R. A. Monty (Eds.), *Choice and perceived control* (pp. 301–313). Hillsdale, N.J.: Erlbaum.

LANGER, E. J. (1981). Old age: An artifact? In S. Kiesler & J. McGaugh (Eds.), *Behavior: Biology and aging* (pp. 255–281). New York: Academic Press.

LANGER, E. J., BECK, P., JANOFF-BULMAN, R., & Timko, C. (1984). An exploration of relationships among mindfulness, longevity, and senility. *Academic Psychology Bulletin, 6,* 211–226.

LANGER, E. J., JANIS, I. L., & WOLFER, J. A. (1975). Reduction of psychological stress in surgical patients. *Journal of Experimental Social Psychology, 11,* 155–165.

LANGER, E. J., & RODIN, J. (1976). The effects of choice and enhanced personal responsibility for the aged: A field experiment in an institutional setting. *Journal of Personality and Social Psychology, 34,* 191–198.

LANGER, E. J., RODIN, J., BECK, P., WEINMEN, C., & SPITZER, L. (1979). Environmental determinants of memory improvement in later adulthood. *Journal of Personality and Social Psychology, 37,* 2003–2013.

LANGER, E. J., CHANOWITZ, B., PALMERINO, M., JACOBS, S., RHODES, M., & TAYLOR, P. (1988). Nonsequential development and aging. In C. N. Alexander & E. J. Langer (Eds.), *Higher stages of human development: Perspectives on adult growth*. New York: Oxford University Press.

LANGSTON, C. A., & CANTOR, N. (1989). Social anxiety and social constraint: When making friends is hard. *Journal of Personality and Social Psychology, 56,* 649–661.

LAZARUS, R. S. (1984a). Puzzles in the study of daily hassles. *Journal of Behavioral Medicine, 7,* 375–389.

LAZARUS, R. S. (1984b). The trivialization of distress. In B. L. Hammonds & C. J. Scheirer (Eds.), *Psychology and health* (pp. 125–144). Washington, D.C.: American Psychological Association.

LAZARUS, R. S., & FOLKMAN, S. (1984). *Stress, appraisal and coping*. New York: Springer.

LEFCOURT, H. M. (1976). *Locus of control: Current trends in theory and research*. New York: Halstead.

LEFCOURT, H. M., MARTIN, R. A., FICK, C. M., & SALEH, W. E. (1985). Locus of control for affiliation and behavior in social interactions. *Journal of Personality and Social Psychology, 48,* 755–759.

LEHMAN, D. R., ELLARD, J. H., & WORTMAN, C. B. (1986). Social support for the bereaved: Recipients' and providers' perspectives on what is helpful. *Journal of Consulting and Clinical Psychology, 54,* 438–446.

LERNER, M. J. (1980). *The belief in a just world: A fundamental delusion*. New York: Plenum.

LEVENTHAL, E. A., LEVENTHAL, H., SHACHAM, S., & EASTERLING, D. V. (1989). Active coping reduces reports of pain from childbirth. *Journal of Consulting and Clinical Psychology, 57,* 365–371.

LEWINSOHN, P. M. (1975). Engagement in pleasant activities and depression level. *Journal of Consulting and Clinical Psychology, 84,* 729–731.

LEWINSOHN, P. M., ANTONUCCIO, D. O., STEINMETZ, J. L., & TERI, L. (1984). *The coping with depression course*. Eugene, Ore.: Castalia.

LEWINSOHN, P. M., MISCHEL, W., CHAPLIN, W., & BARTON, R. (1980). Social competence and depression: The role of illusory self-perceptions. *Journal of Abnormal Psychology, 89,* 203–212.

LIBOW, L. (1977). Medical problems of older people. In A. Bosco & J. Porcino (eds.), *What do we really know about aging*. Stony Brook, N.Y.: State University of New York at Stony Brook.

LIFTON, R. J., & OLSON, E. (1976). The human meaning of total disaster: The Buffalo Creek experience. *Psychiatry, 39,* 1–18.

LINDEMAN, E. (1944). Symptomatology and management of acute grief. *American Journal of Psychiatry, 101,* 141–148.

LINVILLE, P. W. (1987). Self-complexity as a cognitive buffer against stress-related illness and depression. *Journal of Personality and Social Psychology, 52,* 663–676.

LITT, M. D. (1988). Self-efficacy and perceived control: Cognitive mediators of pain tolerance. *Journal of Personality and Social Psychology, 54,* 149–160.

LOHR, J. M., & BONGE, D. (1982). Relationship between assertiveness and factorially validated measures of irrational beliefs. *Cognitive Therapy and Research, 6,* 353–356.

LOHR, J. M., HAMBERGER, L. K., & BONGE, D. (1988). The relationship of factorially validated measures of anger-proneness and irrational beliefs. *Motivation and Emotion, 12,* 171–183.

LOHR, J. M., NIX, J., DUNBAR, D., & MOSESSO, L. (1984). The relationship of assertive behavior in women and a validated measure of irrational beliefs. *Cognitive Therapy and Research, 8,* 287–297.

LONG, B. C. (1984). Aerobic conditioning and stress inoculation: A comparison of stress-management interventions. *Cognitive Therapy and Research, 8,* 517–542.

LONG, B. C., & HANEY, C. J. (1988). Coping strategies for working women: Aerobic exercise and relaxation interventions. *Behavior Therapy, 19,* 75–83.

MACPHERSON, M. (1984). *Long time passing: Vietnam and the haunted generation.* Garden City, N.Y.: Doubleday.

MADDI, S. R., BARTONE, P. T., & PUCCETTI, M. C. (1987). Stressful events are indeed a factor in physical illness: Reply to Schroeder and Costa (1984). *Journal of Personality and Social Psychology, 52,* 833–843.

MANNE, S., & SANDLER, I. (1984). Coping and adjustment to genital herpes. *Journal of Behavioral Medicine, 7,* 391–410.

MARGOLIN, G., TALOVIC, S., & WEINSTEIN, C. D. (1983). Areas of Change Questionnaire: A practical approach to marital assessment. *Journal of Consulting and Clinical Psychology, 51,* 920–931.

MARKMAN, H. J., FLOYD, F. J., STANLEY, S. M., & LEWIS, H. C. (1986). Prevention. In N. S. Jacobson & A. S. Gurman (Eds.), *Clinical handbook of marital therapy* (pp. 173–195). New York: Guilford.

MARKMAN, H. J., FLOYD, F. J., STANLEY, S. M., & STORAASLI, R. D. (1988). Prevention of marital distress: A longitudinal investigation. *Journal of Consulting and Clinical Psychology, 56,* 210–217.

MARMAR, C. R., & HOROWITZ, M. J. (1988). Diagnosis and phase-oriented treatment of post-traumatic stress disorder. In J. P. Wilson, Z. Harel, & B. Kahana (Eds.), *Human adaptation to extreme stress: From the Holocaust to Vietnam* (pp. 81–103). New York: Plenum.

MARTIN, J. E., & DUBBERT, P. M. (1982). Exercise applications and promotion in behavioral medicine: Current status and future directions. *Journal of Consulting and Clinical Psychology, 50,* 1004–1017.

MARTIN, R. A., & LEFCOURT, H. M. (1983). Sense of humor as a moderator of the relation between stress and moods. *Journal of Personality and Social Psychology, 45,* 1313–1324.

MATARAZZO, J. D. (1980). Behavioral health and behavioral medicine: Frontiers for a new health psychology. *American Psychologist, 35,* 807–817.

MATARAZZO, J. D. (1984). Behavioral immunogens. In B. L. Hammonds & C. J. Scheirer (Eds.), *Psychology and health* (pp. 9–43). Washington, D.C.: American Psychological Association.

MATARAZZO, J. D., BAILEY, W. A., KRAUT, A. G., & JONES, J. M. (1988). APA and AIDS: The evolution of a scientific and professional initiative in the public interest. *American Psychologist, 43,* 978–982.

MCARTHUR, D. L., COHEN, M. J., GOTTLIEB, H. J., NALIBOFF, B. D., & SCHANDLER, S. L. (1987a). Treating chronic low back pain. I. Admissions to initial follow-up. *Pain, 29,* 1–22

MCARTHUR, D. L., COHEN, M. J., GOTTLIEB, H. J., NALIBOFF, B. D., & SCHANDLER, S. L. (1987b). Treating chronic low back pain. II. Long-term follow-up. *Pain, 29,* 23–38.

MCCAUL, K. D., & MALOTT, J. M. (1984). Distraction and coping with pain. *Psychological Bulletin, 95,* 516–533.

MCCRAE, R. R., & COSTA, P. T. (1986). Personality, coping, and coping effectiveness in an adult sample. *Journal of Personality, 54,* 385–405.

MCKUSICK, L. (1988). The impact of AIDS on practitioner and client: Notes for the therapeutic relationship. *American Psychologist, 13,* 935–940.

MCMULLIN, R. E. (1986). *Handbook of cognitive therapy techniques.* New York: Norton.

MEAD, M. (1986). Jealousy: Primitive and civilised. In G. Clanton & L. G. Smith (Eds.), *Jealousy* (pp. 115–126). Lanham, Md.: University Press of America.

MEER, J. (1986, June). The reason of age. *Psychology Today,* pp. 60–64.

MEICHENBAUM, D. (1977). *Cognitive-behavior modification.* New York: Plenum.

MEICHENBAUM, D. (1985). *Stress inoculation training.* New York: Pergamon Press.

MELAMED, B. G. (1984). Health intervention: Collaboration for health and science. In B. L. Hammonds & C. J. Scheirer (Eds.), *Psychology and health* (pp. 49–119). Washington, D.C.: American Psychological Association.

MELZACK, R. (1975). The McGill Pain Questionnaire: Major properties and scoring methods. *Pain, 1,* 277–299.

MELZACK, R., JEANS, M. E., Stratford, J. G., & MONKS, R. C. (1980). Ice massage and transcutaneous electrical stimulation: Comparison of treatment for low-back pain. *Pain, 9,* 209–217.

MENAGHAN, E. (1982). Measuring coping effectiveness: A panel analysis of marital problems and coping efforts. *Journal of Health and Social Behavior, 23,* 220–234.

MEYER, C. B., & TAYLOR, S. E. (1986). Adjustment to rape. *Journal of Personality and Social Psychology, 50,* 1226–1234.

MICHELA, J. L., PEPLAU, L. A., & WEEKS, D. G. (1982). Perceived dimensions of attributions for loneliness. *Journal of Personality and Social Psychology, 43,* 929–936.

MILLER, L. C., BERG, J. H., & ARCHER, R. L. (1983). Openers: Individuals who elicit intimate self-disclosure. *Journal of Personality and Social Psychology, 44,* 1234–1244.

MILLER, S. M. (1987). Monitoring and blunting: Validation of a questionnaire to assess styles of information seeking under threat. *Journal of Personality and Social Psychology, 52,* 345–353.

MILLER, S. M., & BIRNBAUM, A. (1988). Putting the life back into 'life events': Toward a cognitive social learning analysis of the coping process. In S. Fisher & J. Reason (Eds.), *Handbook of life stress, cognition and health* (pp. 499–511). New York: Wiley.

MILLER, S. M., BRODY, D. S., & SUMMERTON, J. (1988). Styles of coping with threat: Implications for health. *Journal of Personality and Social Psychology, 54,* 142–148.

MILLER, S. M., LEINBACH, A., & BRODY, D. S. (1989). Coping style in hypertensive patients: Nature and consequences. *Journal of Consulting and Clinical Psychology, 57,* 333–337.

MITCHELL, R. E., BILLINGS, A. G., & MOOS, R. H. (1982). Social support and well-being: Implications for preventive programs. *Journal of Prevention, 3,* 77–98.

MONROE, S. (1983). Major and minor life events as predictors of psychological distress: Further issues and findings. *Journal of Behavioral Medicine, 6,* 189–205.

MOOS, R. H., & BILLINGS, A. G. (1982). Conceptualizing and measuring coping resources and processes. In L. Goldberger & S. Breznitz (Eds.), *Handbook of stress: Theoretical and clinical aspects.* New York: Free Press.

MORIN, S. F. (1988). AIDS: The challenge to psychology. *American Psychologist, 43,* 838–842.

NEWQUIST, D. D. (1985). Voodoo death in the American aged. In J. E. Birren & J. Livingston

(Eds.), *Cognition, stress, and aging* (pp. 111–133). Englewood Cliffs, N.J.: Prentice-Hall.

NEZU, A. M. (1986). Efficacy of a social-problem therapy approach for unipolar depression. *Journal of Consulting and Clinical Psychology, 54,* 196–202.

NEZU, A. M., NEZU, C. M., & BLISSETT, S. E. (1988). Sense of humor as a moderator of the relation between stressful events and psychological distress: A prospective analysis. *Journal of Personality and Social Psychology, 54,* 520–525.

NICHOLLS, J. G. (1984). Achievement motivation: Conceptions of ability, subjective experience, task choice, and performance. *Psychological Review, 91,* 328–346.

NIELSON, W. R., & MACDONALD, M. R. (1988). Attributions of blame and coping following spinal cord injury: Is self-blame adaptive? *Journal of Social and Clinical Psychology, 7,* 163–175.

NOREM, J. K., & CANTOR, N. (1986a). Anticipatory and post-hoc cushioning strategies: Optimism and defensive pessimism in "risky" situations. *Cognitive Therapy and Research, 10,* 347–362.

NOREM, J. K., & CANTOR, N. (1986b). Defensive pessimism: Harnessing anxiety as motivation. *Journal of Personality and Social Psychology, 51,* 1208–1217.

NOVACO, R. W. (1975). *Anger control.* Lexington, Mass.: Heath.

NOVACO, R. W. (1976). Treatment of chronic anger through cognitive and relaxation controls. *Journal of Consulting and Clinical Psychology, 44,* 681.

NOVACO, R. W. (1980). Training of probation counselors for anger problems. *Journal of Counseling Psychology, 27,* 385–390.

NOVACO, R. W. (1985). Anger and its therapeutic regulation. In M. Chesney & R. Roseman (Eds.), *Anger and hostility in cardiovascular disorders* (pp. 203–226). Washington, D.C.: Hemisphere.

NOVACO, R. W. (1986). Anger control as a clinical and social problem. In R. J. Blanchard & D. C. Blanchard (Eds.), *Advances in the study of aggression* (Vol. 3, pp. 1–67). New York: Academic Press.

ORVIS, B. R., KELLEY, H. H., & BUTLER, D. (1976). Attributional conflict in young couples. In J. H. Harvey, W. J. Ickes, & R. F. Kidd (Eds.), *New directions in attribution research* (Vol. 1, pp. 353–386). Hillsdale, N.J.: Erlbaum.

OSMAN, J. D., & JOHNSON, M. F. (1979). *AMJA runner's daily diary.* North Hollywood, Calif.: American Medical Joggers Association.

OSTROVE, N. (1978). Expectations for success on effort-determined tasks as a function of incentive and performance feedback. *Journal of Personality and Social Psychology, 36,* 909–916.

PAULHUS, D. L., & MARTIN, C. L. (1988). Functional flexibility: A new conception of interpersonal flexibility. *Journal of Personality and Social Psychology, 55,* 88–101.

PAULUS, P. B., MCCAIN, G., & COX, V. C. (1978). Death rates, psychiatric commitments, blood pressure and perceived crowding. *Environmental Psychology and Nonverbal Behavior, 3,* 107–116.

PEARLIN, I., & SCHOOLER, C. (1978). The structure of coping. *Journal of Health and Social Behavior, 19,* 2–21.

PECK, R. C. (1968). Psychological developments in the second half of life. In B. L. Neugarten (Ed.), *Middle age and aging: A reader in social psychology* (pp. 88–92). Chicago: University of Chicago Press.

PEPLAU, L. A., RUSSELL, D., & HEIM, M. (1979). The experience of loneliness. In I. H. Frieze, D. Bar-Tal, & J. S. Carroll (Eds.), *New approaches to social problems: Application of attribution theory* (pp. 53–78). San Francisco: Jossey-Bass.

PERLMAN, D., & PEPLAU, L. A. (1981). Toward a social psychology of loneliness. In S. Duck & R. Gilmour (Eds.), *Personal relationships in disorder* (pp. 31–56). London: Academic Press.

PERLMUTER, L. C., & LANGER, E. J. (1983). The effects of behavioral monitoring on the perception of control. *Clinical Gerontologist, 1,* 37–43.

PERLOFF, L. (1987). Social comparison and illusions of invulnerability to negative life events. In C. R. Snyder & C. E. Ford (Eds.), *Coping with negative life events* (pp. 217–242). New York: Plenum.

PETERSON, C. (1988). Explanatory style as a risk factor for illness. *Cognitive Therapy and Research, 12,* 117–130.

PETERSON, C., & BARRETT, L. C. (1987). Explanatory style and academic performance among university freshmen. *Journal of Personality and Social Psychology, 53,* 603–607.

PETERSON, C., & SELIGMAN, M. E. P. (1984). Causal explanations as a risk factor for depression: Theory and evidence. *Psychological Review, 91,* 347–374.

PETERSON, C., & SELIGMAN, M. E. P. (1987). Explanatory style and illness. *Journal of Personality, 55,* 237–265.

PETERSON, C., SELIGMAN, M. E. P., & VAILLANT, G. E. (1988). Pessimistic explanatory style is a risk factor for physical illness: A thirty-five-year longitudinal study. *Journal of Personality and Social Psychology, 55,* 23–27.

PFEIFFER, S. M., & WONG, P. T. P. (1989). Multidimensional jealousy. *Journal of Social and Personal Relationships, 6,* 181–196.

PHARES, E. J. (1976). *Locus of control in personality.* Morristown, N.J.: General Learning Press.

PIETROMONACO, P. R., & MARKUS, H. (1985). The nature of negative thoughts in depression. *Journal of Personality and Social Psychology, 48,* 799–807.

PILKONIS, P. A. (1977). The behavioral consequences of shyness. *Journal of Personality, 45,* 596–611.

PIPER, A. I., & LANGER, E. J. (1987). Aging and mindful control. In M. Baltes & P. Baltes (Eds.), *Aging and mindful control.* Hillsdale, N.J.: Erlbaum.

POLLOCK, M. L., WILMORE, J. H., & FOX, S. M. (1978). *Health and fitness through physical activity.* New York: Wiley.

POMERLEAU, O. F., & RODIN, J. (1986). Behavioral medicine and health psychology. In S. L. Garfield & A. E. Bergin (Eds.), *Handbook of psychotherapy and behavior change* (pp. 483–522). New York: Wiley.

PYSZCZYNSKI, T., & GREENBERG, J. (1987a). Depression, self-focused attention, and self-regulatory perseveration. In C. R. Snyder & C. E. Ford (Eds.), *Coping with negative life events* (pp. 105–129). New York: Plenum.

PYSZCZYNSKI, T., & GREENBERG, J. (1987b). Self-regulatory perseveration and the depressive self-focusing style: A self-awareness theory of reactive depression. *Psychological Bulletin, 102,* 122–138.

RAIMY, V. (1975). *Misunderstandings of the self.* San Francisco: Jossey-Bass.

RANDO, T. A. (1984). *Grief, dying, and death.* Champaign, Ill.: Research Press.

REIS, H. T., WHEELER, L., NEZLEK, J., KERNIS, M. H., & SPIEGEL, N. (1985). On specificity in the impact of social participation on physical and psychological health. *Journal of Personality and Social Psychology, 48,* 456–471.

REKER, G. T. (1985). Toward a holistic model of health, behavior, and aging. In J. E. Birren & J. Livingston (Eds.), *Cognition, stress, and aging* (pp. 47–71). Englewood Cliffs, N.J.: Prentice-Hall.

REKER, G. T., & WONG, P. T. P. (1985). Personal optimism, physical and mental health. In J. E. Birren & J. Livingston (Eds.), *Cognition, stress, and aging* (pp. 134–173). Englewood Cliffs, N.J.: Prentice-Hall.

RESICK, P. A., CALHOUN, K. S., ATKESON, B. M., & ELLIS, E. M. (1981). Social adjustment in victims of sexual assault. *Journal of Consulting and Clinical Psychology, 49,* 705–712.

REVENSON, T. A., & FELTON, B. J. (1989). Disability and coping as predictors of psychological adjustment to rheumatoid arthritis. *Journal of Consulting and Clinical Psychology, 57,* 344–348.

RICHTER, C. P. (1957). On the phenomenon of sudden-death in animals and man. *Psychosomatic Medicine, 19,* 191–198.

RIESMAN, D. (1953). *The lonely crowd.* New Haven, Conn.: Yale University Press.

RODIN, J., & BAUM, A. (1978). Crowding and helplessness: Potential consequences of density and loss of control. In A. Baum & Y. M. Epstein (Eds.), *Human response to crowding.* Hillsdale, N.J.: Erlbaum.

RODIN, J., & LANGER, E. J. (1977). Long-term effects of a control-relevant intervention with the institutionalized aged. *Journal of Personality and Social Psychology, 35,* 897–902.

ROGERS, C. R. (1961). *On becoming a person.* Boston: Houghton Mifflin.

ROOK, K. S. (1984). Promoting social bonding. *American Psychologist, 39,* 1389–1407.

ROOK, K. S. (1987). Social support versus companionship: Effects on life stress, loneliness, and evaluation by others. *Journal of Personality and Social Psychology, 52,* 1132–1147.

ROSENMAN, R. H. (1978). The interview method of assessment of the coronary-prone behavior pattern. In T. M. Dembroski, S. M. Weiss, J. L. Shields, S. G. Haynes, & M. Feinleib (Eds.), *Coronary-prone behavior.* New York: Springer-Verlag, pp. 55–69.

ROTTER, J. B. (1966). Generalized expectancies for internal versus external control of reinforcement [Special issue]. *Psychological Monographs, 80* (1).

ROY, R. (1984). Pain clinics: Reassessment of objectives and outcomes. *Archives of Physical Medicine and Rehabilitation, 65,* 448–451.

RUBENSTEIN, C. M., & SHAVER, P. (1980). Loneliness in two northeastern cities. In J. Hartog, J. R. Audy, & Y. A. Cohen (Eds.), *The anatomy of loneliness* (pp. 319–337). New York: International Universities Press.

RUBENSTEIN, C. M., & SHAVER, P. (1982). The experience of loneliness. In L. A. Peplau & D. Perlman (Eds.), *Loneliness: A sourcebook of theory, research and therapy* (pp. 206–223). New York: Wiley Interscience.

RUBIN, Z., & PEPLAU, L. A. (1975). Who believes in a just world? *Journal of Social Issues, 31,* 65–89.

RUSSELL, C. H. (1989). *Good news about aging.* New York: Wiley.

RUSSELL, D., CUTRONA, C. E., ROSE, J., & YURKO, K. (1984). Social and emotional loneliness: An examination of Weiss's typology of loneliness. *Journal of Personality and Social Psychology, 46,* 1313–1321.

RUSSELL, D., & MCAULEY, E. (1986). Causal attributions, causal dimensions, and affective reactions to success and failure. *Journal of Personality and Social Psychology, 50,* 1174–1185.

RUSSELL, D., PEPLAU, L. A., & CUTRONA, C. E. (1980). The revised UCLA Loneliness Scale: Concurrent and discriminant validity evidence. *Journal of Personality and Social Psychology, 39,* 472–480.

RYAN, W. (1971). *Blaming the victim.* New York: Random House.

SALOVEY, P., & RODIN, J. (1988). Coping with envy and jealousy. *Journal of Social and Clinical Psychology, 7,* 15–33.

SARASON, B. R., SHEARIN, E. N., PIERCE, G. R., & SARASON, I. G. (1987). Interrelations of social support measures: Theoretical and practical implications. *Journal of Personality and Social Psychology, 52,* 813–832.

SARASON, I. G. (1984). Stress, anxiety, and cognitive interference: Reactions to tests. *Journal of Personality and Social Psychology, 46,* 929–938.

SARASON, I. G., LEVINE, H. M., BASHAM, R. B., & SARASON, B. R. (1983). Assessing social support: The Social Support Questionnaire. *Journal of Personality and Social Psychology, 44,* 127–139.

SCHAEFER, C., COYNE, J. C., & LAZARUS, R. S. (1981). The health-related function of social support. *Journal of Behavioral Medicine, 4,* 381–406.

SCHEIER, M. F., & CARVER, C. S. (1985). Optimism, coping, and health: Assessment and implications of generalized outcome expectancies. *Health Psychology, 4,* 219–247.

SCHEIER, M. F., WEINTRAUB, J. K., & CARVER, C. S. (1986). Coping with stress: Divergent strategies of optimists and pessimists. *Journal of Personality and Social Psychology, 51,* 1257–1264.

SCHERER, M., & ADAMS, C. H. (1983). Construct validation of the Self-Efficacy Scale. *Psychological Reports, 53,* 899–902.

SCHERER, M., MADDUX, J. E., MERCANDANTE, B., PRENTICE-DUNN, S., JACOBS, B., & ROGERS, R. R. (1982). The Self-Efficacy Scale: Construction and validation. *Psychological Reports, 51,* 663–671.

SCHLICHTER, K. J., & HORAN, J. J. (1981). Effects of stress inoculation on the anger and aggression management skills of institutionalized juvenile delinquents. *Cognitive Therapy and Research, 5,* 359–365.

SCHOENBERG, B. M. (Ed.). (1980). *Bereavement counseling: A multidisciplinary handbook.* Westport, Conn.: Greenwood Press.

SCHULZ, R., & DECKER, S. (1985). Long-term adjustment to physical disability: The role of social support, perceived control, and self-blame. *Journal of Personality and Social Psychology, 48,* 1162–1172.

SCHUNK, D. H. (1982). Effects of effort attributional feedback on children's perceived self-efficacy and achievement. *Journal of Educational Psychology, 74,* 548–556.

SCHUNK, D. H. (1983). Ability versus effort attributional feedback: Differential effects on self-efficacy and achievement. *Journal of Educational Psychology, 75,* 848–856.

SCHUNK, D. H. (1984). Sequential attributional feedback and children's achievement behaviors. *Journal of Educational Psychology, 76,* 1159–1169.

SCHUNK, D. H., & HANSON, A. R. (1985). Peer models: Influence on children's self-efficacy and achievement. *Journal of Educational Psychology, 77,* 313–322.

SCHUNK, D. H., HANSON, A. R., & COX, P. D. (1987). Peer-model attributes and children's achievement behaviors. *Journal of Educational Psychology, 79,* 54–61.

SCOTT, D. S., & BARBER, T. X. (1977). Cognitive control of pain: Effects of multiple cognitive strategies. *Psychological Record, 27,* 373–383.

SCURFIELD, R. M. (1985). Post-trauma stress assessment and treatment: Overview and formulations. In C. R. Figley (Ed.), *Trauma and its wake* (pp. 219–256). New York: Brunner/Mazel.

SELIGMAN, M. E. P. (1975). *Helplessness: On depression, development, and death.* New York: W. H. Freeman.

SHAVER, P., & RUBENSTEIN, C. M. (1980). Childhood attachment experience and adult loneliness. In L. Wheeler (Ed.), *Review of personality and social psychology* (Vol. 1, pp. 42–73). Beverly Hills, Calif.: Sage.

SHERMAN, S. J., SKOV, R. B., HERVITZ, E. F., & STOCK, C. B. (1981). The effects of explaining hypothetical future events: From possibility to probability to actuality and beyond. *Journal of Experimental Social Psychology, 17,* 142–158.

SHOTLAND, R. L., & CRAIG, J. M. (1988). Can men and women differentiate between friendly and sexually interested behavior? *Social Psychology Quarterly, 51,* 66–73.

SHUPE, D. R. (1985). Perceived control, helplessness, and choice. In J. E. Birren & J. Livingston (Eds.), *Cognition, stress, and aging* (pp. 174–197). Englewood Cliffs, N.J.: Prentice-Hall.

SIBICKY, M., & DOVIDIO, J. F. (1986). Stigma of psychological therapy: Stereotypes, interpersonal reactions, and the self-fulfilling prophecy. *Journal of Counseling Psychology, 33,* 148–154.

SIEGEL, J. M. (1986). The multidimensional anger inventory. *Journal of Personality and Social Psychology, 51,* 191–200.

SILLARS, A. L. (1981). Attributions and interpersonal conflict resolution. In J. H. Harvey, W. J. Ickes, & R. F. Kidd (Eds.), *New directions in attribution research* (Vol. 3, pp. 279–305).

Hillsdale, N.J.: Erlbaum.

SIMON, C. (1987, December). Age-proofing the home. *Psychology Today,* pp. 21, 52–53.

SINGER, J. L. (1974). *Imagery and daydream methods in psychotherapy and behavior modification.* New York: Academic Press.

SKINNER, B. F. (1986). What's wrong with daily life in the western world. *American Psychologist, 41,* 568–574.

SKINNER, B. F., & VAUGHAN, M. E. (1983). *Enjoy old age.* New York: Norton.

SLATER, P. E. (1970). *The pursuit of loneliness.* Boston: Beacon Press.

SMITH, T. W., SNYDER, C. R., & HANDLESMAN, M. M. (1982). On the self-serving function of an academic wooden leg: Test anxiety as a self-handicapping strategy. *Journal of Personality and Social Psychology, 42,* 314–321.

SMITH, T. W., SNYDER, C. R., & PERKINS, S. C. (1983). The self-serving function of hypochondriacal complaints: Physical symptoms as self-handicapping strategies. *Journal of Personality and Social Psychology, 44,* 787–797.

SNYDER, C. R. (1989). Reality negotiation: From excuses to hope and beyond. *Journal of Social and Clinical Psychology, 8,* 130–157.

SNYDER, C. R., HIGGINS, R. L., & STUCKY, R. J. (1983). *Excuses: Masquerades in search of grace.* New York: Wiley Interscience.

SNYDER, C. R., & SMITH, T. W. (1982). Symptoms as self-handicapping strategies: On the virtues of new wine in an old bottle. In G. Weary & H. L. Mirels (Eds.), *Integration of clinical and social psychology* (pp. 104–127). New York: Oxford University Press.

SNYDER, C. R., & SMITH, T. W. (1986). On being "shy like a fox": A self-handicapping analysis. In W. H. Jones, J. M. Cheek, & S. R. Briggs (Eds.), *Shyness: Perspectives on research and treatment* (pp. 161–172). New York: Plenum.

SNYDER, C. R., SMITH, T. .W., AUGELLI, R. W., & INGRAM, R. E. (1985). On the self-serving function of social anxiety: Shyness as a self-handicapping strategy. *Journal of Personality and Social Psychology, 48,* 970–980.

SOLANO, C. H., BATTEN, P. G., & PARISH, E. A. (1982). Loneliness and patterns of self-disclosure. *Journal of Personality and Social Psychology, 43,* 524–531.

SPANOS, N. P., BROWN, J. M., JONES, B., & HORNER, D. (1981). Cognitive activity and suggestions for analgesia in the reduction of reported pain. *Journal of Abnormal Psychology, 90,* 554–561.

SPANOS, N. P., HORTON, C., & CHAVES, J. F. (1975). The effects of two cognitive strategies on pain threshold. *Journal of Abnormal Psychology, 84,* 677–681.

SPANOS, N. P., RADTKE-BODORIK, H. L., FERGUSON, J. D., & JONES, B. (1979). The effects of hypnotic susceptibility, suggestions for analgesia, and the utilization of cognitive strategies on the reduction of pain. *Journal of Abnormal Psychology, 88,* 282–292.

SPANOS, N. P., STAM, H. J., & BRAZIL, K. (1981). The effects of suggestion and distraction on coping ideation and reported pain. *Journal of Mental Imagery, 5,* 75–90.

STALL, R. D., COATES, T. J., & HOFF, C. (1988). Behavioral risk reduction for HIV infection among gay and bisexual men: A review of results from the United States. *American Psychologist, 43,* 878–885.

STAM, H. J., & SPANOS, N. P. (1980). Experimental designs, expectancy effects, and hypnotic analgesia. *Journal of Abnormal Psychology, 89,* 751–762.

STAMPFL, T., & LEWIS, D. (1967). Essentials of implosive therapy: A learning-theory-based psychodynamic behavioral therapy. *Journal of Abnormal Psychology, 72,* 496–503.

STEARNS, C. Z., & STEARNS, P. N. (1986). *Anger: The struggle for emotional control in American history.* Chicago: University of Chicago Press.

STEINMETZ, J. L., LEWINSOHN, P. M., & ANTONUCCIO, D. O. (1983). Prediction of individual outcome in a group intervention for depression. *Journal of Consulting and Clinical Psychology, 51,* 331–337.

STERNBERG, R. J. (1986). A triangular theory of love. *Psychological Review, 93,* 119–135.

STERNBERG, R. J., & GRAJECK, S. (1984). The nature of love. *Journal of Personality and Social Psychology, 47,* 312–329.

STRACK, S., & COYNE, J. C. (1983). Social confirmation of dysphoria: Shared and private reactions to depression. *Journal of Personality and Social Psychology, 44,* 798–806.

STRICKLAND, B. R. (1978). Internal-external expectancies and health-related behaviors. *Journal of Consulting and Clinical Psychology, 46,* 1192–1211.

STUART, R. B. (1980). *Helping couples change.* New York: Guilford.

SULS, J. (1982). Social support, interpersonal relations, and health: Benefits and liabilities. In G. Sanders & J. Suls (Eds.), *Social psychology of health and illness.* Hillsdale, N.J.: Erlbaum.

SULS, J., & FLETCHER, B. (1985). The relative efficacy of avoidant and nonavoidant coping strategies: A meta-analysis. *Health Psychology, 4,* 249–288.

SWEENEY, P. D., ANDERSON, K., & BAILEY, S. (1986). Attributional style in depression: A meta-analytic review. *Psychological Bulletin, 50,* 974–991.

SZASZ, T. S. (1987). *Insanity: The idea and its consequences.* New York: Wiley.

TABACHNIK, N., CROCKER, J., & ALLOY, L. B. (1983). Depression, social comparison, and the false-consensus effect. *Journal of Personality and Social Psychology, 45,* 688–699.

TAIT, R., & SILVER, R. C. (1989). Coming to terms with major negative life events. In J. S. Uleman & J. A. Bargh (Eds.), *Unintended thought* (pp. 351–382). New York: Guilford.

TAYLOR, S. E. (1979). Hospital patient behavior: Reactance, helplessness, or control? *Journal of Social Issues, 35,* 156–184.

TAYLOR, S. E. (1983). Adjustment to threatening events: A theory of cognitive adaptation. *American Psychologist, 38,* 1161–1173.

TAYLOR, S. E. (1986). *Health psychology.* New York: Random House.

TAYLOR, S. E., & BROWN, J. D. (1988). Illusion and well-being: A social psychological perspective on mental health. *Psychological Bulletin, 103,* 193–210.

TAYLOR, S. E., & CLARK, L. F. (1986). Does information improve adjustment to noxious medical procedures? In M. J. Saks & L. Saks (Eds.), *Advances in applied social psychology* (Vol. 3, pp. 1–28). Hillsdale, N.J.: Erlbaum.

TAYLOR, S. E., FALKE, R. L., SHOPTAW, S. J., & LICHTMAN, R. R. (1986). Social support, support groups, and the cancer patient. *Journal of Consulting and Clinical Psychology, 54,* 608–615.

TAYLOR, S. E., LICHTMAN, R. R., & WOOD, J. V. (1984). Attributions, beliefs about control, and adjustment to breast cancer. *Journal of Personality and Social Psychology, 46,* 489–502.

TAYLOR, S. E., & LOBEL, M. (1989). Social comparison activity under threat: Downward evaluation and upward contacts. *Psychological Review, 96,* 569–575.

TAYLOR, S. E., WOOD, J. V., & LICHTMAN, R. R. (1983). It could be worse: Selective evaluation as a response to victimization. *Journal of Social Issues, 39,* 19–40.

TEGLASI, H., & HOFFMAN, M. A. (1982). Causal attributions of shy subjects. *Journal of Research in Personality, 16,* 376–385.

THOMPSON, S. E., & KELLEY, H. H. (1981). Judgments of responsibility for activities in close relationships. *Journal of Personality and Social Psychology, 41,* 469–477.

THORNE, A. (1987). The press of personality: A study of conversations between introverts and extraverts. *Journal of Personality and Social Psychology, 53,* 718–726.

TITCHENER, J. L., & KAPP, F. T. (1976). Family and character change at Buffalo Creek. *American Journal of Psychiatry, 133,* 295–299.

TRIMBLE, M. R. (1985). Post-traumatic stress disorder: History of a concept. In C. R. Figley (Ed.), *Trauma and its wake* (pp. 5–14). New York: Brunner/Mazel.

TROSS, S., & HIRSCH, D. A. (1988). Psychological distress and neuropsychological complications of HIV infections and AIDS. *American Psychologist, 43,* 929–934.

TUCKER, J. A., VUCHINICH, R. E., & SOBELL, M. B. (1981). Alcohol consumption as a self-handicapping strategy. *Journal of Abnormal Psychology, 90,* 220–230.

TURK, D. C., HOLZMAN, A. D., & KERNS, R. D. (1986). Chronic pain. In K. A. Holroyd & T. L. Creer (Eds.), *Self-management of chronic disease* (pp. 441–472). New York: Academic Press.

TURK, D. C., MEICHENBAUM, D., & GENEST, M. (1983). *Pain and behavioral medicine.* New York: Guilford.

TURK, D. C., RUBY, T. E., & SALOVEY, P. (1985). The McGill Pain Questionnaire reconsidered: Confirming the factor structure and examining appropriate uses. *Pain, 21,* 385–397.

U.S. NEWS AND WORLD REPORT. (1987, June 29). Taking the pain out of pain. 50–57.

VELTEN, E. (1968). A laboratory task for induction of mood states. *Behavior Research and Therapy, 6,* 473–482.

VITALIANO, P. P. (1988). *ADS and WCCL manual.* Seattle: University of Washington.

VITALIANO, P. P., KATON, W., MAIURO, R. D., & RUSSO, J. (1989). Coping in chest pain patients with and without psychiatric disorders. *Journal of Consulting and Clinical Psychology, 57,* 338–343.

WALLSTON, B. S., ALAGNA, S. W., DEVELLIS, B. M., & DEVELLIS, R. .F. (1983). Social support and physical health. *Health Psychology, 2,* 367–391.

WALLSTON, B. S., WALLSTON, K. A., KAPLAN, G. D, & MAIDES, S. A. (1976). Development and validation of the Health Locus of Control (HLC) scale. *Journal of Consulting and Clinical Psychology, 44,* 580–585.

WALSTER, E. (1966). Assignment of responsibility for an accident. *Journal of Personality and Social Psychology, 3,* 73–79.

WANDERER, Z., & CABOT, T. (1978). *Letting go.* New York: Warner Books.

WARD, C. (1988). The Attitude Toward Rape Victims Scale. *Psychology of Women Quarterly, 12,* 127–146.

WEINBERGER, D. A., SCHWARTZ, G. E., & DAVIDSON, R. J. (1979). Low-anxious, high-anxious, and repressive coping styles: Psychometric patterns and behavioral and physiological responses to stress. *Journal of Abnormal Psychology, 88,* 369–380.

WEINER, B. (1979). A theory of motivation for some classroom experiences. *Journal of Educational Psychology, 71,* 3–25.

WEINER, B. (1985). An attributional theory of achievement motivation and emotion. *Psychological Review, 92,* 548–573.

WEINER, B., FRIEZE, I., KUKLA, A., REED, L., REST, S., & ROSENBAUM, R. M. (1971). *Perceiving the causes of success and failure.* Morristown, N.J.: General Learning Press.

WEINER, B., PERRY, R. P., & MAGNUSSON, J. (1988). An attributional analysis of reactions to stigmas. *Journal of Personality and Social Psychology, 55,* 738–748.

WEINER, B., RUSSELL, D., & LERMAN, D. (1979). The cognition-emotion process in achievement-related contexts. *Journal of Personality and Social Psychology, 37,* 1211–1220.

WEISS, R. S. (1973). *Loneliness: The experience of emotional and social isolation.* Cambridge, Mass.: MIT Press.

WEISS, R. S. (1974). The provisions of social relationships. In Z. Rubin (Ed.), *Doing unto others.* Englewood Cliffs, N.J.: Prentice-Hall.

WETHINGTON, E., & KESSLER, R. C. (1986). Perceived support, received support, and adjustment to stressful life events. *Journal of Health and Social Behavior, 27,* 78–89.

WHITE, J. (1982). *Rejection.* Reading, Mass.: Addison-Wesley.

WHITE, R. W. (1959). Motivation reconsidered: The concept of competence. *Psychological Review, 66,* 297–333.

WILFLEY, D., & KUNCE, J. (1986). Differential physical and psychological effects of exercise. *Journal of Counseling Psychology, 33,* 337–342.

WILLS, T. A. (1987). Help-seeking as a coping mechanism. In C. R. Snyder & C. E. Ford (Eds.), *Coping with negative life events* (pp. 19–50). New York: Plenum.

WILSON, J. P., SMITH, W. K., & JOHNSON, S. K. (1985). A comparative analysis of PTSD among various survivor groups. In C. R. Figley (Ed.), *Trauma and its wake* (pp. 142–172). New York: Brunner/Mazel.

WILSON, T. D., & LINVILLE, P. W. (1982). Improving the academic performance of college freshmen: Attribution therapy revisited. *Journal of Personality and Social Psychology, 42,* 367–376.

WILSON, T. D., & LINVILLE, P. W. (1985). Improving the performance of college freshmen with attributional techniques. *Journal of Personality and Social Psychology, 49,* 287–293.

WOLPE, J. (1958). *Psychotherapy by reciprocal inhibition.* Palo Alto, Calif.: Stanford University Press.

WOLPE, J. (1969). *The practice of behavior therapy.* New York: Pergamon Press.

WOLPE, J. (1982). *The practice of behavior therapy* (3rd ed.). Elmsford, N.Y.: Pergamon Press.

WOOD, J. V., TAYLOR, S. E., & LICHTMAN, R. R. (1985). Social comparison in adjustment to breast cancer. *Journal of Personality and Social Psychology, 49,* 1169–1183.

WORDEN, J. W. (1982). *Grief counseling and grief therapy.* New York: Springer.

WORTHINGTON, E. L., & SHUMATE, M. (1981). Imagery and verbal counseling methods in stress inoculation training for pain control. *Journal of Counseling Psychology, 28,* 1–6.

WORTMAN, C. B., & SILVER, R. C. (1987). Coping with irrevocable loss. In G. R. VandenBos & B. K. Bryant (Eds.), *Cataclysms, crises, and catastrophes: Psychology in action* (Vol. 6, pp. 189–235). Washington, D.C.: American Psychological Association.

WORTMAN, C. B., & SILVER, R. C. (1989). The myths of coping with loss. *Journal of Consulting and Clinical Psychology, 57,* 349–357.

YOUNG, J. E. (1982). Loneliness, depression, and cognitive therapy: Theory and application. In L. A. Peplau & D. Perlman (Eds.), *Loneliness: A sourcebook of current theory, research, and therapy* (pp. 379–405). New York: Wiley Interscience.

YOUNG, J. E. (1989). *Schema-focused cognitive therapy for personality disorders and difficult patients.* Sarasota, Fl.: Professional Resource Exchange.

ZBOROWSKI, M. (1969). *People in pain.* San Francisco: Jossey-Bass.

ZEISS, A. M., LEWINSOHN, P. M., & MUÑOZ, R. F. (1979). Nonspecific improvement effects in depression using interpersonal skills training, pleasant activity schedule, or cognitive training. *Journal of Consulting and Clinical Psychology, 47,* 427–439.

ZEVON, M. A., KARUZA, J., & BRICKMAN, P. (1982). Responsibility and the elderly: Applications to psychotherapy. *Psychotherapy: Theory, Research, and Practice, 4,* 405–411.

ZIMBARDO, P. G. (1977). *Shyness: What it is, what to do about it.* Reading, Mass.: Addison-Wesley.

ZIMBARDO, P. G., COHEN, A., WEISENBERG, M., DWORKIN, L., & FIRESTONE, I. (1969). The control of experimental pain. In P. G. Zimbardo (Ed.), *The cognitive control of motivation* (pp. 100–122). Glenview, Ill: Scott, Foresman.

Index